SEX,
MURDER,
AND THE
UNWRITTEN
LAW

American Liberty & Justice

Gordon Morris Bakken,
SERIES EDITOR

SEX, MURDER & THE UNWRITTEN LAW

GENDER AND JUDICIAL MAYHEM, TEXAS STYLE

BILL NEAL

FOREWORD BY GORDON MORRIS BAKKEN

TEXAS TECH UNIVERSITY PRESS

This book is typeset in Monotype Perrywood. The paper used in this book
meets the minimum requirements of ANSI/NISO Z39.48–1992 (R1997). ∞

Designed by Lindsay Starr

LIBRARY OF CONGRESS CATALOGING-IN-PUBLICATION DATA
Neal, Bill, 1936–
    Sex, murder, and the unwritten law : courting judicial mayhem, Texas
style / Bill Neal.
        p. cm. — (American liberty and justice)
    Includes bibliographical references and index.
    Summary: "Six Texas trials from 1896 to 1968 illuminate how "unwrit-
ten law" permitted violence toward offenders of Southern notions of female
virtue, male honor, or sanctity of marriage. Explores the maneuvers of defense
lawyers who managed to extricate guilty clients when there appeared no legal
basis for a defense"—Provided by publisher.
    ISBN 978-0-89672-662-8 (hardcover : alk. paper) 1. Trials (Murder)—
Texas. 2. Sex crimes—Texas. 3. Sex discrimination in criminal justice administration—Texas. 4. Sex and law—Texas—Interpretation and construction. 5.
Gender and politics. I. Title.
    KF221.M8N433 2009
    345.764'02523—dc22   2009015357

Printed in the United States of America

10   11   12   13   14   15   16   17   18 / 10   9   8   7   6   5   4   3   2

TEXAS TECH UNIVERSITY PRESS
Box 41037, Lubbock, Texas 79409–1037 USA
800.832.4042 | ttup@ttu.edu | www.ttupress.org

For my children, Monte, Max, and Kay

CONTENTS

ILLUSTRATIONS

FOREWORD

ill Neal's *Sex, Murder, and the Unwritten Law* adds new dimensions to a growing body of literature on criminal trials and the unwritten law. Robert Ireland has written pioneering articles about the unwritten law of the nineteenth century.[1] His 1992 article on women defendants scrutinizes the relationship of sexual dishonor and violence, femininity and insanity, and rage and law.[2] Basing his study on cases from 1843 to 1896, Ireland found the invention of the unwritten law that exonerated male and female killers who avenged sexual dishonor. Ireland's trials evinced an ideology that men had a duty to protect women from "slimy, snake-like libertines" and to punish "Eve-like women who too readily embraced those libertines."[3]

At trial, defense attorneys painted their female clients as "weak and hysterical, whose hysteria rendered them legally insane," and prosecutors painted them "inherently licentious and the purveyors of social evil."[4] Theorists tied female insanity, in turn, to menstrual dysfunction and "an inherent condition of emotional instability."[5] Nineteenth-century physicians labeled it dysmenorrheal. Today it is known as premenstrual syndrome, or PMS.[6] Popular paperbacks keep the issue alive in a broad national setting.[7] Scholarly work on seduction litigation has created a far more nuanced view of marriage, seduction, and violence.[8]

In the twentieth century, a new unwritten law emerged. This new unwritten law provided women the right to use deadly force to resist an abusive partner. The defense argued this unwritten law in terms of self-defense precipitated by wife or partner beating.[9] Appying it in Cook County, Illinois, juries convicted only 16 of 103 women who killed men, and 9 of the 16 defendants were African-American.[10]

Christopher Waldrep, following the work of Richard Hamm on honor and homicide in the South, concluded, "By the end of the nineteenth century, Americans widely understood that an unwritten law existed off the books allowing men to slay the seducers of 'their' women." Looking at a national trend of historical interest in single cases, Waldrep further noted, "The appearance of so many historical crime stories from major, well-established, elite scholars writing for the top publishers, authors that used to write very different books, brings new gravitas to this line of inquiry."[11] Yet, class was often not a factor in the trials except for the very wealthy defendants. Readers will note that Bill Neal deals with a variety of class issues over time and puts them in very specific settings. Further, he asks good historical questions of the evidence.

Historians also have researched race and immigrant status relative to this issue. Clare V. McKanna, Jr., found that cultural conflict, transient populations, Western boomtown attitudes, and the easy availability of firearms and alcohol created a climate of violence in Douglas County, Nebraska; Las Animas County, Colorado; and Gila County, Arizona.[12] McKanna also demonstrated that American Indians were the least likely to receive justice in the American court system.[13]

Kevin J. Mullen detected violence patterns inherent in immigrant communities which traveled to the urban West, and these immigrant communities earned the label of "dangerous."[14] The relationship of crime, the police, and ethnic communities profoundly impacted Mexican-American communities in Los Angeles.[15] In Chicago, juries clearly motivated by race refused to afford the unwritten law to African-American women who killed, because jurors thought that defense was "subversive and dangerous."[16]

In California criminal justice history, Lawrence M. Friedman and Robert Percival's *The Roots of Justice* remains the most important study of the system.[17] Notably, the authors explained the problems of criminal evidence and the jury system. Termed "a giant card house of rules," California criminal law gave the jury great power, but erected a complicated rulebook "to make sure that jurymen eat nothing but the safest, softest Pablum of evidence." The rules in law books had "exceptions, and exceptions to exceptions; and these in turn have exceptions."[18] Judges were at risk of making errors that were grounds for appeal in long trials with skilled defense attorneys. The two most frequent grounds for appeal were errors in the charge to the jury, or on evidence. Evidence error challenged the judge's admission of evidence testimony or physical evidence deemed "incompetent, irrelevant and immaterial."[19] Nineteenth-century and twentieth-century lawyers made their reputations as attorneys by performing before a judge, jury, and audience made up of members of the bar, the press, and the public.[20]

Neal's focus on Texas juries adds a new dimension to prior scholarly studies. Not only does he provide verdicts, but he also contextualizes them and puts them in cultural terms by asking good questions. This book is thought provoking and puts solid case analysis behind scholarly conclusions. In addition to adding to the scholarly literature, Bill Neal makes this history interesting and lively with superbly crafted language that questions meaning and significance.

GORDON MORRIS BAKKEN
California State University, Fullerton

ACKNOWLEDGMENTS

For help on this book, many thanks are owed. To my wife, Gayla, first and foremost—she who is my secretary, research assistant, and doer of all manner of detail work. In addition, she fed me nearly every day. Also special thanks is due to Hanaba Munn Welch, my research assistant and general handyman. Many thanks to a college classmate and fellow author, Mike Cochran, veteran newspaper reporter for the Associate Press and the *Fort Worth Star-Telegram*, who wrote the definitive book on the Cullen Davis murder trials. Another college classmate, Dr. David McPherson, retired University of New Mexico English professor and Shakespeare scholar, lent much encouragement and advice. Also special thanks to Professor Gordon Morris Bakken of California State University, Fullerton, for his encouragement and constructive criticism. Thanks also to my son, Monte Neal, who read the manuscript and made helpful suggestions.

Local historians who have generously shared their stories and material with me include Myna Hicks Potts of Chillicothe, Texas; Peggy Barker Atchison of Quanah, Texas; Joe Brown, columnist for the *Wichita Falls Times Record News;* Edgar Shockley, Wichita County historian; the Hon. Clyde Whiteside, retired district judge; and Lita Watson, archivist of the Museum of North Texas History, all of Wichita Falls; Jeane Pruett of Ranger, Texas, president of the Ranger Historical Society; Dick Vallon of Burkburnett; Marisue Burleson Potts Powell of Matador; and Don Woodard of Fort Worth.

Thanks also to the court clerks in Wichita Falls, Vernon, Quanah, Benjamin, Seymour, Matador, and Abilene for assisting me in research of court records and to personnel at the *Wichita Falls Times Record News* (Deanna Watson, editor), the *Vernon Daily Record* (Jimmy Carr, editor), and the *Quanah Tribune-Chief* (Carol Ann Witmire, editor).

Others whose contributions are appreciated are Allen Kimble of Fort Worth, Woody Brown of Copperas Cove, and David Kent, photographer at the *Fort Worth Star-Telegram*.

Also appreciated are Tai Kreidler and his staff at the Southwest Collections Library at Texas Tech University; Warren Stricker, research center director at the Panhandle-Plains Historical Museum; John Anderson, preservation officer at the Texas State Library and Archives Commission; Robert Palmer, chairman of the Wichita County Historical Commission; Christina Stopka, deputy director of the Texas Ranger Research Center; Patrick Lemmelle, University of Texas at San Antonio's Institute of Texan Cultures; Jill Henderson, librarian at the Taylor County Law Library; personnel at the Jamail Center for Legal Research at the Tarlton Law Library, University of Texas at Austin; and Cathy Spitzenberger at the University of Texas at Arlington Library.

SEX,
MURDER,
AND THE
UNWRITTEN
LAW

Author's collection. Map designed by Hanaba Munn Welch.

Introduction

SEX AND THE LAW, BOTH WRITTEN AND UNWRITTEN

"Neither can he be thought guilty of a Crime greater
[than manslaughter], who, finding a Man in Bed with
his Wife, or being actually struck by him, or pulled by
the Nose, or filliped upon the Forehead, immediately
kills him."

> W. HAWKINS, "A Treatise of the Pleas of the
> Crown" (1716), c. 31, s. 36

I f, in the State of Texas, you want to kill a deer, or a duck, or
a quail, or a turkey, you are first required to buy a hunting
license from the State and then wait until the season opens.
However, if you want to kill some lesser species (predators such as coy-
otes or wild hogs, or common varmints such as possums, coons, rabbits,
and the like), then no permit is required, and the season is always open.
Until the Year of Our Lord 1973, in the State of Texas, human males
fell into that latter category—provided you could catch one between
the sheets *in flagrante delicto* with your wife. However, there was one
difference in the applicable hunting regulations that the manhunter had
to observe: while it is not considered sporting to, say, shoot a quail on
the nest (the bird should be flushed and allowed to take flight before

the hunter attempts to bag it—"sporting chance," they call it), under the pre-1973 Texas law, the manhunter must *not* allow the quarry to rise from the nest. "Pot shooting" was not only permitted, it was mandated! Article 1220 of the *Texas Penal Code* spelled it out: "A homicide is justifiable when committed by the husband upon the person of anyone taken in adultery with the wife; *provided* the killing takes place *before* the parties to the act of adultery *have separated*."[1]

The statute would thus seem to put a premium on the sport's quick-draw ability. However, in 1885 a Texas appellate court provided some latitude for enraged Texas husbands. Anthony Price caught Mrs. Price in a corncrib under suspicious circumstances and with no good explanation for her presence in that corncrib in the middle of the night. Upon further investigation, he dug William Chandler out of the corn and shot him—fatally. Judge White of the Texas Court of Criminal Appeals gave the statutory language "before they separated" a rather broad interpretation. White reasoned that Mr. Price acted as a reasonable man in concluding that Chandler had indeed "taken Mrs. Price in adultery" and held that the requirement "before they have separated" wasn't to be taken too literally. It was enough, Judge White declared, if, under suspicious circumstances, the husband discovered the amorous pair while they were still in the same bed, or still in the same room (or corncrib as it were), or still together in the company of each other when the killing took place.[2]

On the other hand, good marksmanship was imperative. The enraged shootist couldn't afford to miss his target and hit the unfaithful wife. That would be murder! An illogical distinction? Not really. The Supreme Court of Georgia explained the logic this way: "Killing the lover to prevent adultery could be justifiable homicide to protect the marriage, though killing the spouse could not be justifiable because it would terminate the marriage."[3] Shotgun weddings, maybe; shotgun divorces, never! Of course, it goes without saying that wives were not afforded reciprocal shooting rights if they stalked and caught a miscreant husband *in flagrante delicto*—even if potting the husband's floozy would have resulted in salvaging the marriage.[4] If, as has often been contended, truth is the first casualty of traditional warfare, then logic, it appears, is the first casualty of sexual warfare.

There was another rule of which the righteously indignant husband had to be mindful: when he zeroed the prey in his gun sight, he had to make darn sure that he killed him dead (or at least made an earnest and sincere effort to do so). In a 1922 case, the Texas Court of Criminal Appeals made that perfectly clear. A fellow named Sensobaugh caught his wife indulging in most unladylike behavior with a stranger. He pulled his six-shooter, but instead of shooting the defiler of his marital bed, he tied him up, announced he would spare his life, then whipped out a razor and deleted the offending appendage.

Although Sensobaugh had spared his life, nevertheless the fellow (obviously a chronic malcontent) went around whining about the incident to all who would listen, including the Dallas County district Attorney. The DA also failed to appreciate the mercy that Sensobaugh had extended the randy intruder and proceeded to prosecute Sensobaugh successfully for criminal assault. Sensobaugh, of course, immediately appealed and claimed that Article 1220 provided him with a perfect defense. After all, he argued, with considerable logic behind his oar, if one could legally kill somebody caught in sexual congress with his wife, then how could it be a crime for the incensed husband to impose some lesser form of self-help punishment on the offender—like, for instance, making a gelding out of the rogue stallion?

Well, the Court struggled; if only Sensobaugh had just gone ahead and killed him, it would have been okay. Or, had he deleted the organ in question with intent to bleed the victim to death, that would have been okay. But half measures just would not do. The Court appears to have finally concluded that Sensobaugh's cold-blooded forbearance resulted in a fate worse than death and thus imposed a $300 fine and sixty days in jail for Sensobaugh.[5]

In 1856, the Texas Congress enacted another piece of legislation that has to be one of the strangest of all the archaic sex laws, bar none. Under Article 597 of the *Texas Penal Code*, hunting rights were not limited to the outraged husband; the entire family of the wronged woman was deputized. Furthermore, sanctioned retaliation was not limited to cases of adultery. Mere "insulting words or conduct" directed toward a "female relative" entitled any member of the clan to unlimber Old Betsy and dispatch the scoundrel.[6] True, that statute *did* provide that if the scoundrel died, the shooter was guilty of the lesser offense of manslaughter (two to five years) instead of first-degree murder, but by the time frontier defense lawyers got through "interpreting" the law to the jury, it somehow seemed to authorize total exoneration for the insulted defendant.

Texas by no means had a monopoly on the weird or the harsh when it came to the regulation—or perhaps more accurately, the attempted regulation—of human sexual behavior. The legal and moral complexities of sex have pervaded, and bedeviled, every culture and every religion and every system of law throughout time.

In 1889, for instance, the very proper, staid, and esteemed Chief Justice of England, Lord Coleridge, and his panel of appellate jurists descended from their lofty heights of judicial ruminations to review the case of a defendant named Brown who had been convicted of attempting to commit an unnatural act with a "domestic fowl," namely, a duck. The defendant appealed, complaining that he had been convicted of doing something that was physically impossible to do. Lord Coleridge and his fellow jurists expended considerable time and much learned judicial exertion wrestling with this engaging question. In the end, they acted like lawyers: they scuttled this debate by simply ducking the issue. Their Lordships concluded that they really did not have to address the problem of connection after all; it didn't matter whether it was or was not physically possible to do a duck since it was the *attempt*, not the act itself, that was the crux of the crime. The Court's verdict? Guilty, with a sentence of twelve months at hard labor for the amorous Mr. Brown.[7]

In the Brown case, no mention was made of the fate of the put-upon duck. Apparently, the duck got off lucky. However, such was not the case in a much earlier prosecution in the New Jersey colony. In 1692, several children came forward and told officials that they had witnessed the defendant "ride upon a cow" in "the manner of the bull." The jury convicted the defendant of buggery, and the judge then sentenced to death not only the defendant, but also the unfortunate cow.[8] English law was no less lenient when it came to such matters. Sodomy, which was defined to include bestiality as well as homosexual intercourse, had been a capital crime in England since the sixteenth century. Prosecutions increased during the early years of the nineteenth century; in 1806 more men were hanged for sodomy than for murder.[9]

The American colonies also had harsh laws and customs. Public floggings were administered for private masturbation and fornication. In 1664, poor Agnes Taylor was caught fornicating. The County Court in Charles County, Maryland, ordered that she endure twenty lashes "at the whipping post in Public View of the People for having Played the Whore." Men were hanged not only for adultery but also for buggery. It was a crime for a woman to bear a child out of wedlock. In 1702, Delaware sentenced one Hannah Dickens to twenty-one lashes in public for having borne "one bastard male child of her body." On June 10, 1692, Bridget Bishop was hanged in Salem, Massachusetts, after having been convicted of being a witch—the first official execution of the infamous Salem witch trials. Under an 1848 New York law, having "illicit connection with an unmarried female of previously chaste character" earned a man up to five years in the pen.[10]

While Article 1220 of the *Texas Penal Code* authorized a husband to kill his wife's paramour when caught in the act of adultery, the English common law (upon which much of America's jurisprudence is grounded) never went quite that far. Under English common law, the husband in such a case would not be exonerated, but instead would be considered guilty of the lesser offense of manslaughter and not murder.

Even so, William Blackstone, the foremost legal commentator on English law, pointed out that the act of revenge must be spontaneous: "So, if a man takes another in the act of adultery with his wife, and kills him directly upon the spot . . . it is not absolutely ranked in the class of justifiable homicide . . . but it is manslaughter." Blackstone went on to explain that "if there be a sufficient cooling time for passion to subside and reason to interpose, and the person so provoked afterwards kills the other, this is deliberate revenge and not heat of the blood, and accordingly amounts to murder."[11]

Nevertheless, Blackstone further observed that if the killing indeed *had* occurred before the "cooling off" time expired (and therefore was deemed "manslaughter" and not "murder"), this should be considered as the "lowest degree" of manslaughter and therefore a lesser sanction "gently inflicted" would be in order. Blackstone referred to a celebrated 1683 case known as *Maddy's Case*: John Maddy brained Frank Mavers with a stool after surprising him in bed with Mrs. Maddy. He was convicted of manslaughter. However, the judges prescribed the punishment to be the burning of John Maddy's thumb (to indicate that he had used up his share of the king's mercy), but went on to direct the executioner to burn his thumb "gently," since there could not have been a greater provocation than had been suffered by Maddy.[12]

In America, the English common law prevailed, insofar as written statutes were concerned. "Caught-in-the-act-of-adultery" killings were not classified as "justifiable homicide." They were treated as manslaughter cases provided the defendant could convince the jury that the killing was the product of a sudden, passion-driven outrage. At least that was the nineteenth-century written law in all states except two: Texas and Georgia, and the territory of New Mexico. Texas and New Mexico each enacted statutes justifying killings in such circumstances.[13] Such killings were also legally justifiable in Georgia. Although the Georgia Legislature never passed explicit legislation to that effect, the Georgia Supreme Court took it upon itself to exercise some creative judicial activism and reached the same result.[14]

Only Texas, New Mexico, and Georgia had such "justifiable homicide" statutes on the books. Still, until late in the nineteenth century, juries in many other states, including northern and western states, often defied their state's written homicide statutes and acquitted defendants who killed their wives' lovers. More often than not, they did so even though the killings occurred long after any reasonable "cooling off" time had expired.

Toward the end of the nineteenth century and after the cataclysmic social upheavals following the Civil War, attitudes toward marriage, sex, and the rights of women slowly began to change as the traditional patriarchal beliefs came under attack from "feminists," "modernists," and "free love advocates." At least it was so in the North, but not yet in Texas, the southern and the western states. Postbellum Southerners still clung tenaciously to the old values, including the Old South's Code of Chivalry, its Code of Honor, and its Victorian notions of sexuality. Meanwhile, they rejected, resisted, and feared the social revolution taking root in the North with all its permissiveness—notions of free love, the social acceptability of divorce, lightness in women, and the threatened failure of male honor. Southerners viewed this Northern-based social revolution as a direct threat to their traditional concept of the nature of the marriage institution itself, as well as the husband's role as the leader of the family, the protector of his womenfolk, and the rightful owner of proprietary rights in and to all the females in his family.

Nineteenth-century Southerners, including Texans, passed a passel of laws dealing with sexual behavior. Texas and other southern states undertook to criminalize just about every imaginable variety of sexual conduct excepting only marital relations, and then only when it was accomplished in the missionary position, at home, behind locked doors, and in the dark. And every Southern male knew for a fact that lovemaking, after all, was really an outrage inflicted upon reluctant womankind (except, of course, for "that kind of woman") and endured by virtuous ladies only for the purpose of perpetuating the race and quelling those base and lustful urges of husbands who might otherwise kick over the traces and leave the farm unplowed. Ironically, at least in Texas, "that kind of woman" was left free to go about her affairs without risk of running afoul of any criminal law. Until well after the Civil War, prostitution was not a crime in Texas.[15]

Texas law books from the 1880s until after World War I are cluttered with reports of sex prosecutions, headlined by criminal prosecutions for rape, fornication, adultery, seduction, and sodomy. Not only that, but law books were also cluttered with civil litigation cases involving sexual misconduct: damage suits for the breach of a promise to marry, suits filed by a spouse against a third party for the alienation of spousal affection, and divorce actions alleging adultery as a basis therefore. (The very idea of a no-fault divorce would have been, without doubt, inconceivable to a Texan in the 1890s.)

Still, despite all these stringent penal laws on the books threatening dire consequences for all sorts of perceived sexual misconduct, it wasn't enough to satisfy Southerners. When the written law failed to satisfactorily exact the appropriate pound of flesh, resort was made to the unwritten laws that permitted the killing—or at least the maiming—

of almost anyone who somehow or another, by actual physical contact or inappropriate verbal comment, offended the Southerner's notion of female virtue and male honor or somehow threatened their marriages.

Illicit sex figures in all of the upcoming stories of Texas murder trials. (Actually, one turned out to be an attempted murder trial since the victim, although shot four times, had the audacity to survive.) In each tale, the victim—at least in the perception of the shooter—had committed some type of sexual misconduct. In each case, the pistol wielder opened fire on the victim with premeditated intent to kill. In each case, the victim was unarmed when shot. In two of the stories, innocent bystanders were killed when caught in the midst of the revenge-fueled fusillade. In each of the resulting trials, the defense relied, at least in part, on the unwritten law to excuse the attacker's resort to self-help justice.[16]

The honor code, the basis of the unwritten law, is commonly associated with the Old South. But it was by no means limited to the southern states. Until late in the nineteenth century, Victorian America's thirst for the blood of the libertine usually resulted—one way or another—in the granting of a free pass to the slayers of libertines. It appears that the first American murder trial in which "the higher law," insofar as it applied to the killing of a seducer, was skillfully articulated was the sensational 1859 murder trial of Daniel Sickles. Sickles was a congressman from New York City who was residing in a mansion in Washington, D.C., when he learned that his wife, Teresa, had been having an affair with U.S. District Attorney Philip Barton Key[17] and that it had been going on for nearly a year. Sickles set up a vigil, and from a front window of his home he observed Key signaling his wife to meet for still another clandestine rendezvous. Sickles raced out the front door and gunned down Key on a public street near Lafayette Park and the White House. Sickles hired an immensely talented team of lawyers, who proceeded to articulate a definitive statement of "the higher law" as it applied to libertines and thus won an acquittal for their client.[18]

One commentator on the Sickles case noted that it did more than any other case to formulate the basic tenets of the unwritten law. Divine law and historical tradition, it was contended, constituted a major part

of the foundation for the unwritten law, and avengers of sexual dishonor were only agents of God acting as "divine functionaries applying
natural principles which could not be altered by human law."[19]

The Sickles trial advanced another tenet, which held that women
were physically and morally weak, in need of the constant and vigilant
protection of their menfolk. One defense attorney in the Sickles trial
declared that "frailty, thy name is woman," and thus informed the jury
that because a woman could not "resist herself and others," God had
placed her "under the protection of man." Moreover, there was only one
way for a cuckolded husband to redeem his honor: private vengeance—
death to the libertine! When informed that Teresa Sickles's adultery
was public knowledge, one of his advisers told the distraught husband
that "there is but one course left for you as a man of honor."[20]

On the other hand, a fallen woman's honor was not a priority of
the unwritten law, and a debauched woman—whether debauched vol-
untarily or involuntarily—was irredeemably disgraced and unfit for
consideration as a marriage partner by any respectable gentleman.

Although the unwritten law was the basis for defense arguments
in such cases in the northern states until late in the nineteenth century,
it was advocated thereafter primarily in the Old South as a part of its
"Code of Honor." But the southern states did not have a monopoly on
its advocacy. Until well after the turn of the century, lawyers in Texas
and other western states continued to invoke *lex non scripta*.[21] The heavy
migration of Southerners to Texas and the western states both before
and after the Civil War doubtless accounted for this cultural export.[22]
The South's Code of Honor owed much to England's Victorian stereotypes of male dominance in the family, strict differentiation of sex roles,
separate standards of morality for males and females, female coldness in
marriage, and a reluctance to speak of sex. All that coupled with chivalrous notions of the gallant knights in shining armor protecting refined
and defenseless ladies who seemed inclined to faint upon the slightest
of provocations—not to mention excessive prudery. The unwritten law
was constructed on, and nourished by, such stereotypes and notions.

In the presence of juries, defense attorneys carefully avoided speaking the words "the unwritten law," typically referring to it by some
code phrase such as "protecting the home." (Although used in a very
different context, Oscar Wilde's famous phrase, "love that dare not

speak its name," comes to mind.) But jurors of that day knew well what "protecting the home" really meant and realized that the defense attorney was appealing to them to ignore the Texas statutory law, as well as the court's instructions, and thus exonerate his client on the basis of "higher authority."

Such was not always the case. One day in 1896, at a crowded railway station in Texarkana, John Hallum shot an unarmed preacher four times for having an affair with his wife. At his trial, Hallum never denied that he shot the preacher. He didn't deny that he intended to kill him; he didn't beg for mercy, either. He told the jury this: "I shot the baseborn libertine with all the coolness and premeditated deliberation that it is possible for a rational mind to conceive." In his final jury argument, Hallum, who represented himself, urged the jury to ignore those "puny mandates" enacted by the Texas Legislature: "Gentlemen, this case is governed by the higher law; you will render a verdict of not guilty."[23]

However, defense attorneys in the other cases recounted here were more circumspect when they appealed for acquittals by virtue of the unwritten law. Usually, although the unwritten law was their *real* defense, these lawyers would at least make some perfunctory nod in the direction of a statutory justification for the killing—more often than not a strained attempt to claim self-defense even when it turned out that the victim had been unarmed. (The defendant usually took the stand and testified that he *thought* the victim had been armed, and that he *thought* the victim was about to pull that nonexistent weapon on him just before he opened fire.)

It is interesting to note that while all the defendants in the stories relied on the unwritten law, none invoked the Article 1220 statutory defense: "I shot him when I caught him in bed with my wife." The unwritten law as recognized in Texas and the Old South was much broader in scope than either the exonerating Article 1220 defense or the mitigating Article 597 on self-defense discussed above. The honor defense afforded total justification to any male who killed another— even when the victim was unarmed—in cases where the deceased had insulted the defendant's honor or in cases where the deceased had, allegedly at least, compromised the virtue of any of the womenfolk in the shooter's extended family either by rape, adultery, seduction, or "slander against their chastity." As far as public opinion was concerned, only one punishment would do when the virtue of a female relative was concerned: violent personal retribution.

In 1897, a Mr. Kimes of West Virginia shot a Mr. Hail three times for "alienating the affections" of Kimes's wife. Kimes was tried, found guilty of the shooting, sentenced to twenty-four hours in jail, and assessed a nominal fine. But he never served a day or paid a dollar of it. The West Virginia governor immediately pardoned him, saying: "I remit his fine and costs with more pleasure than any word the English language can furnish me to express. My only regret is that Kimes did not kill Hail. He ought to have done so."[24] In 1893, a Mr. Mehan shot and killed a man for insulting his pregnant wife. It took an Atlanta jury less than seven minutes to acquit him. The local newspaper applauded the verdict, noting that it was a popular one with the people, and concluded that "any man less than a saint would have done as Mehan did."[25]

Few Southern men or Texans would have been satisfied with any legal settlement of such wrongs. Mere jingle in the pocket would never salve "the hurt that honor feels."[26] That attitude was illustrated by an incident that occurred when future president Andrew Jackson was a young boy. An older and larger boy gave him a painful whipping. One of the Jackson family wanted to file assault charges, but Jackson's mother forbade it. Wait until Andrew grows up, she counseled, and then let him thrash the culprit, adding: "To go to the law for redress is to confess publicly that you have been wronged, and the demonstration of your vulnerability places your honor in jeopardy. . . . The law affords no remedy that can satisfy the feelings of a true man."[27] The unwritten law corollary to that was, of course, when a man did take the law into his own hands to vindicate an insult to his honor and the matter was placed before a jury, the result would be predictable—and favorable to the defendant.[28] Legalism and "honor" were not compatible, and when Southern juries were presented with that choice, the latter generally prevailed.

As the above-cited Andrew Jackson anecdote evidences, the unwritten law was a Mother Hubbard skirt that covered more than sexually related improprieties. Any act or word interpreted as an attack on one's honor nearly always triggered a violent, and permissible, reaction. In its heyday, the jurisprudence of the unwritten law almost assumed the dignity and symmetry of a legal system. Neither legislative nor judge-made, it amounted to a system of jury-made lawlessness which recognized rights that were forbidden by law and denied rights that were granted by law. Since it was in flagrant violation of man-made statutes, its advocates often referred to it as "The Law Above the Statutes," or "The Higher Law." Its basic foundation rested on public opinion approval in the communities where it prevailed.

In a 1906 address to the American Bar Association, a distinguished jurist, Judge Thomas J. Kernon of Baton Rouge, undertook an onerous and ground-breaking task: he attempted to reduce the "unwritten laws" to writing; to-wit:

LAW I.

Any man who commits rape upon a woman of chaste character shall, without trial or hearing of any kind, be instantly put to death by his captors or other body of respectable citizens, not less than three in number; and they shall have the right to determine the mode of execution, which may be both cruel and unusual, the Constitution and laws of the State and of the United States to the contrary notwithstanding.

LAW II.

Any man who commits adultery may be put to death with impunity by the injured husband, who shall have the right to determine the mode of execution, be it ever so cowardly.

LAW III.

Any man who seduces an innocent girl may, without a hearing, be shot or stabbed to death by her, or any near relative of hers; and, if deemed necessary by the slayer, such shooting or stabbing may be done in the back, or while lying in wait.

LAW IV.

Any man who traduces a virtuous woman's character for chastity may be shot with impunity by her, or her husband, or any near relative; but the offender must first be given an opportunity to deny and disprove the charge, or to retract and apologize.

LAW V.

The survivor of a fatal duel must be acquitted, if the duel was fairly conducted according to the time-honored provisions of the Code of Honor.

LAW VI.

Any man who kills another in a fair fight shall not be found guilty, either of murder or manslaughter, but must be acquitted, even though he is the sole aggressor.

LAW VII.

There lie direct and certain other well-known opprobrious epithets, which constitute mortal insult, are each equal to blow, and any of them justifies an assault.[29]

While Judge Kernon's attempt to codify the unwritten laws was a noble undertaking and does succeed in capturing the fundamental tenets, it is far from comprehensive. As we shall see from some of the upcoming stories, clever pioneer defense lawyers often stretched the boundaries of Judge Kernon's code to accommodate a variety of factual situations.

It is a common assumption that the unwritten law was available only to male defendants who took the law into their own hands. Yet, in two of the tales to come, the killers were outraged women, and in both of their murder trials skillful defense attorneys took full advantage of the unwritten law.[30] Texas was not the only venue where women turned the tables and invoked the unwritten law. In an 1899 California case, Mrs. Katie Cook admitted she shot her husband through the brain while he slept. She had just had enough, she explained to the jury. Mr. Cook had been a serial philanderer, parading a series of his young girlfriends through their home and even forcing her to watch while he "accomplished their ruin." On one occasion he even forced "another young girl and her to sit and listen to the reading of page after page of the vilest poetry known to the tenderloin district." And her attorney's closing argument wherein he painted a portrait of the "depravity of the murdered man . . . while the misery of the trusting wife [was] pathetic," drew "deafening applause" from the courtroom spectators—and a "not guilty" verdict from the jury.[31]

An 1893 Nebraska murder case was similar. Eloise Rudiger, a married woman, was seduced by one Henry Reiser, "the Baron" of South Omaha. Thereafter he abused her, beat her several times, and then he spurned her. That did it. The livid Eloise marched down to the local gun shop and bought an American Bulldog .38 revolver. Later that same day she encountered "the Baron" on a nearby street corner. She drew the revolver and shot him three times. Her husband soon appeared at the scene, whereupon Eloise exclaimed, "I have killed him, killed him, and you should have done it." The jury must have agreed; they found her not guilty.[32]

By far the most sensational case, however, was the 1870 California murder trial of Laura D. Fair. She was the mistress of a prominent San Francisco lawyer, A. P. Crittenden. For several years they had conducted a relatively open affair during which time he repeatedly promised to divorce his wife and marry her. But he always reneged. Finally Laura had had enough. On May 3, 1870, while Crittenden and his wife and two of their children were crossing the San Francisco Bay on a ferryboat and in the presence of several eyewitnesses, Laura approached, pulled a pistol, and shot her lover dead, exclaiming: "You have ruined me and my child." They tried Laura in San Francisco while all the area newspapers, wailing like a Greek chorus in the background, clamored for the blood of the wanton slayer of their esteemed favorite son. A jury convicted her, and she was sentenced to hang. But the conviction was reversed on appeal. Upon a retrial, Laura's attorneys, with the courtroom support of a lively contingent of suffragettes, vigorously contended that Laura was innocent since, at the time she pulled the trigger, she was suffering from "temporary partial moral insanity" brought on by "delayed menstruation." It worked. Not guilty.[33]

With only minor back-peddling, the following accounts of killings and murder trials are told in chronological order beginning in the 1890s and progressing through the 1920s. (The final story, which is a sequel to the preceding one, recounts Texas murder trials in the 1970s and 1980s.)

The stories, when taken together, evidence the waning influence of the Old South's unwritten law over the years as Texas and American culture and values evolved and matured, especially following World War I. However, the last story does suggest that even in the 1970s, vestiges of the unwritten law remained, though moribund—still not totally lifeless in far West Texas.

The imaginative and Herculean struggles of the articulate defense lawyers to extricate their obviously guilty clients from the gallows, when there appeared to be no legal basis upon which to peg a defense, is perhaps the most fascinating narrative appeal to these stories. Typically they outmaneuvered prosecutors who railed at jurors to follow the statutory law, and they frequently overpowered or simply ignored judges who attempted, with only limited success, to rein in their excesses. Those early-day lawyers might have been somewhat shy on logic, reason, facts, and the law (statutory law, that is); but they were mighty long and loud and strong on bombast, hyperbole, declamations, biblical quotes, florid orations that went on and on, and emotional appeals crafted to take full advantage of the popular beliefs, biases, fears, and sexual mores of the jurors they faced. Their remarkable courtroom triumphs, and the underlying winning strategies, are fascinating to lawyer, historian, and lay person alike, view it as one may from a legal, historical, sociological, or psychological perspective.

ONE

John Hallum Tried for Shooting a Preacher
DEFENDS HIMSELF IN AN IRATE COMMUNITY

"Do not as some ungracious pastors do,
Show me the steep and thorny way to heaven,
Whilst, like a puff'd and reckless libertine,
Himself the primrose path of dalliance treads."
WILLIAM SHAKESPEARE, *Hamlet*, Act I, Scene Three

At 8:05 on the morning of July 29, 1896, the Cotton Belt Express rolled into the crowded railroad station at Texarkana, Texas. The Reverend W. A. Forbes alighted and started ascending the platform steps. John W. Hallum, a sixty-three-year-old Confederate veteran, was waiting for him. Right there, in front of God and everybody, Colonel Hallum shot the unsuspecting and unarmed preacher five times (well, *four* times, the fifth shot having gone wild), and left him lying there for dead. It sure seemed like three bullet slugs in the neck and one in the left side should have done the trick. But, whether due to sheer cussedness on the preacher's part or intervention on God's part, or both, the preacher simply refused to cooperate and expire.[1] At least that saved John Hallum from facing a

murder charge. Still, he was a long way from being out of the woods—
an indictment for assault with intent to murder was soon returned
against him.

John W. Hallum was born on January 16, 1833, in Sumner County,
Tennessee, the oldest of eleven children born to Bluford Hallum, a
gunsmith and farmer, and his wife, Minerva Davis Hallum. While he
was still a toddler, his parents moved to a farm near Memphis, where he
spent his early childhood. Formal schooling opportunities were meager
at best, and John spent only a few months each year in a one-room log
schoolhouse where he was taught by "indifferent teachers with meth-
ods that were as primitive as the building."[2] Yet John Hallum was a
child prodigy, and even before he ever saw the inside of a schoolroom,
he had taught himself to read by poring over old copies of the *Memphis
Appeal* newspaper. When he started to school at age six, he was thus
able to read all of the grammar school books as well as to spell every
word in *Webster's Spelling Book*. By virtue of constant home study,
coupled with a voracious appetite for classical literature, he qualified
himself to enter a local community college at age fifteen. To support
himself and pay for his college expenses, Hallum raised tobacco on a
three-acre tract his father cleared for him out of the family farm. Two
years later he landed a job as principal of an academy near Memphis.
While teaching, he spent every spare hour in diligent study of the law,
and without ever having set foot in a law school, he passed the Tennessee bar examination at age twenty-one and received his law license
on May 15, 1854.

John Hallum was an immediate success as a practicing lawyer.
Among his early clients was Texas hero, and later Texas governor,
Sam Houston, who hired Hallum to investigate some land titles for his
brother's widow living in Memphis. Hallum's law practice was interrupted by the outbreak of the Civil War. Although Hallum strongly
opposed secession and recognized the disaster that was likely to result,
he echoed Robert E. Lee's belief that "patriotism has its qualifications
and limitations."[3] He simply couldn't bring himself to take up arms
against his fellow Southerners. He wrote: "I love the Union, but I love
the South and her people more, and am willing to share her fortunes,

misguided though she be in precipitating this conflict before exhausting constitutional remedies."[4]

Accordingly, when war came, he closed his law office and joined the Confederate army as a lieutenant. Two years later he was discharged on account of a disability from protracted illness. But the outspoken John Hallum, even though now a civilian, soon found himself in trouble with the Union military government that occupied Tennessee. For publishing scathing criticisms of "corrupt practices" by the military authorities, he soon found himself—without formal charges, without a hearing, and without a trial—incarcerated in a filthy and disease-infested Fort Pickering blockhouse without proper nourishment or medical treatment.

After the Civil War, Hallum moved to St. Louis and began practicing law in 1870. Then, bitten by wanderlust and intrigued by the new opportunities opening up in the untamed West, he moved to Trinidad, Colorado, and opened a law office in 1874. However, by 1876 his ties to the Southland and its people, its customs, and its way of life became too strong to resist, and he moved back to Arkansas, where he lived for the rest of his life, living and practicing law in Little Rock, Lonoke, Fort Smith, and Texarkana.

It was while Colonel Hallum and his wife were living in Lonoke, Arkansas, that their paths first crossed with Reverend W. A. Forbes.[5] They were communicants in his church in Lonoke for two years and afterward for four years at Texarkana. (Texarkana straddles the Texas-Arkansas boundary; part of the town is situated in Arkansas and part in Texas.) During that time Forbes was a frequent and welcome guest in the Hallum home, even when Colonel Hallum's law practice took him out of town. Colonel Hallum trusted his pastor and his wife; he never suspected any impropriety nor doubted the purity of his minister's intentions until the spring of 1895.

During that spring, the Colonel had been on an extended business trip to Nashville, Tennessee. His financial situation had become precarious, meanwhile, and a judgment lien had been taken on his home in Texarkana. While still in Nashville, his wife notified him that Brother Forbes had generously offered to advance $680 to pay off the mortgage on their home. Forbes was willing to come to the rescue of his dear friends and parishioners. But of course it was only proper that Colonel

John Hallum and his soon-to-be-unfaithful wife. (Public domain.)

Hallum and wife give Forbes a mortgage on their home and also convey to the reverend an additional six hundred acres of nearby land to secure repayment of the $680. Later, with the connivance of his wife, Colonel Hallum was duped into giving the preacher an absolute deed to his home.

When the Colonel began hearing reports from Texarkana that the preacher was paying frequent and extended visits to his home, and was going about Texarkana bragging that he had more influence with the colonel's wife than the colonel did, the Colonel finally made the obvious deduction. Colonel Hallum filed a suit on behalf of himself and his wife to regain title and possession to his property, but his wife refused to give any supporting evidence or in any other way aid in the prosecution of the suit, thus confirming his suspicions that illicit relations existed between Mrs. Hallum and her pastor.

It was at that point that Colonel Hallum sent word to Reverend Forbes that he would kill him on sight. Then he filed for a divorce from his unfaithful wife. Meanwhile, Forbes, who then lived about eighty miles from Texarkana, kept making extended visits to that city without, apparently, having any legitimate business there. However, later disclosures would prove that the preacher did, in fact, have a business interest at that time in Texarkana. But just how "legitimate" was that business interest? That issue would soon be addressed. Meanwhile, preacher Forbes obviously did not take John Hallum's threat seriously.

Although Hallum had reasons aplenty to be justly enraged at the preacher, those reasons were not generally known to the public. It was a sure bet, however, that when, during the trial, the jury did eventually learn about the preacher's scandalous behavior, such testimony was bound to elicit a wave of sympathy for Colonel Hallum. However, the preacher's sins, outrageous as they were, would only amount to "extenuating circumstances," explaining Hallum's rage and why he did what he did. But neither then nor now were extenuating circumstances or mitigating facts alone sufficient to get a defendant all the way to home plate. At least not if the game was played by the statutory rule book. For instance, in a murder case if the jury believed that "extenuating circumstances" (as defined by law) existed, then it might well result in the jury convicting the defendant of a "lesser included offense" such as manslaughter instead of convicting him of first degree murder; or it might serve to inspire a jury to greatly reduce the punishment to be assessed. But such was not, in and of itself, a "get-out-of-jail-free" card under Texas law. No legal open hunting season on human beings existed in Texas even if the target was an unrepentant scoundrel— unless, of course, some judgmental husband happened to catch a libertine between the sheets with his wife. However, that statutory loophole didn't exculpate a brazen ambush at a crowded train station.

The provable facts surrounding the incident did not look favorable from a defense standpoint. The prosecution would have no trouble proving that John Hallum launched the attack without any immediate prior provocation. There were so many eyewitnesses that the district attorney would have to stand them in line to testify. Plus, John Hallum never denied that he shot the preacher or that he intended to kill him. Furthermore, there was abundant proof of malice aforethought. Hallum had not only made prior threats to kill the preacher, but there was also evidence that Forbes had been lured into the Texarkana depot ambush. In reporting the shooting incident, the next day's edition of the *Dallas Morning News* had this to say: "After the shooting, Forbes exhibited a letter signed by a man named Smith, asking [Forbes] to come to Texarkana from New Lewisville [Arkansas], where he was holding a revival, to perform a marriage ceremony."[6]

Hallum himself later admitted that this was, in fact, a "decoy letter." To make matters even worse, the preacher was a well-known and popular religious leader. The *Dallas Morning News* observed that "the Rev. Dr. W. A. Forbes [is] a leading light in the Baptist church."[7] The truth of that observation was validated within a few days after the shooting. Fomented by the religious followers of the wounded preacher, a lynch mob began to form. "Hell was in the air," Hallum later recalled. While he was still under arrest to face the criminal charges, the mob threatened to seize him. Heavily armed officers resisted and even supplied Hallum himself with a double-barrel shotgun and twenty rounds of "blue whistlers." Although the lynch mob was rebuffed, Forbes's congregation clamored for revenge. Hallum recalled: "Those good Christians . . . appointed a committee to intercede with people to prevent my giving bond, and they put a corps of little Baptist preachers in the field, who preached hell and damnation and my funeral in every nook and corner of Bowie County, to prejudice the people and make it impossible for me to get an impartial jury."

Soon the local press joined the crusade, and between the pulpit and the press, local sentiment turned so bitterly against Hallum that the local bar capitulated. No lawyer in the area would agree to defend Hallum, and the local judge refused Hallum's request to change the venue to an impartial site. Hallum was left to defend himself in a most hostile environment. A time-honored dictum in the legal community has it that a lawyer who undertakes to represent himself has a fool for a client. As Hallum's trial plan began to unfold, his strategy seemed doomed to prove the wisdom of that old saw. Although the undisputed facts of the case and the plain language of the applicable Texas law were clearly against him, there still was an extralegal loophole for John Hallum—if he played his hand right. That extralegal loophole being, of course, the terms of the unwritten law that had set free many a man who had killed his wife's lover.

However, to claim the benefit of the unwritten law, the skilled defense attorney of that time never invoked it by name in front of the jury. It was just the 800-pound gorilla in the middle of the room whose presence was never acknowledged, at least not explicitly acknowledged. At best, it was referred to by some code name such as "protecting the sanctity of the home," and then the facts were misrepresented, skewed, or tortured, squeezing them into some statutory mold—statutory self-defense most often. Typically, even when the victim was unarmed and shot down in front of unbiased eyewitnesses, the defendant would climb on the stand and tell the jury that he heard the victim had been threatening his life and that when they met on that fatal occasion he saw the victim make some "suspicious movement," which he interpreted as an attempt to reach for a weapon and carry out those threats, and so to save his own life, he had to shoot first. The fact that none of the unbiased eyewitnesses noticed the victim make any such "suspicious movement" didn't matter. The unwritten law usually triumphed. It almost always did if it could also be shown, or even hinted, that the deceased had committed some illicit sexual act with—or simply uttered insulting words directed toward—the defendant's wife, mother, sister, aunt, or any other female relative.

Undoubtedly, that was the tactic that the courthouse railbirds expected John Hallum to employ when his "assault with intent to murder" case was called for trial by the Bowie County District Court on March 9, 1897, in Boston, Texas.[8] (Boston, although smaller than Texarkana, was the county seat of Bowie County because it was located near the center of the county.)

If that was what the courtroom railbirds expected—and surely they did—they were in for a big surprise. Colonel Hallum, supremely confident of the righteousness of his cause and the correctness of his actions, rested his case squarely on the unwritten law. No cute code words for him; no painful struggle to make a square peg of fact fit into a round statutory hole. He didn't claim that Preacher Forbes had threatened his life. He didn't claim that he thought Forbes was armed. He didn't even claim that he saw Forbes make some "suspiciously threatening movement" just before he drew his pistol and shot him. On the contrary, he admitted he went to the railroad depot that day intending to kill Forbes and then did his best to accomplish that purpose. His only regret was that he hadn't succeeded.

Meanwhile, the Colonel sat back and let the prosecution parade as many eyewitnesses to the depot ambush as it cared to before the jury. He didn't bother to cross-examine any of them, and he didn't contradict any part of their testimony when he eventually testified. However, when the State called the Reverend Forbes to the stand, the Colonel bestirred himself and began taking notes. Forbes, of course, denied having committed adultery with Mrs. Hallum—or anybody else. To explain the purpose of his frequent trips to Texarkana while Colonel Hallum was in Arkansas taking care of legitimate business, preacher Forbes told the jury that he had rented a house in Texarkana during this period—for a completely legitimate purpose, of course. He rented it, he contended, for the benefit of a widow and her *three little children*. This, he claimed, he did as a charity for the widow and her brood, as well as to provide an "auxiliary to the ladies' aid society."

Colonel Hallum cross-examined the preacher very thoroughly about every detail, every event, and every person involved in this supposedly charitable undertaking, thus laying the groundwork for yet another ambush of the preacher, albeit a verbal ambush this time. It was obvious that Colonel Hallum had done his homework.

Later, in rebuttal, he called to the witness stand a Mrs. Howell, who just happened to be a relative of the local sheriff. She was also the owner of the house that Forbes had rented for supposedly charitable purposes. Mrs. Howell had quite a tale to tell about that "charity." When she finished telling her story, the Reverend Forbes's "ladies' aid auxiliary" sounded mighty like a good old-fashioned whorehouse. It turned out that the widow lady's "three little children" were all females, ages sixteen, eighteen, and twenty years. (Just whose children they really were was a question that went unanswered.) Mrs. Howell testified that those "little children" were actually "notoriously lewd women," and when she found out what kind of monkey business was really going on in her rent house, she set about trying to oust Minister Forbes from her

SEX, MURDER, AND THE UNWRITTEN LAW

premises. But the reverend did not go gently. Only after "much trouble and harsh words" with Forbes, who "obstinately persisted in protecting these lewd women," did she succeed in evicting his holiness and his subtenants. The prosecutors wisely, it may well be surmised, declined to recall the Reverend Forbes back to the stand to challenge Mrs. Howell's observations and conclusions.

When the State finally rested its case, Colonel Hallum took the stand and gave the jury "the rest of the story." He told all about the adulterous adventures of his wife and the parson and how they had also swindled him out of his house and land.

Nevertheless, everything that had transpired in the trial before the jury arguments amounted to no more than a few parsley trimmings around the edges of the Thanksgiving turkey. And what a feast that main course was! Some years after the fact, the Colonel had his jury argument printed in a pamphlet. Actually it made a fairly good-sized book, forty-six pages in all, with a wonderfully grand title: "Address to the Jury. Col. John Hallum In Self Defense in the case of the State of Texas Against Him: An Indictment For Shooting A Minister of the Gospel, Together with Extraordinary Facts and Remarkable Incidents Connected With the Trial and Prosecution."[9] With that kind of title, who needed a table of contents?[10]

The oratorical tour de force that the Bowie County jury was about to hear would later be heralded as a classic exposition of *lex non scripta*, the unwritten law, and it certainly captured the spirit of that time and place and described Southern culture in the 1890s. It was like no other jury oration, before or after. To begin with, has any other jury, ever, heard a defendant who was seeking exoneration make any statement like this: "I had resolved with unalterable purpose to kill him, and the fact that I had so stated was communicated to him. I had often visited the depots and places where I expected to find him"?

But that was only a warm-up. Colonel Hallum kicked it into over-drive and in tones of self-righteous indignation thundered:

I would have shot the base born libertine if the angels of heaven had been guarding him when I got within gunshot of him, and I would have camped on his trail a thousand years, if . . . it had required that time to come up with him. And let me say further that I shot him with

all the coolness and premeditated deliberation that it is possible for a
rational mind to conceive. . . . I would repeat the same remedy a thousand times in defiance of all the penal statutes of the world. There are
some things in which I fix my own standards, and this is one of them.
The remedy I applied is certainly more effectual than sacramental wine
or catnip tea.

Nor was the Colonel mealy-mouthed in describing the character of
his target, that "knavish, psalm-singing hypocrite": "I defy and challenge all the records of mankind, all the horrid imps of Dante's Inferno,
and all the records of hell to produce a meaner man than W. A. Forbes.
Down, and downward, forever hellward, the trend of his degradation."
(Oh my, what any modern prosecutor wouldn't give just to hear a
defendant volunteer that priceless gem of candor to a jury!)

During his protracted oratorical triumph, the Colonel, whenever
he had occasion to refer to the preacher or his lynch-minded supporters, soared to heights of hyperbole previously uncharted. In addition
to the above-quoted references ("knavish, psalm-singing hypocrite,"
and "base-born libertine"), he nailed the preacher and his mob with
these choice epithets: "Judas Iscariot in clerical robes," "hero of the
hypocrites," "monster of depravity," "junto of howling dervishes,"
"sanctimonious herd of ghouls," "junto of whoring church hypocrites,"
"polluted priest," "hypocritical corporation of priests and laymen," and
"close corporation of bigots."

The Colonel, on a roll now, wasn't about to cut any slack to anybody
sympathizing with the preacher, including the prosecuting attorney
and the State's witnesses. He proceeded to dismiss prosecution witnesses as "blockheads," and "monsters," and "vultures who disguise
themselves with the plumage of the birds of paradise and sit in judgment of men who are infinitely their superiors." His verbal assault on
the prosecutor was particularly vitriolic, once dismissing him as the
"little howling evolute in our midst." Later he denounced the prosecutor for his employment of the "arts of sophistry and devices of dema-
gogues," and told the jury that the district attorney "and all that class of
hypocrites he represents are like dead bodies thrown into the Ganges,
which rise as they rot and float on the surface, an object of contagion
and contamination."

Having, to his satisfaction, put his adversaries in their place, the Colonel then turned to his patriotic heritage, linking himself (through "gallant and chivalric" family members) to the founding fathers of the Republic of Texas, including those who stood with Sam Houston at the battle of San Jacinto.

Next, the Colonel underscored the enormity of Reverend Forbes's crime:

> If there is one crime transcending all others in enormity, it is that of the clergyman . . . leading a . . . wife and mother down to a rayless night and an endless hell . . . for when the wife yields to the primrose dalliances of Judas Iscariot in clerical robes and consents to become the faded refuse of a violated bed, nothing is left . . . but a wilderness of rayless and hopeless sorrow.

Murder, arson, robbery, and all other crimes are less serious than adultery, the Colonel pointed out, since the perpetrator in all those other crimes still left his victims with their virtue intact: better dead than degraded.

The Colonel then settled into the real task at hand: to prove up the case for the "unwritten law" and its supremacy over statutes concocted by mere mortals. Here he gave a truly amazing performance of epic proportions, demonstrating most impressive elocutive skills and an extraordinary command of the English language, plus much more than a nodding acquaintance with the Bible, world history, and classical literature—all of which he proceeded to expound upon at length. Among the many authorities cited, he named Jesus, Moses, Abraham, King David, and many other biblical heroes of the Old Testament as well as Shakespeare, Dante, Homer, and other literary giants. He also managed somehow to fit Attila the Hun and Mohammed into his mosaic of authorities. The Colonel took the jury on a long historical journey outlining the history of the world from the dawn of civilization, omitting very few nations or tribes of any significance. If his sources and authorities, as well as his interpretations of history, were somewhat skewed to suit his purpose and his logic was a tad flawed here and there, nevertheless his oration constituted a dramatic masterpiece, and certainly one tailored to fit the audience of the twelve chivalrous Southerners to whom it was addressed.

He began with classical literature. Shakespeare was the Colonel's heavy hitter, although now and then he took considerable liberties in improving the bard's verses to suit his purposes:

> As Brutus said to Cassius, "I would rather be a dog and bay at the moon," than live with a woman who would thus desecrate and soil the consecrated joys of home.

> As Othello . . . said . . . "I'd rather be a toad and feed on the vapors of a dungeon" than keep a wife for another man's use.

> Poor Ophelia, in the great tragedy of Hamlet, said "do not as some ungracious pastors do, show me the steep and thorny way to heaven, while he, a puffed and reckless libertine, himself the primrose path of dalliance treads."

Then he turned to the Bible. Here the Colonel proved himself to be quite a scholar, although his biblical scholarship seems to have exhausted itself with the last word in the Old Testament—none of that mushy New Testament "forgiveness" stuff for him. Colonel Hallum instructed:

> I am trying to aid you to a thorough insight to the comprehensive greatness and designs of the Creator in arming his children with divine authority to slay the destroyer of family ties . . . the blood of the libertine drips from the family tree of the Savior. . . .

> You may be surprised when I tell you that strategy, both to prevent and to punish with death the crimes of the libertine, comes to us with divine sanction, and was often practiced by those who are conspicuous in the lineage of the Savior.

Colonel Hallum then gave a number of examples, all peopled with Old Testament heroes, the best of which was the wholesale vengeance rained down upon "the dominions of the Prince of Hamor" by the two sons of Jacob. Colonel Hallum related the story of how Jacob's daughter, Dinah, was defiled by Prince Hamor's son, and when Dinah's two brothers discovered it, they took up the sword and "smote to death . . .

the seducer and his retinue of abettors . . . and burned the city." When Jacob expressed fear of retaliation by Hamor's tribe, the two sons rebuked their father. Colonel Hallum commented:

> The reply of the noble sons has come sounding down the corridors
> of time, emblazoned in the tragic heraldry which gave the Savior to
> mankind. "Shall he deal with our sister as with a harlot?" That was all.
> It was enough. From that tree of life drips the blood of the libertine.
> Long may their example animate the generous and chivalrous sons of
> my native soil.

It got better when the Colonel reached the part about Moses ascending to the "flaming clouds around the summit of Mount Sinai" to receive the Ten Commandments. The Colonel seemed to have overlooked that part about the "Thou Shalt Not Kill," but he latched onto the "No Adultery" part with a vengeance—except his version of the wording of that commandment differed somewhat from the King James version of the Bible. The Colonel's version went like this:

> God wrote with his own finger on the tablets of stone a commission
> to all the children of man to destroy the libertine priest who enters the
> household and uproots hallowed family ties and associations.

Having concluded his literary and biblical dissertations, the Colonel then turned to the history of the world—more specifically, the rise and fall of every significant tribe of mankind. The Colonel undertook to prove thereby that the fall of each and every tribe could be traced to one root cause: an increasing laxity in that society's vigilance in protecting the virtue, chastity, and purity of its women. Argued the Colonel: "I will contrast those peoples and nations who hold in the highest esteem the virtue of their women with those peoples who have tolerated either a laxity or a want of virtue in their women."

The Colonel then claimed that in all ascending societies, a "higher type of man" had been primarily responsible for its elevation—a "higher type of man" who was primarily concerned with protecting the virtue of women.

Look over the vast landscape of human history in every age and development of man, and wherever you find him ["the higher type of man"]
treading the highways of greatness . . . you will find that . . . at any sacrifice [he] will protect the virtue of women. . . . These primal elements in
all the higher types of men luminously mark the upward and downward
trends of nations.

. . . [A]ll the higher types of man . . . will [maintain the integrity of the
home] as long as they can pull a trigger or drive a dagger into the heart
of a libertine. Yes, they will do it in defiance of all the puny mandates
of man, as long as rivers flow to the sea and until the ocean heaves her
last billow to the storm.

Of course, "Exhibit A" on the Colonel's list of great nations that
failed was the Roman Empire. The fortunes of the empire ascended,
Colonel Hallum contended, as long as "its foundation was planted in
the enduring chastity of its women." However: "courage and patriotism
in the men declined in a ratio with the loss of virtue in their women,
until the great and powerful Rome . . . crumbled into one vast chaotic
mass of ruin."

Having finally completed his world tour, Colonel Hallum returned
to the shores of his native Southland, the cradle of Old South chivalry—and the home of all twelve jurors.

You have made the solemn proclamation to your wife, and all wives and
mothers and daughters and sisters of this great Southland, that the successful arts of the seducer of their virtue, the destroyer of happy homes
and families should themselves be destroyed. . . .

[O]ur native Southland, laboring yet under the accumulated misfor-
tunes of a long and terrible civil war; borne down as it is by the accumulated evils engendered by such a conflict is yet the home of a nobler
sentiment in the nursery of chivalrous devotion to their women and
the rights of man.

Generously, the Colonel then broadened his scope to include the
rest of America, contending that threats to the "sanctity of the home"

were the underlying rallying cry of the Revolutionary War. Colonel Hallum claimed that the motto, "a man's home is his castle," was proudly displayed from the masthead of the Mayflower.

Finally winding down, the Colonel confided in the jury the fact that time was running short for him; that all this struggle was not about him. It was all about the honor of his progeny:

> I am left in advanced age with but one dominant desire on earth—the honor of my children and lineage. The future holds nothing in store for me this side of the dark river. I'm this hour fighting my last battle for more than an empire is worth.[11]

Yet, the Colonel, upon further reflection, realized that his heroic struggles for justice extended far beyond himself and his progeny—in fact, he reflected, the fate of society itself hinged on the outcome of this noble battle, a familiar refrain that has been heard over and over down through subsequent decades and that is often sung to this day:

> Society itself is on trial, at a critical period when virtue and morality is on a fearful downward trend, without any apparent protest against the advance of the social revolution which threatens so much to the sanctity of the home and to the state itself. We are yet fighting the battle of civilization; my struggles today may be yours tomorrow.

Then a final plea for the application and supremacy of "the unwritten law" was made. He told the jury about a similar case—a murder trial in Kentucky. According to the Colonel, the Kentucky judge, "Judge Donaldson," ordered the jury to render a verdict according to "the higher law."

> Such men [as Judge Donaldson] are the heritage of the state. His name ought to be carved in letters of gold on the columns of the Pantheon. . . . [H]e ascended the rugged heights of Sinai, and on its flaming summit, shook hands with God.

> Judge Donaldson said to the jury: "Gentlemen, this case is governed by the higher law, you will render a verdict of not guilty."

With him, the puny statute of man repealing an ordinance of God for the government of the world was not of primal sanction.

With the jury's rapt and riveted attention, the Colonel was now ready to launch his appeal for application of the unwritten law to the case at hand—ignore those "puny mandates of man" and find him not guilty of the felony offense of assault with intent to murder. God expected the jury to do its duty!

Had Judge Donaldson of Kentucky (cited above) been presiding at this trial, he might have agreed with Colonel Hallum and instructed the jury to disregard Texas law and follow "the higher law," but Bowie County District Judge Tolbert, apparently still earthbound, was not so inclined. He instructed the jury to follow "the puny mandates" as enacted by the Texas Legislature. In view of Colonel Hallum's own testimony, had the jury done so it surely would have been compelled to find Hallum guilty.

However, the Colonel made another startling recommendation to the jury: while the jury should find him not guilty of the felony offense of assault with intent to murder, still the jury *should find him guilty* of the misdemeanor offense of simple assault and assess only the minimum fine of $50. That recommendation left one logical question unaddressed: Why was it that God's supreme unwritten law protected the Colonel from the felony offense of assault with intent to murder, yet somehow petered out when it came to excusing the misdemeanor offense of simple assault? But then logic, after all, had very little to do with these proceedings. Or, perhaps the Almighty just didn't want to be bothered with misdemeanors.

Colonel Hallum's suggestion to the jury that they find him guilty of a minor, misdemeanor offense with no jail time and a small fine stemmed from a very practical and worldly consideration. Hallum was probably concerned that one or more of the jurors might have balked at letting him go "scot-free" with a simple not-guilty verdict.

If so, then the holdout juror or jurors might have caused a hung jury and thus a mistrial. If that had happened then Colonel Hallum would face another trial and be in jeopardy of spending a long vacation in the Texas Bastille. However, if the jury found him guilty of even a minor misdemeanor with a minimal fine, then the prosecution would be forever blocked from retrying Hallum pursuant to those puny man-made laws contained in the U.S. and Texas Constitutions prohibiting "double jeopardy." At any rate, after such a masterful performance by the Colonel, who among the jurors was inclined to bother with such a minor, nit-picking inconsistency in logic?

And so the jury—as directed by Colonel Hallum—found him not guilty of assault with intent to murder but guilty of misdemeanor assault upon the preacher and assessed a $50 fine, a fine which was paid in full by his supporters before he left the courtroom. Thus, the Colonel got the best of both worlds—heaven and earth.

Plus, as a bonus, the district court granted Colonel Hallum a divorce from his wayward wife. (She did not see fit to contest it.)

Epilogue

John Hallum might have been a self-educated scholar and a lawyer, but he certainly taught himself well.

While his astounding defense in the Forbes trial was abysmally lacking in statutory law and his logic was less than flawless, it was nevertheless a masterpiece of 1890s courtroom strategy and brilliance. His oratorical skills were superb, and his knowledge of the Bible, classical literature, and world history were awesome even though he did pick and choose which parts of those sources to rely on and which parts to ignore. John Hallum knew his audience and he knew what resonated well with them, and he strummed their emotional strings like a master guitarist. His audience—Old South rural, provincial, and poorly educated—were highly susceptible to blatantly maudlin emotional appeals and the soaring hyperbole of the snake-oil salesman, the carnival barker, and the hell-fire-and-brimstone preacher. In sum, the jurors proved to be the perfect student body, and Colonel Hallum proved himself to be the perfect and perfectly spellbinding professor to instruct them. One scholar of that era, reflecting on honor and homicide in the South, said this: "By the end of the nineteenth century, Americans widely understood that an unwritten law existed off the books allowing men to slay the seducers of 'their' women."[12]

An 1897 commentator, Thomas Crosby, who wrote the foreword to Hallum's forty-six-page pamphlet, said this of his oration: "It is considered by the Bar of the South as the greatest exposition of the Unwritten Law," adding that it "certainly belongs to the higher class of forensic literature and for purity of diction, grandeur of thought and general excellence, is unsurpassed in legal literature."[13]

A modern commentator said that it "evokes the spirit" of that age, and that it helps us "retain a sense of who we are and where we come from," concluding that it "conveys, in a voice that has outlived its author, the full humanity of the law."[14]

Colonel Hallum died July 11, 1906, as a result of a fall from the steps of a hotel in Pine Bluff, Arkansas.

In his later years Hallum devoted much of his time and talent to writing. He authored several books, including *The Diary of an Old Lawyer: Scenes Behind the Curtain*; *Reminiscences of the Confederacy*; *The Bench and Bar of Arkansas*; and *The History of Arkansas*. Of particular note are certain anecdotes and observations contained in his book *The Diary of an Old Lawyer*.[15] In it he adds further insight into the culture of the Old South and its Victorian mindset as well as the Code of Honor. Here follow a few samples.

The Colonel was always at his eloquent best when rhapsodizing about the Old South and its aristocratic upper class—every gentleman a Knight in Shining Armor, standing ever ready to rush to the rescue of those trembling and defenseless Southern Belles. He exhilarated:

> The Southern people, whose hearts and natures are as warm and genial as the sunbeams that dance in the foliage around their homes, have always loved and admired intellectual conflicts, true eloquence, chivalric manhood, refined and noble womanhood. And those traits will continue to distinguish them as long as the sun exerts climatic influence over physical and mental organism.[16]

He never missed an opportunity to exalt the South's Code of Honor:

> Every gentleman was expected to resent any impugning of his courage or integrity, and the man who disregarded these primal laws became at once a back number. When the glove and gage of battle was thrown

in his face, there were but two ways to meet it, bravely like a man, or cowardly like a cur.[17]

It only followed then that any statutory prohibitions against dueling be automatically condemned: no debate countenanced. Colonel Hallum was a champion of the Code Duello. Hallum noted that "*The Code Duello* was recognized as a part of the *lex non scripta* of gentlemen." He continued:

> *The Code Duello* was of primal obligation with a class of man who adorned the highest class of society. . . . [S]o far as these penal laws [against dueling] are concerned, they belong to that class of dead letter law which lie buried under the frowns of public opinion, and justly so.[18]

In the nineteenth-century American South, a man was charged with two sacred duties: to protect the chastity of his womenfolk and to vindicate any real or perceived insult to his honor—and that by personally taking the law into his own hands and dispatching the offender. Or at least seriously maiming him. Failure to do so was a disgrace, a fate worse than death. Honor was considered more valuable than life itself, and what a man appeared to be to his community was more important than what he really was. The character and rectitude of the inner man took a back seat to outward appearances. At the same time, instances of general violence and mayhem or even killing for nearly any reason seemed to have been shrugged off as just a part of everyday life. During his early legal career, Hallum once served as a prosecutor *pro tem* in an assault with intent to murder case in which the defendant shot and wounded (although not seriously, as it turned out) an unarmed elderly man. According to Hallum, the defendant shot the old man "on impulse" during a dispute over a debt. He obviously did not pursue the prosecution very vigorously. He explained:

> Although it was a clear violation of the law, it was not attended with other presumptive malice, and was not one of those cases for which jurors of the South would readily impose a degrading sentence by sending the defendant to the penitentiary, and I did not expect a conviction.[19]

Eloquence was the Colonel's long suit. Consistency, however, was not one of his priorities. When discussing the high moral standards of the legal profession, Hallum noted that the legal profession "above all others, demands the exposition and probing of fraud . . . an offense never forgiven when robust Saxon is indulged in exposing it."[20] Yet, at another part of his *Diary of a Old Lawyer*, he recounts an episode when he was defending a counterfeiter. The counterfeiter had stashed $300,000 in bogus bills in his home. Colonel Hallum became aware that law officers had a search warrant for his client's home and were about to execute it. Hallum beat the officers to his client's stash and managed to burn up the evidence just in the nick of time. "I acted right from every legal standpoint," he explained.[21]

Although, as we have seen, Colonel Hallum's vitriolic castigation of Reverend Forbes as well as anybody who supported him knew no bounds, he nevertheless wrote this in his diary: "He who too severely criticizes the frailties of his fellow man, blasphemes God. . . . Frailty came with man into the world as a primal law."[22]

Another earmark of the Colonel's lectures was his reliance upon a very selective reading of his sources. As demonstrated by his jury argument in the Forbes case, he relied upon certain biblical injunctions when convenient to his purpose ("Thou Shalt Not Commit Adultery") while choosing to ignore those passages that were not so favorable to his cause ("Thou Shall Not Kill"). Likewise, he wholeheartedly endorsed Old Testament scriptures such as "an eye for an eye," but completely— vigorously—rejected weak-kneed New Testament notions of mercy and forgiveness such as "turning the other cheek."[23] In another biblical bypass, the Colonel said this:

> Humanitarians and theologians and professed Christians who are more conversant with theory than practice, may preach and teach until Gabriel sounds his trumpet that when one cheek is slapped we must turn the other in meekness, and yet there always has been and always will be a chivalrous class of men who will fight upon terms of equality in defense of their reputations and honor.[24]

Which brings to mind a familiar observation: even the devil can quote the Bible to his own purposes.

How the aristocracy of the Old South viewed the differences between the sexes has never been described any better than Hallum did. Men (of the better class, that is) could be brave and chivalrous and high-minded, but men (of the lower class) were likely to be vile and cruel and exploitive. Women (of the better class), on the other hand, were always gentle, fragile, refined, noble, naïve to the ways of men and the world, gullible, and virtually helpless when approached by an unprincipled seducer. Also, those refined Southern Belles were simply incapable of experiencing sexual lust or, for that matter, of committing any foul deed unless forced or tricked into doing so by an unscrupulous male. Ever sweet they were, sweet and pure as magnolia blossoms in springtime.[25] Note that during Hallum's jury argument, he called that "base-born libertine" Forbes almost every nasty epithet invented by man, but not his unfaithful wife. Even though she was a willing participant in the adulterous affair, and even though she connived with that villainous cur Forbes to steal her husband's home and land, nevertheless Colonel Hallum did not contend that she was culpable. Well, at least not much. She was just the poor, naïve, helpless pawn who was seduced and ruined by that "monster of depravity in clerical robes."

In the few references he made to his wife during his jury argument, and even later in his references to their divorce, Hallum depicts her not as a greedy and lewd Jezebel, but rather as an unwilling and unfortunate victim, a soiled and malodorous piece of refuse fit only to be discarded. He seems to infer that discarding her was a duty imposed on him by the South's Code of Honor, a duty he was forced to perform however unpleasant it might have been to him personally. After all, his honor was at stake. The supporters of the unwritten law expected the wronged husband who dutifully killed his wife's paramour to then dutifully cast off his debauched wife. A graphic example of what happened to a husband who failed to do so is what happened to Daniel Sickles, who as mentioned in the Introduction, killed his wife's lover, Philip Barton Key, in 1859 in Washington, D.C., and was thereafter acquitted by reliance upon the unwritten law. However, a few months later, Daniel Sickles took back his wife, and, as a result, suffered public ridicule and humiliation.[26]

An even better example of the Colonel's view of the sexes is set out in his *Diary*. He tells of a murder case he tried earlier in his career. Hallum was the prosecutor in the trial. A wife and her lover had killed the husband, and the wife was being tried for murder. She took the stand in her own defense and, according to Hallum, delivered a consummate performance during which she denied having anything to do with the death of her husband. Hallum didn't believe her. In his *Diary*, he made this astounding—and very revealing—comment: "I was then as convinced of that woman's guilt as at first, *still I did not want to add to the weight of her sorrow.*"[27]

Poor thing.

From this time distance, Colonel Hallum's portrayal of the Old South's culture, and particularly prevalent attitudes about sex and the differences between the sexes, seems more than just quaint. In the end, whatever else may be said of him, John Hallum was a son of the Old South, his views and beliefs molded by the culture of his time and place. And he did succeed grandly—if rather unintentionally—in depicting that culture. He accomplished that with eloquent brilliance.

# TWO

The Seduction of Verna Ware

THE 1909 GATESVILLE COURTHOUSE MASSACRE

At the dawning of the twentieth century, when the mindset of the typical Texan on matters sexual was still decidedly Victorian, it must have seemed strange that Verna Ware's parents would have allowed their fourteen-year-old daughter to go out with a boy, unchaperoned, and stay out until all hours of the night. Even so, what happened that spring night more than a century ago probably didn't seem to be of earth-shaking importance to anyone—perhaps not even to Verna and her date. Yet what happened that night would soon become of earth-shaking importance, and not only to the young couple and to their families. As events spun out of control over the next two years, they shook the whole frontier community from center to circumference. In that short time-frame, the naïve country girl was destined to become a much wiser sixteen-year-old who was to become the central figure in two sensational criminal trials, one of which would be a murder trial. The Old South's unwritten laws would backdrop not only the trials, but also the community's perception of the whole affair.

Verna was the youngest child of George Matt Ware and Margaret Riddling Ware,[1] a hardscrabble farm family struggling to wrest a living from the stubborn soil about halfway between the central Texas towns of Gatesville and Jonesboro. Something of the difficult times, as well as the character of the Wares, may be deduced from a rather curious and intriguing remark made by one of their neighbors. Of the Wares, he said this: "In all their dealings, they drive you for a hard bargain."[2]

One of Verna's acquaintances in the Jonesboro community was John J. Hanes—a handsome, personable fellow of medium height and slender build who, at age twenty-one, was seven years older than Verna. John was a favorite in the community with both young and old alike. Years later, a Jonesboro classmate was to recall that when she arrived at school each morning, John ran out and helped her dismount and then tied up her horse while she proceeded into the schoolhouse. "He was always cheerful—always had something nice to say to everybody."[3]

John was the youngest of five children of Henry Hanes and his wife, Julia "Josie" Allen Hanes. The Hanes family was among the elite of the Jonesboro community. They had large landholdings in the area as well as other business interests, including a thriving freight line. Henry was also a community leader who helped establish and build schools, churches, and tabernacles and "took care of all preachers regardless of their denomination."[4]

While John was a very attractive boy, Verna was not as well endowed physically. Robert W. Brown, a Gatesville lawyer, now deceased, sat down in 1970 and penned some (heretofore unpublished) notes on the tragic events to follow. He described Verna Ware as follows:

She was short, and heavy, with a thick chest, big arms, big legs and very dark, and might be called the wrestler type from her general appearance. She was not altogether unattractive, but she would not be classified as a beauty, and she did have some dates with boyfriends besides John Hanes.[5]

On March 24, 1907, John Hanes invited Verna to a party near the little village of Ireland, a journey of several hours by horse and buggy. However, those attending the party that night later told authorities that the couple never showed up. About daylight the next morning John brought Verna back to the Ware home.

A short time later, Verna discovered that she was pregnant. She asked John to make good on his promise to marry her. John refused, claiming that he was not responsible for her pregnancy. In despair and disgrace, Verna finally went to what was then called a "rescue home" in Fort Worth, a place where unmarried women, in a plight such as Verna found herself, could retreat to have their babies and then put them up for adoption. Afterward she came home and once again beseeched John to marry her and save her from ruin by "making an honest woman of her." He again refused.

By now, of course, Verna's disgrace was the talk of the county. There were about as many versions of the incident as there were tellers of the tale, with some sympathizing with John, others with Verna— although, at fourteen years of age, she was already stigmatized as a "ruined woman" regardless of whose version was to be credited. One story had it that John had drugged her into submission by spiking chocolate candy favors he brought along on the fateful night. However, Verna never claimed that she was drugged or forced into submission. (Commentator Robert W. Brown notes that few people would have believed Verna, had she claimed that John physically overpowered her and forced himself upon her, since she was considerably larger and stronger than John.) Meanwhile, Verna never wavered from her story. She maintained that she had submitted to John only because she relied upon his promise to marry her.

When John continued to spurn her, Verna decided to file a criminal seduction charge against him, and in January 1909 she appeared before the Coryell County Grand Jury and told her tale. John Hanes also appeared before the same grand jury and testified upon his own behalf. He produced several letters for the Grand Jury's consideration—one written by a fellow classmate, Pope Young, to another classmate, J. Y.

Lovelace, Jr., and one or more letters Verna had written to John. Since the Grand Jury proceedings were secret, the content of these letters was not disclosed. However, it appears that, either directly or indirectly, they must have supported John in one of two ways: either tending to show that John had never promised to marry Verna, or tending to prove that someone other than John was, or may have been, responsible for Verna's pregnancy. (Unfortunately, the case was presented to the Grand Jury years before DNA technology was available, which, had it been available, could have removed all doubt as to who was responsible for her pregnancy.) Actually, as we shall soon see, there was a third possibility—another way in which the contents of those letters might have helped John defeat Verna's seduction charge.

Regardless of those letters, the Coryell County Grand Jury thought there was sufficient evidence of seduction to warrant bringing the case to court to be decided by a petit jury after a full airing of the evidence, and so on January 23, 1909, the Grand Jury returned a felony indictment against John J. Hanes, charging him with the seduction of Verna Ware on or about March 24, 1907.[6]

The seduction of unmarried females and the breach of a man's promise to marry were matters not taken lightly by early-day Texans. On the criminal side of the docket, a seduction conviction could earn a term of two to ten years in the penitentiary. On the civil side, a "breach of promise to marry" could put a serious dent in a man's bank account.

In an 1898 seduction case, the Texas Court of Criminal Appeals explained the offense as follows:

> The offense consists in enticing a woman [an unmarried virgin under the age of 25 years] from the path of virtue, and obtaining her consent to illicit intercourse by promises [to marry her] made at the time. The promise and yielding her virtue in consequence thereof is the gist of the offense.

In a telling note on the sexual viewpoint of the times, the court went on to emphasize what it considered to be the obvious: "No one can, with any degree of plausibility, contend that a virtuous female could be seduced without any of those arts, wiles and blandishments so necessary to win the hearts of the weaker sex."[7]

The Supreme Court of Michigan, in an earlier case (1888), elaborated on a similar Michigan statute:

> Debauchery and carnal intercourse without seduction, is no offense under this statute. [In Texas, however, it was a criminal offense, albeit a lesser offense, under the fornication statute.] The offense which this statute is aimed at is the seduction and debauchery accomplished by the promises and blandishments the man brings to his aid in effecting the ruin and disgrace of the female; and where the seduction and debauchery is accomplished by promises of marriage, upon which the female relies, and thus surrenders her person, and gives to the man the brightest jewel in the crown of her womanhood. It is the broken promise which the law will regard as the [essence] of the offense.[8]

When the Texas Legislature passed the "Seduction and Breach of Promise to Marry" laws, it also became necessary for the lawmakers to pass an enabling evidentiary statute in the Code of Criminal Procedure.

The amending of rules of evidence is not normally a subject that rivets the attention of anyone except law professors. Yet this one has an interesting history. Odd as it may seem, it was once the law in every U.S. jurisdiction that "interested parties," in civil suits as well as defendants in criminal trials, were absolutely disqualified to become a witness in their own cases, and that included both men and women. For example, a defendant in a criminal case was forbidden to take the stand and testify—couldn't tell his or her side of the story, not even to present an alibi. Any defense had to be raised by the testimony of third-party witnesses.[9] In 1864, Maine became the first state to abolish this blanket "interested party" prohibition, with many other states and territories, including Texas, soon following suit.[10]

Texas, however, didn't go all the way down that path. Women, like idiots or children too young to understand the meaning of an oath to tell the truth, were still deemed incompetent to testify in any court proceeding. Therefore, when the Texas Legislature passed the "Seduction and Breach of Promise to Marry" law, the evidentiary statute had to be amended to allow the complaining witness to testify in her own behalf. Even so, the Texas lawmakers still did not go all the way. They tacked on a qualification: the victim's testimony, standing alone, couldn't carry the day. Her testimony had to be corroborated by some independent source before the case was entitled to be submitted to a jury.[11]

In 1892, a fellow named W. C. Wright barely escaped spending four years in the Texas pen for an admitted seduction. He succeeded by squeezing through a novel, though onerous, escape hatch thoughtfully provided by the innovative Texas Legislature. Under this most interesting statute, a man guilty of seduction could, nevertheless, "King's X" the proscribed criminal sanction if, prior to making a plea to a seduction indictment, he promised "in good faith" to marry the damsel in distress and thus "make an honest woman" of her. However, that did not automatically get him off the hook. Instead of simply dismissing the indictment, the trial court was required to continue (postpone) the seduction trial for a period of two years. If, at the end of the two-year period the couple was still married and still living together and (presumably) enjoying marital bliss, then, and only then, would the seduction indictment be dismissed.[12] The good faith marriage, though tardy and under duress, retroactively erased the seduction and thus, at least insofar as the law was concerned, miraculously cleansed the new wife who had previously been branded as a loose and immoral woman.

In the 1892 seduction case, the defendant W. C. Wright took advantage of this strange and archaic loophole in the Texas seduction statute in a move that caught everyone by surprise. Before the startled onlookers—the jury, the judge, the lawyers, the witnesses, and the spectators—Wright took the stand before trial, produced a marriage license, and swore that "in good faith" he would, then and there, marry the complaining witness, a Miss Nesbitt, and requested the trial judge to immediately perform the ceremony. However, the district attorney objected and offered witnesses who challenged the defendant's "good faith." They testified that the defendant had previously told them that he would not marry or live with Miss Nesbitt under any circumstances.

Wright again took the witness stand and reiterated his offer of marriage, and further promised not to desert Miss Nesbitt thereafter. At that point, Miss Nesbitt had had enough. She jumped up and declaimed: "I most positively will not marry you or live with you. I would not marry any man who treated a woman as you have done me."

The trial judge refused to dismiss the indictment or to continue the trial, whereupon the jury convicted Wright and sentenced him to four years in the pen. But the Texas Court of Criminal Appeals came to Wright's rescue and reversed the conviction. The court observed that there could be "no earthly doubt" about his good-faith offer to marry the victim: "The penitentiary towering above him was the strongest guaranty of the sincerity of his offer."

After all, the court went on to reason, by suggesting that the trial judge perform the marriage ceremony on the spot, Wright guaranteed that Nesbitt would again be made "an honest woman." (Didn't matter a whit to the court or anyone else—except Miss Nesbitt—what kind of husband the rascal might turn out to be.)[13]

In view of the Texas seduction statute in effect in 1909, John Hanes had four possible avenues of escape: he could (1) offer "in good faith" to marry Verna and do so, or (2) choose to defend the seduction charges by convincing the jury that he never had sexual intercourse with Verna, or (3) convince a jury that, even if he had intercourse with her, he never promised to marry Verna in exchange for her sexual favors, or (4) convince a jury that, even if he lied when he promised to marry her, and by that stratagem succeeded in having sex with her, and even if he did then impregnate her, still, she was not a "virtuous" woman at the time.

John chose not to marry Verna. He and his attorneys elected to defend the seduction charge. But which line, or lines, of defense would he assert? And what did the letters prove? Did she admit that she had not had sex with him, or at least not in reliance on his promise to marry? Did she admit that she had sex with others? Did one of her classmates' letters state that he had previously had sex with her? Those tantalizing questions kept the entire community on the edge of its collective seats.

It takes little imagination to grasp what enormous mental distress and emotional turmoil sixteen-year-old Verna Ware was then experiencing. In many similar Texas cases, the girl's father or brothers took up arms and intervened on her behalf, exacting self-help justice, or otherwise initiated some action in retaliation or vindication. In the Verna Ware case, there is no mention of such support from her family. Support from the community, if any, was meager. Plus, the fact that the Haneses were the elite of the community while the Wares were lower-class folks didn't help Verna's cause. Revenge, retaliation, and/or the rectification of the perceived wrong therefore rested solely on the youthful shoulders of Verna herself. She had already been thoroughly shamed by having been run through the gossip mill of that straitlaced small town and adjudged thereby as a loose—and thus "ruined"—woman, and this even if they believed that John Hanes might have taken undue advantage of her.[14] Now she was about to face an equal—if not worse—ordeal. She might have already been run through the gossip mill of Coryell County, but now she was about to be run through the county's legal mill even though she, at least nominally, was the complaining witness and not the defendant in the upcoming seduction case. Every seat and every aisle in the courtroom would be filled by gawking adults eagerly waiting to hear all the sordid details—allegations and counter allegations. She knew that she would have to testify—have to take the stand, face a courtroom packed with a generous helping of judgmental puritans, and, under oath, admit that she had consented to sexual intercourse, had become pregnant, had the baby, and then placed it up for adoption. She would have to look John J. Hanes in the face and accuse him of being her impregnator and of having tricked her into yielding to him while relying on his promise to marry her.

But that would be the easy part. Verna well knew that after her direct testimony ended, she, herself, would be put on trial by the defendant. She would have to defend her "prior virtue" against the inevitable assault that would be launched during cross examination, carried forward by the testimony of John Hanes and other defense witnesses and, very likely, by those damnable letters—one or more of which she herself had written. John J. Hanes could admit that he had had sex with Verna on the night of March 24, 1907; he could even admit that he had accomplished this by a false promise to marry her and even admit that he was the one who impregnated her. He could admit all of that and still win acquittal if he could prove (or even raise a reasonable doubt in the jury's mind) that prior to March 24, 1907, Verna was not a virgin—that she had had prior sexual intercourse with others, or even with himself. The prosecution and the defense had subpoenaed around one hundred witnesses who, as Verna well knew, would be paraded through the courtroom and, before God and everybody else, tell what they knew of the facts of the case and the character of Verna Ware and John Hanes.

Was Verna's tale true? Did John trick her into having sex with him and thus impregnate her by promising marriage? Or was Verna already pregnant by somebody else and, on that fateful night, did she try to trick John into marriage by submitting herself to him in an effort to save herself, plus, at the same time, land the most handsome, likeable, and wealthy bachelor on the horizon? Answers to those questions were to be addressed in the upcoming seduction trial. Meanwhile, speculation was the talk of the county. Everybody had his or her own theory.

Either way, right or wrong, and with the seduction trial looming ever closer, sixteen-year-old Verna must have felt very much alone, overwhelmed, and desperate. Verna, not all that attractive to begin with, as well as being the child of a socially inferior family, would soon be faced with confronting handsome John Hanes, who would be surrounded by his esteemed family and supported by a host of friendly witnesses as well as by a battery of the best trial lawyers in the area.

Nathaniel Hawthorne's classic *The Scarlet Letter* was set in seventeenth-century America, an era made infamous by the Salem witch trials. Verna Ware's desperate plight mirrors the painful and humiliating fate of Hawthorne's heroine, Hester Prynne. When a child was born to Hester during her husband's long absence, Boston's self-righteous Puritan leaders put her on trial for adultery, convicted her, and sent her to prison. Not only that, but to ensure that forever after she would be branded in disgrace, the pompous community condemned her to wear a bright red "A" over her heart wherever she went. Still not satisfied, upon her release from prison the townsfolk paraded her through the streets to the town square and then forced her—babe in arms—to ascend a scaffold, where she suffered scorn and public ridicule. One "good woman" loudly decried the elaborate letter "A" Hester had embroidered and proudly sewn into her frock in defiance of the hypocrites. A minister in the crowd denounced her and demanded that she reveal the identity of her partner in adultery. (Her partner was another minister who stood silently in the crowd.) She refused. Thereafter she was socially ostracized and banished to a lonely cottage by the sea, where she eked out a living for herself and her daughter by sewing.

Barely literate, Verna Ware could never have described her feelings with the eloquence of Hawthorne, but she must have experienced feelings very similar to those Hawthorne attributed to Hester Prynne:

> Walking to and fro, with those lonely footsteps in the little world with which she was outwardly connected . . . she felt . . . that the scarlet letter endowed her with a new sense. She . . . could not help believing that . . . the outward guise of purity [in others] was but a lie, and that, if truth were everywhere to be shown, a scarlet letter would blaze forth on many a bosom besides Hester Prynne's.[15]

One thing for sure, however, Verna Ware would soon exhibit some of the same spunk and backbone that Hester Prynne displayed when she refused to be shamed but instead wore a beautifully adorned "A" on her breast in defiance of her self-righteous accusers. The folks in Coryell County, Texas, were about to learn that Verna Ware was far from the cowering Southern belle most Southern males of the day expected of their womenfolk; they were about to learn that Verna Ware was much more a thorny Texas mesquite than a tender magnolia blossom. Both the fictional Hester Prynne and the very real Verna Ware defied the judgmental communities which shunned them. But their tactics of defiance differed drastically.

The seduction case against John Hanes was set for a jury trial on February 17, 1909, in the district courtroom of Coryell County, Texas, at Gatesville. The grand old Coryell County courthouse, built in 1897, still stands today, and it is one of the most impressive and majestic pieces of courthouse architecture in Texas—three stories of gray limestone and red sandstone with columns and statues and crowned with a cupola upon which a golden eagle perches.

To understand the tale of murder and mayhem to follow, the reader needs to envision the interior of the courthouse. The district courtroom is today just as it was in 1909. It is located on the second floor, and the second floor has a rotunda with open space in the middle. A circular corridor around the rotunda well allows visitors to look down on the first floor (much like that in the Texas capitol building in Austin). From the circular corridor on the second floor, doors open into the various offices, and two doors open into the district courtroom. The courtroom is located on the north side of the building, and it may be entered from the corridor by either the east door or the west door. Between these two doors, in 1909, there was a large double window, which enabled people walking around the corridor to look directly into the courtroom. By looking through those windows it was equivalent to having a seat on the last row of spectators in the exact rear center of the courtroom—looking directly at the district judge, who would be peering down from the bench. The observer would also be looking at the backs of all the spectators in the center section of the courtroom.

Although the John Hanes seduction trial had been set for February 17, 1909, a pretrial hearing had been scheduled for the afternoon of February 2, 1909. Before the pretrial, however, the court was considering other matters, and the participants and a large number of spectators were seated in the courtroom awaiting a preview of this, the most dramatic and discussed trial in the little county's short history. The Hanes family was all there, including, of course, John Hanes, and they were seated in the rear center of the spectator section of the courtroom—right in front of those double windows.

Verna Ware was also in the courthouse that day—she and an older brother, Ezra, and a sister. (No mention has been recorded of Verna's father or mother being present. Was Verna also to suffer renunciation from shamed parents?) Nevertheless, Verna and her siblings were outside the courtroom in the circular corridor. When they looked into the courtroom from outside the glass windows, there was John Hanes seated immediately in front of Verna, his back turned to them.

Coryell County Courthouse, Gatesville, Texas. (Author's collection.)

When Verna Ware returned from Fort Worth after having her baby, she returned without the baby—but she did return with something else: a consuming passion. For justice. Or revenge. One or the other. Or both.

As a testament to her unswerving determination and simmering rage, Verna Ware somehow obtained a .38-caliber Colt semiautomatic pistol. That took some doing, because in 1909 few people had even heard of a semiautomatic pistol. Most lawmen, including Coryell County officers, still carried revolvers—six-shooters. Single-action revolvers required the shooter to stop and recock the weapon after each shot. But not so with the semiautomatics—just keep on pulling the trigger and firing away. Plus, the semiautomatic pistoleer didn't have to stop and reload after firing six shots.

The tantalizing question was, how did Verna Ware get that semiautomatic pistol? Those weapons were expensive, and Verna Ware was dirt poor. Somebody had to have given that pistol to her. But who? Probably not her father, since he was also dirt poor, and more than that, he seemed to have taken no interest in Verna's plight. If he had bought the pistol, wouldn't he have taken matters into his own hands? Who then? Perhaps there was a clue in those letters that John Hanes had produced in the secret grand jury proceedings, the contents of which had still not been revealed. One of the letters was written by one male classmate to another, and one or more were written by Verna to John. Obviously the letters had something to do with Verna's sexual history, and John must have believed that they tended to exonerate him. It is more than possible that the letters pointed an incriminating finger in the direction of another man. If so, that man would have had a compelling motive to prevent a public trial during which those letters surely would have surfaced. That person most certainly didn't want to risk ending up as the target of another seduction prosecution. Meanwhile, there can be no doubt at all that Verna Ware did not want those letters to be publicly aired. In any event, somehow she got her hands on that .38-caliber semiautomatic pistol.

Verna's rage, though monumental, was nevertheless controlled, cool, and calculating. When, on February 2, 1909, she looked through those windows in the back of the Coryell County Courthouse and saw John Hanes seated directly in front of her, she hesitated not a moment before calmly reaching into her purse and pulling out that cocked and loaded automatic. She shattered the glass windows by firing four shots at John before her brother Ezra could grab her arm in an attempt to stop the assault. Verna didn't miss a shot: two shots penetrated John's back and two more shots hit him in his right leg. But Verna wasn't through yet! Even though Ezra grabbed her shooting arm, she kept pulling the trigger on that automatic, determined to make sure John J. Hanes was dead. Ezra's effort to end the fusillade, however well-intentioned, only made things worse, much worse. Verna jerked off three more shots, and although they all went wild, all three hit innocent bystanders. As a result, two spectators, Dave Ross and J. J. Smith, were fatally wounded, and A. P. Wiley was hit in the heel. (Wiley was a Gatesville schoolboy who had played hooky that day in order to witness the drama.)

District courtroom in the Coryell County courthouse. John J. Hanes was seated on the back row, center, when Verna Ware shot through the rear window of the courtroom and killed him. (Author's collection.)

Rotunda on second floor of the Coryell County Courthouse. Verna Ware stood on the rotunda and shot through the rear courtroom window. (Author's collection.)

Coryell County District Judge Phillip Ziegler points to bullet hole in wall of district courtroom made in 1909 by one of Verna Ware's .38-caliber slugs. (Author's collection.)

There was no order in the court that day. There was total bedlam. One terrified spectator even jumped out of a second-story window and broke his leg. One of those seven deadly shots not only penetrated a human body, but also a door on the north side of the courtroom just to the east of the judge's bench, leaving a bullet hole still in evidence there to this day.

John Hanes died shortly thereafter, but not before once again proclaiming his innocence. "I am an innocent man!"[16]

Thus ended the seduction case against John Hanes. District Judge J. H. Arnold noted on the docket, "death of defendant suggested, dismissed." But the end of the seduction case was only the beginning of three murder cases—all indictments being returned against Verna Ware for the murders of John Hanes, J. J. Smith, and Dave Ross.[17]

The murder case for the killing of John Hanes was called first—called almost one year to the day after the Coryell County Courthouse massacre. District Judge J. H. Arnold presided. District Attorney J. H. McMillan was the prosecutor, assisted by a special prosecutor (undoubtedly hired by the Hanes family), a noted local attorney named Sterling Pratt Sadler. Verna's defense was entrusted to the firm of Morgan and Miller assisted by Judge Jenkins of Brownwood, Texas.

Unfortunately, the transcript of trial testimony is not available, and the news accounts of the trial are skimpy—to put the best face on it. In those days, Victorian delicacy dictated no recital of the real facts of scandalous cases should be reported; "the least said the better" was the dictum of turn-of-the-century journalism. The total trial summary reported by *The Gatesville Messenger* reads as follows:

> Many pathetic scenes took place during progress of the trial that moved the jury and spectators alike to tears. It is not necessary to rehearse at this time the account of the shocking tragedy for the details of the affair are familiar to our readers, the sadness of which has not yet been lifted from the minds of our people.

The Gatesville Messenger's account of the trial tactics of the opposing attorneys is also sadly lacking, dubbing it off as follows:

> Judge Arnold in delivering his charge to the jury dealt only with first degree murder, second degree murder, manslaughter and self defense.

A plea of insanity and irrepressible impulse characterized the attempts of defense counsel before the court and jury throughout the trial.[18]

If, as implied by the above accounts, Judge Arnold ruled out insanity and irrepressible impulse (the latter, in any event, was not recognized as a legal justification for a homicide), then it appears that if the jury were to acquit Verna Ware, it had to be on grounds of "self-defense." That is, *if* the jury followed the court's instruction setting out the written laws of Texas applicable to this particular case. If the jury did so, then what a mind-boggling stretch it must have been for the jurors to conclude that a shooter could, with premeditation, sneak up behind an intended victim—an unarmed victim—seated quietly in a courtroom and shoot him to death in the back, four times, all in order to protect herself from an anticipated, perilous, looming, and threatened lethal attack about to be launched by the victim.

Surprisingly—well, perhaps not so surprisingly, considering the time, the place, and the culture—the jury found Verna Ware not guilty on the second ballot and without any extended debate. The *Gatesville Messenger* observed:

> Citizens from all parts of this county who had been attracted . . . to hear the trial of Miss Verna Ware . . . and who had heard the progress of the trial were not surprised yesterday morning at the verdict of not guilty.[19]

It was obvious that Verna Ware was not set free by reason of any provision found in the law books of the State of Texas; the unwritten law had saved her.

The jury acquitted Verna Ware of the murder of John J. Hanes on January 31, 1910. On the same date, Judge Arnold, on the motion of District Attorney McMillan, dismissed the two remaining indictments charging Verna with the murders of Dave Ross and J. J. Smith, thus raising many more issues and speculations about justice and the law in 1909 Texas.

A month later, however, on March 1, 1909, Verna Ware pled guilty in the Coryell County Court to the misdemeanor offense of unlawfully carrying a pistol and was fined $100.[20] Significantly, on the same date, and in the very next case on the docket, Charley Hanes, brother of the deceased John J. Hanes, also pled guilty to unlawfully carrying a pistol, and he also was fined $100.[21] If the Ware tribe didn't contemplate armed retaliation against the Haneses, it appears that at least one of the Hanes tribe might have had that in mind insofar as the Wares were concerned. But apparently tempers cooled, most likely due to the wise counsel on the part of some Coryell County elders, and thus further bloodshed was avoided.

Although, in the parlance of the day, Verna Ware had been "ruined"—a soiled dove that no honorable man would have—she nevertheless managed to live a long and apparently fruitful life after her acquittal. And she did in fact get married, to William Raymond Eck in Fort Worth on November 12, 1912, and they had a daughter, Opal. Verna died of natural causes in 1973, at age eighty, in Ogden, Utah, where Opal resided. Meanwhile, in the roughly sixty years after the tragedy, and before her death, Verna lived in Cleburne, Texas, and Tulsa, Oklahoma, where she was a saleswoman—and later a buyer—for a clothing store. She was a member of the First Baptist Church and the Business and Professional Women's Club.[22] Her daughter, Opal, from all accounts, also led a long and successful life.

John J. Hanes lies buried in the Jonesboro, Texas, cemetery: born June 20, 1885, died February 9, 1909. A large tombstone with a lamb lying across the top bears this inscription: "Here is one who is sleeping in faith and love with hope that is treasured all in heaven above."

Epilogue

When Verna Ware opened fire on February 2, 1909, in the crowded Coryell County district courtroom, one of her stray bullets hit and killed a spectator named J. J. (Jim) Smith, a farmer who lived a few miles west of Gatesville. Smith's nineteen-year-old son, J. Earl Smith, was also in the courtroom that day and witnessed his father slump to the courtroom floor, fatally wounded. Shortly afterward, J. Earl Smith moved to Arizona. He didn't return to Gatesville for seventy years. Finally, at age eighty-nine, at the urging of his family, he returned to the tragic scene. A reporter for the local weekly newspaper, *The Gatesville Messenger*, interviewed him, the story appearing in the December 13, 1979, edition. In it, J. Earl Smith was quoted as follows:

She [Verna Ware] was justified in shooting him [John Hanes], and the [shooting of the three other victims was] accidental. If her father would have shot [Hanes], he'd never been convicted either. Things were so much different in those days. A woman's honor was next to God, and that young man had trampled her honor.

Two earlier California trials featured almost identical factual bases to Verna Ware's story. On March 16, 1881, on a Los Angeles street, Lastencia Abarta, an eighteen-year-old beauty, shot her lover, Francisco "Chico" Forster, scion of a prominent family. She shot him from a distance of about ten feet and hit him in the right eye. "You are not going to fool another woman again," was the comment heard as she calmly strolled to the courthouse to give herself up. To the bystander who disarmed her, she said, "Why don't you let me have another shot at him?" He described her as being "perfectly cool and collected." She explained that Chico had promised to marry her and she had been seduced by him, believing marriage to be certain. In court, she produced a note from Chico that read: "Come quick, I am waiting for you, don't be afraid, I am going to marry you." But he "ruined" her and then retracted his promise to marry. Although during the trial Lastencia's attorney tossed a hodgepodge of defenses at the jury, including insanity, his final jury argument sounded mighty like an appeal to the unwritten law. He painted a "glowing picture of the girl [who had] been wronged, and the horror attending her future." He was interrupted by spectator applause. He asked the jury to remember how Chico had used his "arts" to "ruin Lastencia," and then wrapped it all up by saying that Lastencia did no wrong in killing Forster. It took the jury only fifty-four minutes to return with its verdict: "Not guilty by reason of insanity." A cheer, "long and loud," went up from the assembled crowd.[23]

A "not guilty" verdict was also returned by another turn-of-the-century California jury at the conclusion of the trial of Clara Fallmer, a pregnant fifteen-year-old girl who killed her lover, a much older man, when he refused to marry her. Not only did he refuse to marry her, but even after he had seduced, impregnated, and abandoned her, he laughed at her and began seeing another woman. The facts of the case smacked of premeditation, and Clara had pulled the trigger in front of credible eyewitnesses. Self-defense was out of the question. Although the defense made a feeble thrust at temporary insanity, it was clear that Clara was as guilty as homemade sin. At least if measured by statutory standards. Instead, Clara's attorneys turned the courtroom into a stage upon which they skillfully scripted a classic Greek tragedy focusing the spotlight on the dastardly deeds of the defendant and the desperate plight of the "ruined" victim. When the curtain finally rang down—when all was said and done—the whole production, and its outcome, told more about the audience than it did about the actors or the play.[24]

Similarly, the Verna Ware story was a Victorian melodrama that spoke volumes, not only about the state of the criminal justice system of 1909 Texas, but also of the culture of that society—one that was unwilling (or, at least for the most part, reluctant) to forgive Verna Ware for her sexual sin. Even if they believed that John Hanes was responsible for her seduction and thus the author of her ruin, still the society of that time and place stamped Verna Ware as "soiled goods," not fit to be seriously considered for marriage by any respectable gentleman. Yet, ironically, the same prudish society that shunned Verna Ware on sexual grounds was quite willing to excuse her from any culpability for her multiple murders. The unwritten laws proved to be a double-edged sword for Verna Ware: she was condemned, but then ultimately rescued, by the provisions of the Old South's Code of Honor.

A final but very important postscript to the Verna Ware saga: For decades, male defendants in Texas and the Deep South had relied upon the unwritten laws to trump statutory law and thus justify the premeditated killing of another man even when the target was unarmed—particularly in cases where the victim was guilty of some real or fancied illicit sexual misadventure with the defendant's wife, daughter, or close female relative. Yet Verna Ware and her lawyers turned the judicial tables around and proved that the unwritten laws could also be relied upon to exonerate a female killer.

THREE

Miss Winnie's Revenge
THE FAMILY MURDER

This is a story about a sensational murder trial that happened a long time ago in my hometown: Quanah, Texas. The killing and the ensuing trial rocked the foundation of our north central Texas village. The time was 1916, and even though that was a couple of decades before I was born, still, for me, there's a personal twist to the tale.

The principal characters in the story are Winnie Jo Morris and Garland Radford, but, more than just their story, it is also the tale of two early-day Hardeman County families: the blue-blood Radford clan and the blue-collar Morris family.

The G. W. Radford family was, arguably, the most prominent family in the county. They arrived in 1890 shortly after the Fort Worth &

Denver City Railroad laid tracks through that horse-and-buggy village. Garland William Radford, the senior, bought a ranch in southern Hardeman County that became widely known as "the old Radford ranch." He and his wife, Anna Elizabeth Randell Radford, had four children, one of whom, Garland William Radford, Jr., became a medical doctor and practiced in the community for many years. One of the most colorful and respected of the Hardeman County pioneers, Dr. Radford was cut from the mold of the old-time "horse-and-buggy" doctors. No night was too cold, no storm too intimidating, no hour too late for Dr. Radford to grab his little black medicine bag, harness his horse to the buggy, and travel to some distant part of the county to deliver a baby or treat a cowboy busted up trying to tame a green bronco. Only four years after the Radford family arrived in Hardeman County, the elder Radford died, leaving Dr. Radford in charge of the family estate. Somehow Dr. Radford found time not only to practice medicine and manage the family estate, including the ranch, but also to become an enterprising and successful businessman. With the help of his family, he opened a general merchandise store and a drug store and founded a bank, the First Guaranty State Bank of Quanah, forerunner of the present town's largest bank, the First National Bank. He also founded an insurance and land title company in Quanah.

Meanwhile, Dr. Radford and his wife, Hannah Bill Robertson Radford, had five children, one of whom was Garland W. Radford III (often called G. W. Radford, Jr., or Garland).[1] Garland was assigned the task of managing the family insurance and land title office.

Prior to the stunning events of July 8, 1915, had you asked neighbors of the Bob Morris family to describe them, you undoubtedly would have heard adjectives like "hard-working," "law-abiding," "honest," and "salt-of-the-earth." Indeed, nothing in the records suggests that— either before or after that tragic day—any of the Morris clan were anything other than honest, hard-working, law-abiding, and salt-of-the-earth folks. They were molded from the same common clay as most of the other pioneer-stock working families who were striving to eke out a living on the windswept prairies of north central Texas shortly after the turn of the century.

At that time, the Morris family lived in a modest house on the western edge of Quanah adjacent to the railroad tracks. Bob, then about forty-five years old, was employed as foreman of the railroad shop of a short-line railroad bearing a wonderfully grand name: the "Quanah, Acme & Pacific Railroad." (Acme—now almost a ghost town—was even smaller than Quanah and was located only six miles to its west, both villages being quite distant from the Pacific Ocean. Local wags irreverently referred to the QA&P Railroad as the "Quit Achin' & Push" line.) Bob's son Ewell, eighteen, was also employed by the QA&P as a motorcar brakeman. In addition to Bob and Ewell, others living in the Morris household were Bob's wife and their two unmarried daughters, the eldest being Winnie Jo Morris, then about twenty years of age.[2] The family's home was only a stone's throw from the railroad "roundhouse" where locomotives were housed and repaired. Winnie Jo had first obtained employment as an assistant to the town's commercial photographer. Later, she got a job as stenographer and bookkeeper for the local insurance and land title ("abstract") company managed by Garland Radford.

About six o'clock on the evening of July 18, 1915, the entire Morris family (excepting only the youngest daughter) went on a revenge-crazed, blood-splattering rampage and killed Garland Radford in the yard of their home. Winnie shot him with a pistol. Ewell shot him with a pistol, and father Bob let him have it with a shotgun. They all kept firing until they ran out of bullets. Then Momma Morris, who didn't have a gun, ran to where the prostrate victim lay, shouting for a hatchet.

After the dust settled, Bob Morris calmly called Hardeman County sheriff B. F. Walker and reported the killing of Garland Radford: "I guess I'm the guy you are wanting," he added. When Sheriff Walker arrived at the scene shortly thereafter, he found Garland Radford, very much deceased, lying in the dust by the yard gate where he had fallen. Bob Morris and Miss Winnie were standing beside the body. Miss Winnie said, "You better take me to jail, for I am the one who did it." Sheriff Walker, after making a cursory investigation, duly jailed Bob and Miss Winnie. The next day, after hearing the whole story, he returned to the Morris home and arrested Ewell Morris. He did not, however, arrest Momma Morris, as no one had seen fit to fetch her the requested hatchet.

———

Although murder indictments were promptly returned by the Hardeman County District Court Grand Jury in Quanah against Miss Winnie, Bob, and Ewell Morris,[3] it was not until the next March (1916) that the case was called for jury trial. Tensions between the opposing families and their partisans had only grown more heated during the interim. An extra-large jury panel had to be called for the trial on account of the sensationalism of the case and the partisanship of many prospective jurors. District Judge J. A. Nabors felt compelled to order Sheriff Walker to search any court spectator he suspected of being armed. And, because of the salacious nature of the anticipated testimony, he also ordered all would-be spectators under the age of eighteen to be barred from the courtroom.

When the trial date arrived, the courtroom, although spacious for the size of the community and endowed with a balcony, could not accommodate the large crowd of spectators. The courthouse halls were packed. Many tried to squeeze into the aisles and spaces between the walls and the seats, although that meant they would have to stand throughout the entire trial to witness the proceedings. Some folks who showed up early and claimed seats either went without lunch or brought their own sack lunches to avoid having to vacate and chance losing their seats. That spectator interest was intense and the proceedings were charged with emotions is evidenced by an observation in the local weekly newspaper, the *Quanah Tribune-Chief*: "Henry Wall, who had been attending the trial, became very hysterical yesterday, and his condition has been very serious ever since." The same edition headlined the story all over the front page, noting that this "celebrated murder case" was "attracting great attention all over the country."[4] (The only other story of the time that came even close to vying for front-page attention was one that updated readers on the progress—or lack thereof—of General Blackjack Pershing, who was conducting a punitive raid into Mexico in a futile search for the wily Mexican bandit Pancho Villa.)

———

The 1915 indictment returned by the Hardeman County District
Court Grand Jury charging Winnie with slaying Garland Radford
by "shooting him with a pistol" on July 8, 1915. (*State v. Winnie Jo
Morris*, No. 891, Hardeman County, Texas District Court.)

District Judge Nabors ordered the murder cases severed, and he put
Miss Winnie to trial first.

An all-star cast of attorneys was assembled to prosecute and defend
Miss Winnie. District Attorney W. D. Berry of Vernon was the lead
prosecutor, assisted by attorneys M. M. Hankins, longtime Quanah
attorney, and O. T. Warlick of Paducah, Texas. Hankins was one of
the first residents of Quanah, arriving in 1885 with a brand-new law
license. That same year, he was appointed as the first county attorney
of Hardeman County and later was elected county judge, a position he
held for several years before going into private law practice. The for-
midable Amos J. Fires of Childress headed up Miss Winnie's defense

A.J. Fires, an early-day bulldog of a defense lawyer, lost only 4 of the 123 murder cases wherein he defended the accused. He often associated with Temple Houston (son of Texas hero Sam Houston) on the defense. Whatever Fires may have lacked in Houstonian eloquence, he made up for in tenacity, toughness, and total dedication to his client. (Image courtesy of the Panhandle-Plains Historical Museum, Special Collections, Canyon, Texas.)

team, ably assisted by Fires's partner, Davis E. Decker (himself a noted defense lawyer) and R. V. Crowder of Quanah, who, no doubt, was most helpful in selecting a favorable jury.

A. J. Fires and his friend and frequent cocounsel in celebrated murder trials, Temple Houston—youngest son of the revered Texas hero Sam Houston—were two of the most famous and successful criminal defense lawyers of their era.[5] Fires may not have been as brilliant or as eloquent as Houston, but he made up for it with unswerving tenacity, bulldog determination, exhaustive trial preparation, and an earthy demeanor that played well to rural jurors. Murder trials were his specialty. In defending those accused of murder, he seldom lost a case during his long career.[6]

Once during Fires's salad days, a stranger woke Fires up early one morning in a state of panic and blurted out this tale: He had just killed another man with whom he had been feuding for several years. The two had chanced to meet on a country road somewhere near Childress; tempers flared, and matters escalated from bad to worse, culminating in Fires's client-to-be grabbing his 12-gauge shotgun and blasting his antagonist into kingdom come. The victim had been unarmed. The shooter left his victim lying beside the road, and immediately rushed to town to consult with Fires. He told Fires that there were no witnesses to the incident except himself and the victim.

After digesting all this, Fires loaded up his new client and raced to the crime scene. Sure enough, there was the body. Nobody had discovered it. While examining the area, Fires noticed a broken wagon wheel spoke about the size of a small baseball bat down the road some distance. He called his client to bring his shotgun. Then he had the client shoot the wagon spoke from about the same distance he had been from the victim when he fatally wounded him. Then he seized the wagon spoke (now sprinkled with several shotgun pellets), and threw it down beside the body, whereupon Fires and client departed in haste. Fires directed the client to immediately rush into the sheriff's office and breathlessly report the killing, adding that he had no choice but to shoot the fellow since he was coming at him with a club and threatening to beat his brains out. Sure enough, when the sheriff arrived on the scene and conducted his investigation, he discovered the body and the wagon spoke club lying beside it—both liberally punctured by the same size shotgun pellets. Fires then encountered little difficulty making a self-defense plea stand up in court.[7]

In a time when trials, rodeos, and revivals were about the only form of public entertainment available, folks would gather from miles around, camp out on the courthouse lawn, and pack the courtroom when they learned that A. J. Fires was the defendant's attorney in a murder case.

The high-caliber legal talent on both sides did not escape the notice of the *Tribune-Chief* reporter, who during the ensuing trial took time out to share these observations with his readers:

> A royal battle of wits is going on between these two brilliant members of the bar, Judge Berry and Fires who are respectively conducting the prosecution and defense. Berry, imperturbable and urbane; Fires, quick as lightning and sharp as a Damascene blade. The two have met in many a legal battle, and to watch their attack and parry is a feast of the mind.[8]

And so, in that packed, emotionally charged courtroom, the trial finally began. The State made known that it was seeking the death penalty—probably a grave tactical mistake on the part of the prosecution given the mores of the time relating to the "gentler, kinder" sex.

Promptly at ten o'clock the Morris family arrived. Miss Winnie was wearing a black toque, a black dress, and a light blue coat. Her hair hung down in ringlets. The reporter noted that she "looked very slight and young." While District Attorney Berry read the indictment charging her with killing Garland W. Radford "with malice aforethought . . . by shooting him with a pistol," she rose and stood before the jury "pale but perfectly composed." Fires answered for his client, Miss Winnie: "Not guilty."

Jury selection then began. From the juror examinations it became apparent there were two cross-currents churning beneath the surface: sex and class. In those times, class distinction was more pronounced than today; the prominent and well-off Radford family versus the Morris family, the blue-collar manual laborers. Some prospective jurors were excused when they disclosed that they were obligated on loans from the Radfords' First Guaranty State Bank. Other men said they would find it difficult to be a juror in a case where a woman was accused of murder, especially where the State was seeking the death penalty. Another admitted that he would not convict a woman as quickly as a man, and he was promptly challenged by the prosecution.

Finally a jury was seated, and District Attorney W. D. Berry of Vernon, a skilled and veteran trial lawyer, began the proceedings by reminding the jury that the State was seeking the death penalty. Then he got down to business. The State's case was simple and direct, and there was no real dispute about the facts.

The State called four eyewitnesses to the killing: Oscar Simpson, J. O. Yates, A. Z. Stevens, and Duncan Greenleaf. All testified to essentially the same thing. On the day of the shooting they, together with Garland Radford, had been employed by A. F. Decker to thresh wheat on "the Crowder place." The Crowder place was located only about a half mile west of the Morris home on the western edge of Quanah. Garland Radford was driving the horse-drawn water wagon for the threshing crew that day. Sometime during the day, a pivotal event occurred in that wheat field—a confrontation between Bob Morris and Garland Radford.

At quitting time that afternoon, the whole crew formed a caravan of horse-drawn wagons and headed back to Quanah. They had to go through the yard at the Morris home. They were almost to the yard gate when they saw Miss Winnie, pistol in hand, walk out of Morris's barn. She got within about forty feet and attempted to shoot Garland, but she apparently had difficulty releasing the safety on her pistol. Meanwhile, even though Radford had a loaded .38 pistol under the wagon seat, he did not attempt to reach for it. Instead, Yates yelled for him to jump off and run—in hindsight, a really bad piece of advice. Garland tried to do just that, but his foot caught in the harness, delaying him briefly. When he finally got untangled and started to run, Miss Winnie began firing. She hit him in the back and knocked him down. But Garland jumped up and started running away again. About that time the threshing crew saw her brother, Ewell, emerge from the barn and begin firing with another pistol, and then father Bob appeared with a shotgun. They all began shooting at Garland. Radford was knocked down again. This time he didn't get up. But the shooting continued. Meanwhile, they heard Bob Morris yell, "Shoot the sonofabitch." About that time, they saw Mrs. Morris run out of the barn and join in the blood-frenzied free-for-all. She ran over to the fallen man and shouted, "Bring the hatchet and let me cut his damned head off."

Two doctors testified. One identified twenty-seven bullet wounds on the body, seven apparently from pistol shots and the other twenty were from medium-size shotgun pellets. Any one of several wounds would have proven fatal according to their testimony. Next, the State called Sheriff Walker, who recited the confession Miss Winnie had made just after the shooting. The State then rested its case. Now it was the defense's turn.

Miss Winnie's defense was in the able hands of old A. J. Fires, the battle-scarred lion of the defense bar who in a long and colorful career in West Texas courtrooms had persuaded 119 out of 123 juries in murder cases to acquit his client. Still, what could he do? Miss Winnie never recanted the confession she made to Sheriff Walker, never claimed it was made involuntarily. She could hardly claim insanity. She had no history of mental illness, and Sheriff Walker testified that when he took her confession less than half an hour after the killing, she was calm and rational. Self-defense? Hardly. The unarmed Garland Radford had been shot repeatedly in the back as he ran away from his attackers. Lesser defense attorneys might have thrown in the towel at this juncture and persuaded their client to plead guilty and beg the district attorney or the jury for mercy and a lenient sentence. After all, there were some extremely emotionally potent arguments to be made in favor of miti-gation; few and far between are the defendants who, confronted with such bull-stout evidence against them while standing in the shadow of the gallows, wouldn't have jumped at the chance to do light time—and thank God and the Tooth Fairy for the favor. Besides, Miss Winnie was bucking the powerful and prominent Radford family.

But wily old A. J. Fires wasn't about to start throwing in towels or running up white flags. He was in to win.

Thinking trial strategy, two things were clear from the outset. First, the State would have no difficulty proving up beyond *any* doubt by uncontested testimony that Miss Winnie, in concert with father and brother, intentionally killed Garland Radford. Second, that being the case, A. J. Fires could not afford to sit back and simply try to pick at the State's case, hoping to raise reasonable doubt as to Miss Winnie's guilt. In addition, he couldn't afford to exercise the defendant's right not to testify. It was clear even to neophytes that Miss Winnie would eventually have to take the stand and testify. But what would she say? Indeed, what *could* she say?

Fires called A. F. Decker, the threshing crew boss, as his first wit-ness. Decker testified that he knew there was some trouble between the Morris family and Radford before the shooting. On the fateful day, Radford was in charge of hauling water for the crew. He proposed to get the water from a source near the railroad roundhouse only about 150 yards from the Morris home. Decker said he told Radford not to go there, but instead get the water from another source farther from the wheat field, as "I didn't want any trouble." But Radford refused, saying that "it didn't bother him," and he was going there anyway. After the killing, Decker said he removed Radford's fully loaded .38-caliber pistol from under the wagon seat where Radford had been seated.

Now it was time for Fires to get down to the real business of defense. He set the stage by calling Mrs. Morris, Miss Winnie's mother. She was crying and became hysterical when put on the stand, and it took some time to get her calmed down sufficiently to begin her testimony. She told this story: She and Bob Morris were married in Dallas in 1890. They had lived in Cleburne, Johnson County, Texas, until about six years earlier when they moved to Quanah upon Bob's employment as the railroad's shop foreman. She told that Miss Winnie was not yet twenty-one years of age. She had gone to school in Johnson County and in Quanah but was always frail, so she never could attend regularly. Finally, after the tenth grade, she had to drop out of school because the family could no longer afford tuition and books. She told of Miss Winnie's employment with the photographer beginning in September 1913. Then, in December 1913 she was hired by Garland Radford as a stenographer and bookkeeper at his land title office in Quanah, and held that job until late spring of 1914, when she quit, complaining of being sick. Unlike her usual "jolly" self, she now became despondent. She went to Tolbert, Texas (about twenty-five miles east of Quanah), and visited friends or relatives for a time, and then went to stay with her grandmother in Fort Worth. When she returned to Quanah in the fall of 1914, she was a "physical wreck." Finally, on about December 12, 1914, Miss Winnie broke down and told her mother that she was "in a family way" and that Garland Radford was responsible.

Unwisely—very unwisely—District Attorney Berry then elected to cross-examine Miss Winnie's weeping mother. Mrs. Morris gave her account of the day of the killing. In a most tantalizing and cryptic bit of testimony, she related that on the morning of the shooting her husband, Bob, took Miss Winnie's baby and went out to the wheat field where the threshing crew was working and confronted Garland Radford. Mrs. Morris simply added that Bob "did not stay [in the wheat field] very long."

At the time of the shooting, Mrs. Morris continued, Miss Winnie weighed only about seventy-five pounds. She said that after supper that day, about five o'clock (after Bob had confronted Garland in the wheat field with the baby), she sent Miss Winnie to slop the hogs. Mrs. Morris went to the barn to "look for some setting hens" and later, when she looked up, she saw Miss Winnie approach Garland Radford on the water wagon. She saw him jump off the wagon and saw Winnie shoot while he was looking at her. On further cross-examination by Berry, Mrs. Morris claimed she didn't recall making the remark: "Bring the hatchet, and let me cut his damned head off." She added that she did not hear anybody say, "Kill the sonofabitch."

The stage was now set for Miss Winnie to testify—Fires's trump card. Trump card, well, maybe. But it still looked very much like an open-and-shut, airtight case, whatever Winnie might say. No legal defense seemed viable. The operative word there, however, was *legal*. The defense A. J. Fires had in mind for Miss Winnie had very little to do with the written laws of the State of Texas.

Fires was an astute observer of people and human nature. He knew his audience, and he knew what resonated with them. He well understood the strict Victorian mores and sexual taboos of the times. Plus, he was absolutely tireless and thorough in his trial preparation. He orchestrated every defense as meticulously as if it were a Broadway production, and he thoroughly rehearsed every witness—over and over again. And in this case, his star witness was, of course, Miss Winnie herself. Dressed plainly in black, she appeared shy and nervous and trembled slightly when she took the stand. She was pale and frail, weighing less than one hundred pounds. But Miss Winnie's fate now rested squarely on those frail shoulders.

Miss Winnie did very well on the stand. Really well. This is the story she told:

She had not been able to finish high school because her parents were too poor to pay for her tuition and books, so she had to drop out of school and find a job. In December 1913 Garland Radford hired her as his secretary in his land title and insurance business. She was eighteen and unmarried at the time. Garland was then twenty-two years old, married, and the father of an infant daughter. A few months later she had to quit that job because she had become pregnant with Garland Radford's child. Garland insisted she move to her grandmother's home in Fort Worth before it became apparent to the community that she was pregnant. And who, besides Winnie, was responsible? The answer to that question would be as apparent as Winnie's condition. Garland vowed his love for her and promised that he would divorce his wife, marry her, and they would move to California. Miss Winnie told the

jury that she fell under his influence and firmly believed in his honorable intentions.

Months went by, but somehow Radford didn't get around to filing for
a divorce. He occasionally wrote her love letters, but always insisted that
she destroy them. In addition, he mailed her some medicine—medicine
for "headaches," he said. He prescribed the dosages she should take.

Unfortunately for Garland Radford, Miss Winnie was becoming
increasingly suspicious. Instead of taking the prescribed dosages, she
took only a tiny bit of the headache medicine. She testified that she felt
"drugged" at the time and feared Garland was trying to poison her and
so refused to take anymore.

Also unfortunately for Garland, Miss Winnie did not destroy Garland's letters, but instead produced them at the time of trial and read
them to the jury. One read, in part:

> Don't be foolish. Take the medicine like I told you, only take three big
> doses two hours apart and then four. Remember you are not the only
> one to lose if you don't play straight. If you haven't any of the dope
> write to me and I will send more. . . . Be careful. Someone almost got
> your letter. Keep a stiff upper lip and everything will be alright. Tear
> this letter up. Someone may get a hold of it. Keep quiet and things will
> be all OK . . . I want to make it as easy as possible for you.

Thoughtfully, Garland even enclosed an envelope for her to use
when she replied. It was a business stationary envelope ("German Alli-
ance Insurance Company") with Garland's name and address typed on
it. Instead, Miss Winnie kept it and produced it in court.

Meanwhile, time went by, and with each day Winnie's suspicions
as to the sincerity of Garland's repeated assurances of his undying love
for her continued to grow. Sometime in the fall of 1914, he promised
to come to Fort Worth for her. He failed to show. Finally, it dawned
on Miss Winnie that she had been deceived, and that was when, a
few months later in December, she tearfully returned to Quanah and
confessed to her humiliated parents. Then she returned to her grandmother's home in Fort Worth, and there, on February 1, 1915, her baby
was born. It was a boy.

Letters introduced into evidence in the trial of "Miss Winnie" Morris for the murder of Garland Radford, the (married) father of her illegitimate child. (*State v. Winnie Jo Morris*, No 891 in the Hardeman County, Texas District Court.)

Dont be foolish, Take that medicine
like I told you only take three
big doses two hours apart and
then four. Remember you
are not the only one to loose
it if you don't play straight if
you havent any of the dope
write me and I will send
you more. Let me know
just before you go to
Ft. Worth. Be careful some
one almost got your letter. Keep
a stiff upper lip and every
thing will be alright.
Tear this letter up someone
may get a hold of it. Just
Keep quiet and things will
be all o.k. Be sure and let
me know before you go
to Fort Worth. I know you
will get out of it alright
but I want to make it as
easy as possible for you.

Garland Radford's letter to Miss Winnie, introduced into evidence in her trial.

About two weeks later, Garland finally did show up in Fort Worth. They had a fateful encounter on a downtown Fort Worth street corner—hardly the romantic setting she had envisioned for his return; hardly the hearts-and-flowers elopement to sunny California where they would live happily ever after. It was definitely not the future she had dreamed of all those lonely nights—not at all what he had been promising. Instead, Garland now had a new plan.

He wanted her and the baby to go to Houston, where he said he had "influential relatives" who would get her a good job. Winnie stubbornly insisted that she would not go anywhere without him—and then only as his wife. And if he wouldn't marry her, she would return to Quanah and live with her parents. Garland ordered her not to return to Quanah, saying that it would be impossible for both of them to live there. Then he threatened to steal or kill the baby if she brought it back to Quanah.

But Garland's threats and scare tactics didn't work. In fact they backfired. Winnie was not only humiliated, she was enraged. And, as the saying goes, "hell hath no fury like . . ."

Sure enough, babe in arms, Winnie returned to her family. Her appearance with the baby publicly shamed them in that small Victorian-era community. They also were humiliated—and enraged.

At that point, the court recessed for the day. The next day, Miss Winnie resumed her testimony, and the *Tribune-Chief* editor gave this account:

> On Wednesday Miss Winnie continued the recital of her wrongs, saying that after she came back to Quanah in the spring of 1915, she saw Radford several times under the window of her room. She was frightened, and began carrying a revolver that her father had given her.[9]

To an experienced trial lawyer of today, viewing those proceedings that took place almost a century ago and in a very different culture, Miss Winnie's testimony that the newspaper recounted sounds a tad off-key. It sounds, suspiciously, a lot more like A. J. Fires than Miss Winnie Morris. The assertion that Garland Radford was surreptitiously and repeatedly creeping around Miss Winnie's seems most suspect, at best. What, pray tell, would have been his purpose? Recall that by then the whole town was already aware of the situation. To argue that Garland planned to steal a baby he never wanted in the first place, or that he wanted to kill Miss Winnie and thereby almost certainly earn himself an immediate murder indictment, sounds ludicrous. Was he trying to intimidate Miss Winnie? Hardly. He must have learned from the Fort Worth encounter that the enraged Miss Winnie was not about to be intimidated, and especially now that the secret was out and she was lodged in the bosom of her family. And, had Garland really been skulking around the Morris home, wouldn't Bob Morris have reported it to the local sheriff—or worse, taken matters into his own hands?

On the other hand, A. J. Fires was in desperate need of some *legal* peg upon which to hang a defense in a case that seemed open-and-shut in favor of the prosecution. At the outset of the trial, "self-defense" must have seemed a most unlikely peg. Yet perhaps Fires was grasping for any old straw at that point. The portion of Miss Winnie's testimony reported in the newspaper seems like a rather flimsy platform upon which to construct a self-defense plea, but then it was better than nothing at all. If the jury could be made to believe that Garland really was stalking her with God knows what evil intent, then maybe the jury would believe her when she said the whole family was frightened of Garland to the extent that they all started packing pistols. Then when Garland later showed up at their gate (with a loaded .38 pistol within arm's reach), the Morris family believed he was about to launch some lethal attack. Therefore, they had to make a preemptive strike to protect themselves. Sounds pretty far-fetched, but it at least provided Fires with some basis, however weak, to make a legal self-defense argument. The bottom line was that if the jury returned with the "not guilty" verdict that Fires sought, it was not obligated to specify whether the verdict was based on legal self-defense or based on the actual, if unstated, defense that Fires was advocating—the unwritten law.

In any event that part of Miss Winnie's recital does not have a truthful ring to it.

Winnie next told the jury what happened on the early afternoon of that tragic day in July, 1915. She said her father took his baby grandson in his arms and marched out into the wheat field where Garland and the threshing crew were working. He confronted Garland before the entire crew. Exactly what was said has not been recorded, but whatever

Garland told him, it was the wrong thing to say—dead wrong, as it turned out. Then he turned his back on Bob and the baby and shunned them. That mental image of Bob Morris, in the wheat field, infant in arms, confronting the arrogant scion of a blue-blood family, the author of his daughter's ruin, and then being rebuffed before all those men. . . . Well, it must have had considerable visceral impact on the jurors.

A furious Bob Morris slowly returned from the wheat field that afternoon and told Miss Winnie, Ewell, and his wife what had just transpired.

As a finale to her performance on the witness stand, Fires had Miss Winnie produce the love letters written to her by Garland, and then he had her read them to the jury. However, Judge Nabors had to stop the proceedings and clear the overflow from the courtroom. The courtroom was designed to seat about 300 people, but when the time arrived to read those love letters, some 450 more had managed to squeeze in around the edges. Judge Nabors ordered all who could not find seats to vacate the courtroom, plus anybody else who was eighteen years of age or younger.

Unfortunately, the content of those love letters, as well as what Bob Morris told his family upon his return from the wheat field confrontation with Garland Radford, and other scandalous portions of Miss Winnie's story are not available. No trial transcript exists now, and the only report we have of trial testimony is what the local newspaper saw fit to print, and in that Victorian era, all sexually explicit testimony was ignored. (Can anyone imagine modern media informing its readers or viewers: "Sorry, her testimony was too salacious to report"?)

That Miss Winnie's performance was worth an Academy Award is beyond doubt, as evidenced by the *Quanah Tribune-Chief* editor's take on her performance—a report that also provides us with a most revealing, though unintended, comment on the sexual mores of the day. The local editor wrote this:

> Miss Winnie Morris, the defendant, was then put on the stand and as much of her testimony is unprintable, we shall not attempt to give all. Suffice it to say, that the story she told was the old, sordid tale of a lustful, unscrupulous man's duplicity and cruelty towards a helpless, tiny bit of a girl. The recital was dramatic, and even among the jurymen

there was a suspicious amount of sniffling, and a surreptitious use of handkerchiefs. At the height of the recital the witness slid out of her chair and fainted.[10]

The editor might have added: "Right on cue! Perfect! Just dead solid perfect!"

And so ended Miss Winnie's tale.

But A. J. Fires was not finished yet. Emphasizing Mrs. Morris's testimony of her daughter's physical and emotional devastation as well as Miss Winnie's own testimony of being intentionally "drugged" by Garland Radford, Fires then called Dr. J. T. Horton to the stand. The *Tribune-Chief* reporter did not favor his readers with Dr. Horton's credentials or expertise, if any. Nevertheless, Dr. Horton was allowed to testify that in his opinion the mental and physical condition of Miss Winnie, in addition to want of sleep, at the time of the killing made her "irresponsible" for any act. Furthermore, he continued, in his opinion the drugs Garland gave Miss Winnie must have contained morphine, and that had she taken them as Garland directed, it would have been a "fatal dose." He admitted on cross-examination that he had never seen the drugs or any analysis of their contents. He admitted that he was simply relying upon Miss Winnie's description of the drug and its effect. However, that didn't deter Dr. Horton from insisting that in his opinion the drug "probably" contained morphine and that the suggested dosage "probably" would have proven fatal.

Lawyer Fires then attempted, unsuccessfully, to put some icing on the defense cake by calling two witnesses to testify as to Garland Radford's promiscuous womanizing and his lack of character. The prosecution objected to their testimony before it was given in open court, and so Judge Nabors had the jury removed from the courtroom and heard their testimony outside the jury's presence and hearing in order to rule on its admissibility.

Fires first called Miss Gustine Brayzi of Fort Worth. She was Garland Radford's attending nurse at St. Joseph's Hospital in Fort Worth during his two-week recovery from an appendectomy in 1912—all this occurring less than three months after Garland's marriage. Garland must have made a very quick and vigorous recovery, because Miss Brayzi testified that she became engaged to him, unaware that he was a married man. The other proffered defense witness was Dock Wilson. He related a conversation between himself and Garland Radford that occurred in the fall of 1914. According to Wilson, Radford told him that he "was in trouble over a woman, not the first by any means, but that he was caught up now." However, Wilson testified, Radford told him that he "intended to lay it on somebody else." Wilson said he advised Radford to get out of town.

But Judge Nabors ruled that the testimony of both of these two witnesses was unfairly prejudicial and thus inadmissible, and so the jury never got to hear either testify.

Here the defense rested and turned the courtroom back to the prosecution for rebuttal. The only rebuttal witness called by the State was the widow of the slain victim, Mrs. Garland W. Radford III. She testified that she and Garland were married in Weatherford, Texas, on September 15, 1912, and they had one child. Her testimony was obviously intended to portray Miss Winnie as something less than the pure, innocent little lamb that Fires had depicted. She said she took her baby to her husband's abstract office often, and that Miss Winnie would play with the baby—this at a time when the duplicitous Miss Winnie was having an affair with her husband. She also said that although the Morris house was a considerable distance from the Radford home, she once saw Miss Winnie walk by their house three times in one afternoon.

At that point, the case was over except for jury arguments—which were extensive. All six of the trial lawyers got to address the jury: Warlick and Hankins opened the fireworks for the prosecution, then Decker, Crowder, and Fires, in that order, took it to the jury for the defense. They were followed by the State's closing argument articulated by District Attorney Berry.

The *Tribune-Chief* reporter, unfortunately, failed to give us the benefit of these orations. He simply summed it up thusly:

> It would be too much to try to give their speeches . . . suffice it to say that the arguments produced were strong, and the points well taken, and that the eloquence displayed by prosecution and defense both were of a high order, fully up to anything ever heard in the Hardeman temple of justice before.[11]

Although Fires made a faint nod toward the legal defenses of "temporary insanity" and "self-defense," it was clear his real defense was emotional, not legal. Read: "the-scoundrel-deserved-a-damn-good-killing-anyway" defense. In his requests to the trial judge for jury instructions, Fires asked the judge to tell the jury that it should find Miss Winnie not guilty if the jurors believed she was temporarily insane on account of being "seduced . . . under false representations" by the deceased, thus causing her to be incapable of "cool reflection" and thus not "knowing the difference between right or wrong." Also, Fires asked the judge to tell the jury that it should acquit her if it believed the deceased "violated her chastity" and then, by threatening her life or the life of her child, had caused her to labor under the delusion that the deceased was actually about to carry out his earlier threat and thus making it appear to her that it was necessary for her to kill the deceased in order to preserve her own life or the life of the child. Although the trial judge properly refused to give the jury Fires's inflammatory instructions, he nevertheless did charge it on the statutory wording of the defenses of insanity and self-defense. The jury then retired—but not for long. They returned shortly with a verdict finding Miss Winnie not guilty.

The *Tribune-Chief*'s take on the verdict again reflected the usual turn-of-the-century journalistic mix. The headline contained a not-so-subtle clue as to the editor's personal view. It read, simply: "Satisfactory Verdict." The editor's account followed:

> Seldom has a verdict been received with greater satisfaction here than the news that the jury on Friday morning had pronounced Winnie Morris not guilty. Everybody seemed pleased, and we are told that ten members of the jury at the first ballot were in favor of acquittal, and that it took only three ballots in all to bring complete unanimity.[12]

Well, maybe not quite everybody was elated with the verdict. It appeared that a substantial number of folks were not thrilled. The Radford family, after all, was very prominent and had many supporters. In fact, quite a hubbub seems to have occurred after the verdict. Under a heading of "Wild Rumors" in the following week's edition of the

Tribune-Chief the editor reported that Judge Nabors had received a letter from a wife of one of the jurors who was distressed for the safety of her husband. He had received an anonymous letter from someone threatening to kill him and all the other jurors. Although the reporter dismissed this as being just another "silly report" in the trial's aftermath, Judge Nabors decided to change the venue of the upcoming murder trial of Bob and Ewell Morris to Wichita Falls, some eighty miles to the southeast of Quanah.

It was more than a year later (May 1917) when Bob and Ewell Morris were put to trial in the 78th Judicial District Court of Wichita County, Texas, in Wichita Falls. Both defendants were tried together by mutual agreement of the State and prosecution.[13] Once more, A. J. Fires, this time assisted by the Wichita Falls firm of Carrigan, Montgomery & Britain, headed up the Morris defense. This time the State did not seek the death penalty, and wisely so. First, the case against Bob and Ewell Morris was not nearly as strong as that against Miss Winnie, who, after all, was the one who led the charge. Second, the State had taken its best shot—and missed. Much of the steam was obviously taken out of the prosecution's resolve and performance. Plus, the defense now had an additional arrow in its quiver: "Miss Winnie did it!"[14]

Neither Bob nor Ewell had testified in Miss Winnie's trial. Fires also wanted to avoid putting either on the stand during their own trial, thereby dodging some embarrassing, and very likely incriminating, cross-examination probes. Fortunately for the defendants, he didn't have to. Miss Winnie, a tried, true, and potent weapon, was there to carry the ball for them: "I did it," she told the jury. Or course since she had already been tried and acquitted of the murder, she could shoulder the blame with impunity. "King's X": double jeopardy.

Miss Winnie had considerable latitude to tell the defense story and to elaborate so long as she didn't contradict her prior testimony. She was free to deny that there had been any prior common plan or scheme between herself and her father and brother to kill Radford. Plus, Winnie added that when she came out of the barn shooting and chasing Garland, she wasn't looking behind her and therefore couldn't see what her father and brother were doing. She had started shooting first and assumed that Bob and Ewell, hearing the gunshots, must have thought that Garland was attacking her, and that's why they then came out of the barn, guns blazing—all in an attempt to protect her.

While Miss Winnie was on the stand, Fires didn't miss the golden opportunity to let her recount in detail to the jury her sordid tale of woe and mistreatment at the hands of a lustful and unscrupulous scoundrel. She did so and, once again, with great effect. The prosecution objected to the trial judge's allowing Winnie to go into the "tale of sordid sexual exploitation," but the court allowed it to come into evidence—but for a limited purpose. Garland's "sordid sexual exploitation"—even if believed by the jury—did not amount to a *legal justification* for Bob and Ewell to kill him, the judge instructed the jury. However, the court continued, if the jury believed that even if Bob and Ewell intentionally killed Radford, but if jurors further believed that the attack was motivated not by cold premeditation but by a heated "sudden passion" caused by "adequate cause," then, even though it was still a crime, it would be a lesser offense: manslaughter. From a practical standpoint, however, once the stench of that sordid tale was aired, it is doubtful that any jury of that day would have been inclined to struggle with those fine judicial distinctions.

Finally, due to the sensational nature of Miss Winnie's trial and all the publicity it had previously received across Texas, and since it is only a short distance between Quanah and Wichita Falls, it is impossible to believe that at least most jurors weren't already aware that Miss Winnie had already been tried and acquitted. The jurors might well have wondered this: if Miss Winnie was the main gun and she had already been acquitted, then why was the State now prosecuting her father and brother?

In the end, the judge gave the jury a choice of four possible verdicts: (1) guilty of murder: five years to life, or death; (2) guilty of manslaughter: two to five years; (3) guilty of aggravated assault: one month to two years in the county jail; or (4) not guilty.

The jury took only about five hours to consider the matter before returning its verdict, finding both Bob and Ewell not guilty. The reporter for the *Wichita [Falls] Daily Times* noted that "those who heard the testimony in the case were not surprised at the verdict of acquittal."[15]

Ellabelle Radford, beloved Quanah,
Texas, high school teacher and daughter
of homicide victim Garland Radford.
(Author's collection.)

Soon after the trial—and after the dust finally settled—the Morris
family moved away from Quanah, never to be heard from again. Years
later, a lifelong resident of Quanah mentioned that she once heard
one of the Radford family descendants say that Dr. Radford, Garland's
father, discreetly made financial arrangements for the Morris family to
move far away and obtain employment.[16] If true—and it seems likely
that it was—what a soul-wrenching endeavor it must have been for Dr.
Radford to assist the family responsible for the murder of his son and,
at least in part, for the shocking scandal that brought such shame to the
Radford family. It was, after all, a time when a public sex scandal was
considered a family misfortune worse than death.

Epilogue

As appears in the foregoing story, at the time he was killed in 1915,
Garland Radford was the father of an infant daughter. The baby's name
was Ellabelle. Ellabelle Radford grew up to be an exceptional woman.
Other than her college years, she spent her entire life in her hometown
of Quanah. And, perhaps because of the nature of the tragedy that

ended her father's life, she never married. Intelligent, personable, and endowed with a wry and earthy sense of humor, Ellabelle was much beloved by the students she taught for many years in Quanah High School and nearly everybody else in town—including the author of this tale. Ellabelle, now deceased, was my high school algebra teacher, my tennis coach, and a very dear friend for the rest of her life. She used to call me "Lightnin'." Why, I can't imagine.

FOUR

A Valentine's Day Tragedy

THE BOY FROM THE WRONG SIDE OF THE TRACKS

"Oh, how they danced
On the night they were wed.
They vowed their true love,
Though a word wasn't said."

"THE ANNIVERSARY SONG," paraphrase
of lyrics by Jolson and Chaplin, 1946

olks said that Buster was the best dancer in town, and
when he and the mayor's daughter took the floor, everybody stood back and watched. Watched while they gyrated
to the jazzy rhythm of the Charleston, that outrageous new dance that
was sweeping the nation.[1] And what a couple they made! Mary Frances,
seventeen, was beautiful, vibrant, artistically talented, and headstrong.
Buster, only two years older, was handsome, energetic, optimistic, and
determined.

They were deeply, desperately in love. Her parents thought—hoped,
at least—that it was only a teenage crush, or perhaps both were just
crazy about dancing. What they did not know—what nobody knew
except the young couple—was that Buster Robertson and Mary Fran-

Elzie "Buster" Robertson, taken from February 16, 1925, *Wichita Falls Record News.* (Image courtesy of *Wichita Falls Times Record News.*)

Mary Frances Collier, taken from July 31, 2005, *Wichita Falls Times Record News.* (Image courtesy of *Wichita Falls Times Record News.*)

ces Collier were married and had been for several months. One night in June 1924 they had eloped—slipped out of their hometown of Wichita Falls, Texas, and crossed the Red River into Oklahoma, where they lied about their ages, got a marriage license, and then found a Methodist minister to perform the ceremony. The blissful couple never regretted it: it was a marriage made in heaven, and it would last forever. And "forever" would last for a very long time.

The carefree lovers danced long into the night in the fancy ballroom of Wichita Falls' new 225-room Kemp Hotel. It had been built only four years earlier and soon would become the first hotel in the United States to boast wall-to-wall air-conditioning from the lobby to the penthouse.[2]

The world of Buster and Mary Frances was filled with gaiety and laughter. And indeed the world they inhabited was blessed with a serendipitous confluence of a very special place with a very special time. It was 1925, right in the midst of the Roarin' Twenties. World War I was over, and the world was now safe for democracy—and the Jazz Age, which was just beginning to heat up. What in the world was to be done with this New Generation? "Shocking" just didn't quite cover all the unholy stuff that was going around—and sometimes those scandalous skirts the flappers were wearing just didn't quite cover, well . . . hardly anything . . . including all those most unladylike wigglings-around that were going on when the flappers danced the Charleston or the Black Bottom.[3] And, Lordy, some of those brassy flappers were even glimpsed smoking cigarettes. And in public no less![4] Some folks even drove those Model T Ford automobiles.[5] Of course, not everyone was thrilled with such carryings-on, especially south of the Mason-Dixon Line, where Victorian notions of propriety and restraint still held sway, particularly when it came to sex and the proper roles of conduct for ladies and gentlemen. Notions of chivalry were still very much alive and well, particularly in upper-class society, and especially if, as did many Texans of that time, they shared an Old South heritage. While women were now allowed to vote, still only men could serve on juries and smoke openly in public. Nevertheless, life was lighter and more fun in the 1920s. But, in addition to being a special *time*, 1925 Wichita Falls was also a special *place*—a place of promise, a vibrant place bursting with enthusiasm and industry. There was excitement in the air because Wichita Falls was a boomtown. Oil! Big oil!

Only a few years earlier this site had been a sparsely populated buffalo grass cow pasture in the rolling plains of North Texas some 150 miles northwest of Dallas. Some settlers cleared small fields to grow wheat and cotton, but mostly it was cow country, and only a handful of cattle barons like Burk Burnett and Dan Waggoner and his son, W. T. Waggoner, boasted much wealth. Wichita Falls was first linked to the outside world in 1882, when the Fort Worth & Denver City Railroad Company's tracks reached the city limits. Still, even then it was a horse-and-buggy place until well after the turn of the century. In 1900, the village counted only 2,400 adventurous souls as residents.[6]

The first hint of big things to come was noted in 1903, when cattle baron W. T. Waggoner dug a shallow water well on his half-million-acre ranch near the present-day village of Electra some twenty-five miles west of Wichita Falls. At least Waggoner thought he was drilling a water well. He was disgusted when, instead of water, some slimy black stuff started oozing out of the hole. "Cows can't drink that gunk," he grumbled. W. T. was somewhat mollified when he discovered that

The Electra oil field located near the town of Electra, Texas (approximately twenty-five miles west of Wichita Falls) opened up in 1911 with the discovery of the Clayco No. 1 well. Here a team of mules pulls a wagon load of oil through the muddy streets of downtown Electra shortly after the field began producing. (Image courtesy of Wichita County Historical Commission.)

he could dip his cows in the nasty stuff and thus rid them of disease-bearing ticks.[7] However, some eight years later, oil men caught the scent and opened up the rich Electra oil field with the discovery of a gusher called the Clayco No. 1.[8] That shifted the economic base of the whole county. But the boom didn't really skyrocket until July 26, 1918, when the Fowler No. 1 gusher sprayed oil all over the countryside just a few miles north of Wichita Falls in the Burkburnett community (named for cattle baron Burk Burnett).[9] The massive Burkburnett oil field caused Wichita Falls bank deposits to skyrocket by 400 percent in 1919. Oil refineries and factories began to spring up. By 1926, there were thirty-three oil refineries and seven gas plants in the community and some 122 manufacturing companies supplying the petroleum industry with oil field supplies from pumps to drilling equipment to nitroglycerin.[10] According to Wichita Falls historian Edgar Shockley, by 1925, "there were more millionaires per square mile in Wichita Falls than anywhere else in the world."[11] Wichita Falls had rapidly become an economic and social hub in the Red River country located approxi-

mately halfway between Fort Worth to the east and Amarillo to the west, all three cities being linked by the FW&DC Railroad.

The 1926 Wichita Falls city directory, in keeping with the happy-face chamber of commerce boosterism so typical of frontier villages, declared that the population had swelled from 2,400 in 1900 to 55,000 in 1926, and that all its 55,000 inhabitants were "happy, loyal, contented and home-loving people." Undoubtedly, some were. There were, after all, thirty-seven churches, a 260-acre park, an eighteen-hole golf course, and "a bathing beach" at 2,900-acre Lake Wichita, as well as the fancy 225-room Kemp Hotel and other downtown buildings that kept popping up and springing skyward.[12]

On the other hand, more than a few local residents didn't quite fit that "happy, contented and home-loving" mold. Historian Shockley chuckled, "It was about as wild and woolly as you can get."[13] And Wichita Falls archivist Lita Watson later reflected that the boom "brought in all kinds of people eager to make money in oil or off the people who did. Brawls and gunfights were common. Wages for workers were high by the standards of the day, but many diversions could separate a man from his money":[14] a thriving red-light district sprang up in the "dogpatch" part of town. Cards, dice, shell games, and get-rich-

The huge Burkburnett oil field located near Burkburnett, Texas (approximately ten miles north of Wichita Falls), came to life with the discovery of the Fowler No. 1 well on July 26, 1918. (Image courtesy of Wichita County Historical Commission.)

opposite page: Shortly after the discovery of the Fowler No. 1 well, the Burkburnett field turned into a forest of oil derricks. (Image courtesy of Wichita County Historical Commission.)

quick oil promotional scams—not to mention the old standbys of dope, loose women, and bootleg whiskey (which, despite Prohibition laws, was readily available). And it wasn't just the oil-patch roughnecks who quenched their thirst with illegal booze. Some of those happy, home-loving folks who held prominent stations in the community were occasionally glimpsed furtively toting around vessels containing liquids other than coffee or tea, all concealed in plain brown paper bags.

Even cold sober, though, times were good. Excitement crackled. Unbridled optimism reigned. Model T Fords, oil trucks, and streetcars rattled up and down the streets, and men from all walks of life scurried about. Wealthy bankers, shrewd businessmen, contentious lawyers, and hustling oil operators rubbed shoulders and traded jokes with roughnecks, roustabouts, toolpushers, drillers, promoters, shysters, gamblers, and conmen.

Speaking of the last, J. D. McMahon comes to mind. J. D. McMahon was a man who recognized a bird's nest on the ground when he saw one. When the slick Philadelphia promoter stepped off the train and surveyed the frenzied 1919 Wichita Falls scene where the recent discovery of black gold had turned thousands of town folk into millionaires . . . well, he knew he was in huckster heaven. Folks with pockets

Shortly after the Electra oil field began producing in 1911 and the Burkburnett oil field followed suit in 1918, Wichita Falls became a crowded, frenzied boomtown. Above scene is downtown Wichita Falls, 1919. (Image courtesy of Wichita County Historical Commission.)

full of cash were scurrying about the streets making deals right and left—big deals, too. Oil lease deals, mineral rights deals, drilling deals. Deals were made on street corners and in the shade of tents that served oil operators as company headquarters. "What we need here," J. D. thought, "is a gigantic office building where all these high-rollers can locate." He had identified a desperate need, and J. D. McMahon was a man with a plan—complete with blueprints.

Blueprints for such a building in hand, it didn't take a talented talker like our hero long to raise $200,000 from eager investors caught up in the get-rich-quick fever of the day. Quite a sum that, considering that a fellow could buy a barrel of oil for two dollars, give or take. McMahon promised his investors that he would build a multistory office building at the corner of Seventh Street and LaSalle, just across the street from the thriving St. James Hotel.

McMahon did, in fact, build a "multistory office building," but his skyscraper hardly soared to the stratosphere—it barely graced the

Boomtown Wichita Falls proved a fertile field for con men and shysters of all descriptions. In 1919 J. D. McMahon scammed gullible investors out of $200,000 by promising to build a "skyscraper" office building. He then proceeded to build what became known as "the world's littlest skyscraper" which, when completed, reached skyward only forty feet high and was about the size of a large elevator shaft—eleven feet wide by nineteen feet in length, to be exact. (Author's collection.)

Wichita Falls skyline. In fact, it was later dubbed "the World's Littlest Skyscraper." When completed, it looked more like an elevator shaft than a high-rise office complex. This four-story freak was only forty feet tall with a total of only 118 square feet of office space per floor. The outside dimensions were only eleven feet by nineteen feet, and the stairwell that led to the upstairs floors occupied a good twenty-five percent of the interior.

When the startled investors finally recognized that something was drastically wrong, they pulled out the contract they had signed with McMahon. The blueprints for the building were attached to the contract. Upon closer examination of the blueprints, the duped investors discovered that the scale of those blueprints was in inches—not feet. They had no legal recourse, since McMahon had constructed the architectural dwarf according to the specifications given in the contract. It didn't make much difference anyhow, since by that time J. D. McMahon was long gone and gone for good. Meanwhile, McMahon's skyscraper earned a place in *Ripley's Believe It Or Not* book, and it still stands in downtown Wichita Falls—a paradoxical monument to the oil boom years.[15]

Although prominent community leaders might mix and mingle freely with common folks on the streets during the daytime, there was a distinct and growing sense of class when it came to private lives. When the first settlers began trickling into the area after the Civil War, nearly all were poor, land-hungry pioneers—common folks struggling just to survive. Within a few years, however, as more merchants, professional types, and promoters moved into the settlements, class distinctions began to take root and grow.

Wichita Falls, like most other frontier towns in the West that survived and prospered, was located along a railroad line. Typically, that led to a rather remarkable demographic phenomenon. The richer, more prominent townspeople tended to settle on one side of those railroad tracks, while the poor "common" folks were relegated to the other side of the tracks—"the wrong side of the tracks," as it became known in almost every settlement. Thus, saying that somebody was from "the wrong side of the tracks" became a shorthand way of dismissing the subject as a lower-class person not welcome in polite society. In 1925 Wichita Falls, the "wrong side of the tracks" became known as the "dogpatch" or "No-Man's-Land"[16]—a piece of real estate so unattractive that no one cared if squatters of whatever race threw up any kind of shack or shelter to keep out of the weather.

Meanwhile, on the "right side of the tracks," Wichita Falls was booming. Downtown, new buildings kept popping up, and more mansions graced residential areas. In fact, according to historian Shockley, when Commodore Vanderbilt visited Wichita Falls during the twenties, he commented that there were more opulent mansions in Wichita Falls than he had ever before seen in one place. Brothers-in-law Frank Kell and Joseph Alexander Kemp were the richest oilmen in town, and it was the latter (with associates) who built the Kemp Hotel. The lobby of the Kemp Hotel was *the* place to be if you wanted to do an oil deal, and it was *the* place to be seen if you wanted to impress anybody.[17] (Today, the two main thoroughfares in town are named Kemp and Kell.

Some Wichita Falls oldtimers still quote the local formula for success: "Think like Kemp; work like Kell.")

In 1925, Wichita Falls was indeed that magical and unprecedented blend of the best of times with the best of places. Then, multiply that by ten, if you happened to be a young couple, newly married, much in love, and dancing to heart's content in that fancy ballroom. Buster and Mary Frances were so looking forward to their first Valentine's Day together as a married couple. It was a fairy tale almost too good to come true.

For readers of classic English literature, however, the story of the romance of Buster and Mary Frances—and its aftermath—bears an eerily familiar ring to a tale of star-crossed lovers told some five centuries earlier by a bard named William Shakespeare. He entitled his tale *Romeo and Juliet.*

———

The beautiful and talented Mary Frances was the daughter, and only child, of Wichita Falls mayor Frank Collier and his wife, Dorothy McCauley Collier. Frank himself had rather humble beginnings.[18] He was seven years old when he and his mother came to Wichita Falls in about 1884. None of the accounts of his family or background mention his father, leaving a suspicion that perhaps there had been a divorce or scandal involving him. (Divorce itself *was* a scandal in that day.) However, the young Collier was determined to make something of himself. He soon found part-time employment delivering groceries and ice. (No refrigerators in those days; folks bought "ice boxes," which had to be reloaded with a new block of ice every few days.) Frank was obliged to drop out of school after the tenth grade, but he soon landed a job as a fireman on the FW&DC Railroad. About that time it was discovered that Frank had great athletic talent. He was an outstanding baseball pitcher, and that was how he first gained prominence in the community. In those times when entertainment opportunities were limited, baseball was *the* game and practically the *only* game in town. All the players were local boys, and they were community heroes. Minor league baseball was a primary source of entertainment for small cities and continued to be so even into the late 1940s and early 1950s, when television finally doomed hometown baseball teams across the nation.

Baseball was so popular, and devotion to the home team was so great, that almost everybody in town supported the team. Frank Collier would later recall that "merchants would close their stores and come to the games, or if we were playing out of town, they'd charter a special train and go with us."[19]

Frank was the star of the team, the ace pitcher for the Wichita Falls Cremos (named for a cigar brand) and later for the Wichita Falls Spudders (named for the oil field workers who "spudded" a new oil well). For twenty years he played semipro and professional baseball for Wichita Falls teams. In 1905 he pitched nineteen innings against a Fort Worth team. The game was finally called on account of darkness with the score tied, 1–1. He was so popular that for years, even after he retired from the team, he was accorded the honor of throwing out the first pitch to open every new season. Taking advantage of his popularity, Frank Collier later opened a successful clothing store, which he operated for thirteen years, and then started a sporting goods business. His prominence in the community continued to grow, as evidenced by the fact that he was elected as the second grand potentate of the Maskat Temple of the Masonic Lodge. It is almost impossible to overestimate the power and influence of the Masonic Lodge in those days. As historian Shockley, who is himself a 33rd degree Mason, observed: "Back in those days, if you wanted to get elected to anything or if you wanted to get ahead in your job or your business, it was almost essential that you be a Mason."[20] To be elected as the "grand potentate" of the lodge was an honor coveted beyond all others by most men in the community.

In 1922, Wichita Falls voters accorded forty-five-year-old hometown hero Frank Collier yet another coveted honor: they elected him the new mayor of Wichita Falls. In 1924, Frank was still the mayor and the father of his beloved daughter, Mary Frances, age seventeen. The boy with humble beginnings who came to town with a single mother and who first lived in Wichita Falls's "No-Man's-Land" and who started his career by delivering groceries had come a long way, and he was rightfully proud of his hard-earned prominence in the community.

Frank Collier's wife, Dorothy, also gloried in Frank's position and the family's exalted social status. Her father, John Henry McCauley, was a

TENDERS RESIGNATION

FRANK COLLIER

Frank Collier, 1925 mayor of Wichita Falls, taken from *Wichita Daily Times*, February 18, 1925. (Image courtesy of the *Wichita Falls Times Record News*.)

The "Cremos," Wichita Falls semi-professional baseball team, early 1900s. Frank Collier, the star pitcher for the team, is shown third from the left. (Image courtesy of *Wichita Falls Times Record News*.)

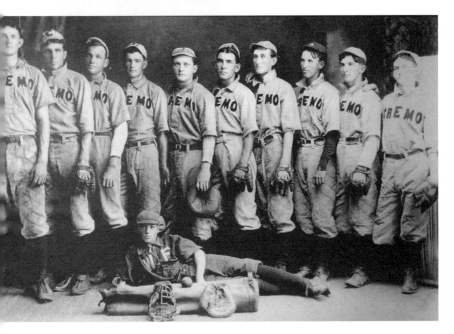

Confederate hero during the Civil War, having served with distinction as captain of Company E of the Tenth Texas Cavalry. After the war he was an active member of the Stonewall Jackson Camp of Confederate Veterans.[21] He was also an active member of the Wichita Falls Masonic Lodge. Dorothy's mother, Mary McCauley, was the sister of famed Texas Ranger Captain William Jess "Bill" McDonald.[22] Bill McDonald and his sister, Mary, had an almost idyllic Old South childhood for a time. Then came the devastation of the Civil War. Their father, Major Enoch McDonald, enlisted in the Confederate Army and was killed in 1862 in the battle at Corinth, Mississippi. In the tumultuous and desperate days following the Civil War, Mrs. McDonald gathered up her two children and migrated to Texas. Much later, Bill McDonald would become one of the four famous Texas Ranger captains of the late nineteenth century. In 1891 Governor James Stephen Hogg appointed McDonald to command Company B of the Frontier Battalion of the Texas Rangers.[23]

Meanwhile, Bill McDonald's sister, Mary, married J. H. McCauley, and they, together with their five children, including Dorothy McCauley, moved to Wichita Falls in 1884, the same year that seven-year-old Frank Collier and his mother moved to town. Dorothy was four years old at the time. Dorothy's older brother, William J. "Billy" McCauley, also became a Texas Ranger and served in his uncle Bill McDonald's ranger company. He served in that company for fifteen years, rising to the rank of lieutenant.

Almost three decades before the principal events of this story, Capt. McDonald played a major role in the early history of Wichita Falls. On February 25, 1896, while McDonald commanded Company B of the Frontier Battalion, two Oklahoma Territory outlaws, Foster Crawford and Elmer "Kid" Lewis, robbed the Citizens National Bank in Wichita Falls, during which they killed a cashier, Frank Dorsey. Later that same day, with the assistance of an impromptu citizens' posse, McDonald and several of his rangers (including Private Billy McCauley) ran the culprits to ground, captured them, and jailed them in Wichita Falls. The next morning, even though lynch fever was rampant, McDonald loaded up his rangers and departed, leaving the jail guarded by only one

Captain Bill McDonald, commander of Company B, Frontier Battalion of the Texas Rangers. (Image courtesy of the Texas Ranger Research Center, and Texas Ranger Hall of Fame and Museum, Waco, Texas.)

Company B, Frontier Battalion, Texas Rangers, was commanded by Captain W. J. (Bill) McDonald. This picture was made in 1893 at Amarillo. Back row (*left to right*): Jack Harwell, Sergeant W. John L. Sullivan, Bob Pease, Arthur Jones, Ed Connell, and Lee Queen. Front row: (*left to right*): Billy McCauley, Bob McClure, Wes Carter, and [first name unknown] Owens. Billy McCauley was Captain McDonald's nephew, the son of his sister, Mary McDonald McCauley of Wichita Falls. Billy McCauley was also the brother of Dorothy McCauley Collier, wife of Wichita Falls mayor Frank Collier. (Image courtesy of the Panhandle-Plains Historical Museum, Special Collections, Canyon, Texas.)

Bank robbers Foster Crawford *(left)* and Elmer "Kid" Lewis, on February 26, 1896, shortly after they were lynch-mobbed and hanged in downtown Wichita Falls, Texas, for robbing the City National Bank and killing cashier Frank Dorsey. Picture taken from the December 3, 2005, edition of the *Wichita Falls Times Record News*. (Image courtesy of the *Wichita Falls Times Record News*.)

deputy sheriff. That afternoon a mob stormed the jail, overpowered the deputy, seized the prisoners, and hanged them from a telegraph pole in front of the bank they had robbed.[24]

———

In 1925, Captain McDonald's niece, Dorothy McDonald McCauley, was not only proud to be the mayor's wife, she was also very proud of her aristocratic heritage—a heritage rooted in the Old South and nourished in its customs and traditions, including strict adherence to the Code of Honor and its view of the sexes: chivalrous men protecting the virtue and chastity of their refined and noble womenfolk. Dorothy was also proud of her position as one of the socially elite of the town.

Then along came Buster.

Buster was a classmate of Mary Frances Collier at Wichita Falls High School. That's where they met, started dating, and fell in love. Buster Robertson, however, was not a blue-blood. Not even close. The uppercrust of Wichita Falls society had a name for folks like the Robertson family: "common," sniffed dismissively. Buster was next to the oldest of Hattie Robertson's large brood. She was married at age thirteen and had borne ten children, seven of whom were still surviving in 1924. Six of those (including Buster) were living with Hattie; the

THE WESTERN UNION TELEGRAPH COMPANY.
INCORPORATED
21,000 OFFICES IN AMERICA.   CABLE SERVICE TO ALL THE WORLD.

This Company TRANSMITS and DELIVERS messages only on conditions limiting its liability, which have been assented to by the sender of the following message. Errors can be guarded against only by repeating a message back to the sending station for comparison, and the Company will not hold itself liable for errors or delays in transmission or delivery of Unrepeated Messages, beyond the amount of tolls paid thereon, nor in any case where the claim is not presented in writing within sixty days after the message is filed with the Company for transmission. This is an UNREPEATED MESSAGE, and is delivered by request of the sender, under the conditions named above.

THOS. T. ECKERT, President and General Manager.

NUMBER	SENT BY	REC'D BY	CHECK
	12 Da ALL't	148 paid 2 ex via Ft Worth 240 pm	

RECEIVED at Austin, Tex. } 104-106 WEST SIXTH ST.   189

Dated   Wichita Falls Tex 28 Feby 96

To   Gen W H Mabry, Austin

I would Say that In justice to privates McClure and McCauley, who went into thicket with me and arrested robbers were the only ones that did go in, the papers called other names that was not present and also stated that we got there at ten oclock when in fact we got to where they quit their horses, at five and took the trail afoot wading lakes and rivers where robbers did, and followed same till night and captured them three miles below where they quit their

66-1

THE WESTERN UNION TELEGRAPH COMPANY.
INCORPORATED
21,000 OFFICES IN AMERICA.   CABLE SERVICE TO ALL THE WORLD.

This Company TRANSMITS and DELIVERS messages only on conditions limiting its liability, which have been assented to by the sender of the following message. Errors can be guarded against only by repeating a message back to the sending station for comparison, and the Company will not hold itself liable for errors or delays in transmission or delivery of Unrepeated Messages, beyond the amount of tolls paid thereon, nor in any case where the claim is not presented in writing within sixty days after the message is filed with the Company for transmission. This is an UNREPEATED MESSAGE, and is delivered by request of the sender, under the conditions named above.

THOS. T. ECKERT, President and General Manager.

NUMBER	SENT BY	REC'D BY	CHECK

RECEIVED at Austin, Tex. } 104-106 WEST SIXTH ST.   189

Dated

To   (2)   12 Da

horses : However we give the citizens posse credit for doing good work in following them, yet it is due the boys that they faced the dangerous looking thicket while others refused to do so, everything is quiet here I fail to find anybody that knows anything about the hanging except that they were strangers or women in disguise. I go to headquarters today.

W S. McDonald
Capt Co B

Shortly after the 1896 lynching in Wichita Falls, Captain McDonald was requested by his superior, Texas Adjutant General W. H. Mabry, to report the identity of those responsible for the lynching. In response, on February 28, 1896, Captain Bill McDonald filed one of the strangest investigative reports of all times. He telegraphed Mabry: "I fail to find anybody that knows anything about the hanging except that they were strangers or women in disguise." Since none of the mob bothered to wear a mask, and since McDonald, a former resident of Wichita Falls, was well acquainted with most of the prominent citizens of the town, and since his nephew, Henry McCauley, was later identified as one of those present at the lynching, it is tempting to conclude that Ranger McDonald's investigation was less than exhaustive. (Adjutant General Correspondence Files, box 401-438-12. Image courtesy of Texas State Library and Archives Commission, Austin, Texas.)

1. B. F. Crawford
2. Bob Daggs
3. C. W. Ward
4. Henry McCauley — [first one to see them]
5. Judge Dupuy
6. C. K. Thomas + [went for Rangers]
7. M. A. Talbot — Ranger
8. Lee McMurtry
9. Lem Chastel
10. Sonnamaker
11. Tony Thornberry

Marion Potter } [climbed up pole]
Jim Avis } Put rope over neck
F. M. Davis — Ex Sheriff led mob

Mose Sheriff
Hardady — Jailer
McMurtry — Deputy Sheriff

Foster Crawford — Weatherford
Kid Lewis (Slaughter)

Veteran Wichita Falls newspaper editor/publisher Rhea Howard, on March 23, 1964, took time to record a handwritten historical memorandum listing the names of some of the prominent Wichitans who were present February 26, 1896, when bank robbers Foster Crawford and Elmer "Kid" Lewis were lynched in downtown Wichita Falls. (The information contained in the memorandum has never before been published or otherwise publicly disclosed). Howard states that ex-sheriff F. M. Davis "led mob" and that Marion Potter "climbed the pole" from which the outlaws were hanged, and that Potter and Jim Avis "put ropes over necks." Of particular importance to this story is the listing of Henry McCauley as being present at the hanging. Rhea Howard wrote that he was also "the first one to see them," apparently meaning that Henry McCauley was one of the citizens' posse which helped the Texas Rangers run the outlaws to ground in a thicket north of Wichita Falls the day before they were lynched. Henry McCauley, a Wichita Falls resident, was a nephew of Captain Bill McDonald and a brother of Ranger Private Billy McCauley, who was in McDonald's Ranger posse when they and the citizens' posse captured the duo. Henry McCauley and Billy McCauley were brothers of Dorothy McCauley, all of whom were the children of McDonald's sister, Mary McDonald McCauley. Dorothy McCauley later married Frank Collier, who, in 1924, was mayor of Wichita Falls. Memorandum discovered in files of the *Wichita Falls Times Record News*. (Image courtesy of the *Wichita Falls Times Record News*.)

oldest son, Irvin, was serving in the U.S. Navy. Two years earlier, her husband had disappeared after some squabble. Some said it involved a shooting scrape, but apparently, if true, neither was hit. In any event, he was providing no support for the family. When they first moved to Wichita Falls several years earlier, virtually penniless, Hattie moved her family into a shack on the wrong side of the tracks: "No Man's Land." She eked out a meager existence by taking in washing and doing sewing alterations. Finally, somehow, she managed to move across the tracks and rent a shabby boardinghouse. She rented out rooms to common laborers—oil field workers, mostly.[25]

The one luxury that Hattie was able to afford was a Victrola. It was the best of the line of record players available at that time. A crank on the side of the Victrola powered the machine as it spun 78 rpm platters round and round and filled Hattie's home with popular tunes. Apparently Hattie, her boarders, and their guests enjoyed dancing in Hattie's living room, and perhaps that's where Buster became such a dancing fool. (Incidentally, Mayor Collier also had a Victrola in his living room.)

Dancing was an activity that cut across class lines in 1925 Wichita Falls. Not only Hattie and her oil patch tenants enjoyed "cuttin' a rug," as they put it, but also the upper-class Wichitans enjoyed society dances at the Kemp Hotel ballroom. (Admittedly, the dress code was noticeably different.) However—and this is a pretty significant "however"—not all 1924 Wichitans viewed dancing as a pleasurable and wholesome pastime. The sizable and politically potent Baptist church-going contingent, as well as other religious groups, viewed dancing as a sin second only to unmarried sex—which, of course, they contended it invariably led to. A newspaper story of the day sheds much light on the Baptist view of dancing. In 1926, the Baptist General Convention of Texas passed a resolution opposing dancing, not only in Baptist colleges but also in any state school or state-owned facility. The resolution recited: "[It] has come to the attention of the members of the convention that dances are held regularly in the buildings owned by the State, and since the convention looks with alarm upon this evil everywhere, it feels it is its duty to protest against it."[26]

Not satisfied with that, the convention proposed another anti-dancing resolution—this one directed at governor-elect Dan Moody. It directed Moody not to hold an inaugural ball when he took office as governor of Texas, since such irreverent revelry would undoubtedly involve dancing. It was further reported that Baylor University president B. P. Brooks mounted the podium and tackled head-on those pernicious rumors that some Baylor University professors "were inclined to the Darwinian theory of evolution." He went on to assure the delegates that "no one was employed [by Baylor] whose orthodoxy could be questioned."

Wichita Falls newspapers meanwhile bravely straddled the dancing issue. While the newspapers frequently printed stories reporting the denunciations by fundamentalist ministers condemning dancing, they often (sometimes in the same issue) ran stories extolling the virtues of dancing. In a 1924 issue of the *Wichita Falls Record News*, two stories were run side-by-side. The heading on the first was "Fear of God Is Almost Gone . . . Evangelist at First Baptist Church Deplores Prevailing Sin," juxtaposed to which was this headline: "Arms Makes [*sic*] the Woman and Dancing Makes the Arms, Says Gloria Gould Bishop." That was followed by a subsequent society page article by the same author under this heading: "Gloria Gould, 'Million-Dollar Bride,' Urges Wichitans to Dance If They Would Be Happy and Beautiful at Same Time." Gloria kicked off her story with this verse:

> To dance is to be happy
> To dance is to be beautiful,
> Buoyancy of Step
> Means buoyancy of Soul.[27]

While there existed a significant divergence among the ranks of Wichitans as to the benefits or the evils of dancing, most Wichitans (excluding, of course, some of those scandalous Jazz Age "flappers," free-thinkers, and rebels, as well as many on the lower rung of society) seemed basically united in their view of sex and the accepted roles of each gender. And that view definitely was distinctively Victorian in flavor. In a March 28, 1926, article in the *Wichita Falls Record News* under a heading informing readers that Dr. Lincoln McConnel had attacked "Flappers' Ills," the *News* reported that Dr. McConnel declared that "The Age of Chivalry Is Gone." In a "women only" lecture, Dr. McConnel confided this to the ladies:

Your sex, instead of being a protection to you is a menace to you. The age of chivalry is gone. You women might as well face the facts. Women have become much more common and ordinary parts of life than they were yesterday. They equal men politically, and economically, and they compete with him in the business world. Woman no longer depends on man for protection, she competes with him. In grandmother's day, a girl's body and mind were more protected and shielded from the heavy burdens of life than now. She was thought to be much finer physically and psychologically than man. Her very sex and nature were her appeal for regard and protection. Girls then seemed more refined, cleaner and more moral than men. And in the shattering of that belief has come the danger for women and girls.[28]

McConnel went on to explain that there was "something about a man's makeup that made it almost impossible for him to remain chaste." However, he continued, "once upon a time" there was something in a woman's makeup that "made it impossible for her to become unchaste." "Modern times," McConnel concluded, have now made it possible for a girl "to become unchaste." He claimed that "promiscuous turning loose of girls unchaperoned and untaught to jazzy dances and suggestive shows is to blame for all this. . . . Youth today are wild, unrestrained, and free." In closing, he advised the women that "kissing, necking, hugging and spooning isn't a safe proposition." (One wonders if the women in the audience—all of whom were married—were meticulously taking notes.)

There was little doubt about the fact that some of those "jazzy dances" were going on over in Hattie Robertson's living room when she and/or some of her boarders cranked up that old Victrola. Rumors were whispered about that some of her boarders and visitors often quaffed down a snort or more of bootleg booze. Possibly, even, some loose women had entered, which—considering the fact that many of Hattie's boarders were young, unmarried, raucous, vigorous, and red-blooded oil patch roughnecks and roustabouts—should not have come as a shock even to McConnel's church ladies.

Meanwhile, in order to help support his mother and siblings, Buster had to drop out of high school a year before he was to graduate. He got a job at a local refinery, the Texhoma Oil and Refining Company.

It came as no shock to anyone that the status-conscious mayor and his wife took a dim view of their only daughter going out with a boy from the wrong side of the tracks. At first, they assumed that Mary Frances would soon "come to her senses" and dump Buster in favor of boys of her own class. "Just give it time," they decided. But Mary Frances kept on dating Buster—and nobody else. They tried lecturing her, but that didn't work. Then they decided it must be that "dancing thing." She was going with Buster because he was such a good dancer, and they both loved to dance. So they laid down the law: "No dancing!" That didn't work either. They kept slipping out and going to dances. Then the angry mayor whipped Mary Frances. He put his foot down. "No more dates with Buster!" She disobeyed. He whipped her again, and then a third time. Still, the headstrong Mary Frances would not obey. He didn't have much better luck trying to intimidate Buster. Once at the Collier home, he slapped Buster a few times and ordered him out of the house. Another time, outside the Robertson home, Frank Collier, an automobile crank in hand, threatened Buster with mayhem if he went with Mary Frances again. Meanwhile, Dorothy Collier became almost frantic with alarm when she became aware that in the better circles of Wichita Falls society whispers were being circulated that Mary Frances was head-over-heels in love with that trashy Robertson boy and that she had been seen in Hattie's boarding house, where it was rumored that whiskey and "those kind of women" were available. It didn't improve Dorothy's state of mind the day that Mary Frances mentioned that once when she was in Hattie Robertson's home they played some records, and Hattie asked Mary Frances if she knew how to dance "the shimmy," that being the name of one of those scandalously suggestive Jazz Age dances. Dorothy was horrified. She had little doubt that if all this continued, Hattie and her crowd of degenerates would soon turn Mary Frances into a common prostitute.

In early January 1925, Frank Collier borrowed enough money to send Mary Frances to a fancy girls' school in Missouri the next school year. (She was then in her first year at a local community college.) That, he reckoned, would put her far beyond the reach of Buster Robertson. But when he told Mary Frances of his plan, she flatly refused and said she would not go.

Then things got worse—a lot worse. They headed downhill like a runaway train.

It happened later that same month when Frank spent a few days at the state capitol in Austin on city business. One night while he was away, Dorothy Collier woke up at about three in the morning. She decided to go check on Mary Frances, who was sleeping on a second-story "sleeping porch." She found Mary Frances in bed all right—but not alone. Buster was there too. Naked. Dorothy screamed and then grabbed Buster by the hair. In subsequent testimony, she testified that Buster said to her, "Wait a minute, I want to talk to you." Dorothy testified that she replied, "I'll talk to you. Wait till I get my gun." By the time Dorothy returned with her pistol, Buster was gone. Clad only in his shorts, Buster had jumped out a window and was then racing across the yard. Dorothy managed to fire off one shot before Buster disappeared into the night.[29] Then, in a classic case of slamming the barn door shut after the horse had been stolen, Dorothy Collier got a hammer and nailed down all the windows. However, while Dorothy ran to fetch a hammer, Mary Frances took advantage of an opportunity to toss Buster's clothes out the window into the backyard, where Buster later sneaked back and retrieved them.

Dorothy Collier must have come mighty close to having a heart attack that night when she pulled the covers back and discovered a naked truth she had hoped and prayed didn't exist. Little did she dream that before the next morning sun she would be in for yet another jolt.

When her mother got through nailing shut the windows and had regained her coherence, Mary Frances calmly informed her that she and Buster were married and had been since last June, June 17, 1924, to be exact. When on January 14, 1925, Frank Collier returned from Austin, Dorothy Collier broke the news to him. Even though it was near midnight when he found out, Frank jumped out of bed and went to confront Buster. Mrs. Robertson met him at her front door, and, sensing danger, lied and told Frank that Buster was not home.

At first blush, knowing the customs and mores of the day, one might have supposed that since Buster had "done the right thing" by marrying his girlfriend and thus "making an honest woman out of her" (thereby reinstating her reputation for virtue—if not for chastity), then her parents' main concern (their reputation) had been satisfied even if they didn't approve of Mary Frances's marrying way below her class. After all, "shotgun weddings" were the prescribed remedy for a premature loss of virginity at that time and for many years thereafter. But Frank and Dorothy Collier were not even close to being mollified or appeased. The class issue was just too much for them to overcome.

Three days later, Mayor Collier collared Buster and marched him down to the law office of Frank's attorney, where he ordered the lawyer to draw up an annulment petition. He made Buster sign a waiver, thus allowing the annulment suit to proceed without further notice to him or contest by him. An annulment of the marriage could have been successfully prosecuted, since both Buster and Mary Frances were under the legal age to get married without parental consent in Oklahoma. Mary Frances was only seventeen at the time, and Buster was only nineteen. To obtain a marriage permit in Oklahoma at that time without parental consent, the bride had to be at least eighteen and the groom at least twenty-one. However, the Oklahoma law further provided that if the couple did obtain a marriage license (even though they were not legally entitled to do so) and proceeded to get married and consummated that marriage, then the couple was legally married although the marriage was "voidable" if an annulment suit was successfully prosecuted.[30]

After seeing that the annulment suit was duly filed in the Wichita Falls district court, Mayor Collier then went to both the local newspaper offices and saw to it that nothing about his daughter's marriage or the annulment suit hit the press. It would have seemed therefore that the scandal was contained. Yet the Colliers's anger continued to seethe just beneath the surface while the young couple's love—though forbidden—was beyond denial and stronger than ever.

After the annulment suit was filed, the Colliers succeeded in keeping Buster and Mary Frances apart for a week, but on Friday, February 13, 1925, Buster telephoned Mary Frances. They had a long talk. Mary Frances would later recall this: "We decided we could not be apart any longer, and Buster asked me, 'You'll stay by me this time, won't you, Mary Frances?' I promised I would and got everything ready to meet him Saturday night."[31]

The next day was Saturday, February 14, 1925—Valentine's Day. Buster and Mary Frances had eagerly anticipated their first Valentine's Day together as a married couple, and they were determined that nobody was going to keep them apart. Not even Frank and Dorothy

Collier. They clung to a hope that differences between the two families could somehow be reconciled.

It all came to a head on that Saturday—Valentine's Day, 1925. Early in the evening, Mary Frances told her mother she intended to see Buster. Dorothy flew into a rage. She again grabbed the family pistol and screamed that if Buster came over she would "blow his brains out." (Later, Dorothy would claim that she only meant to scare Mary Frances.) The Colliers then loaded Mary Frances into the family car and drove several blocks to the home of Dorothy's sister, Mrs. Eula Mae McCauley Duke. Again Mary Frances insisted that she wanted to see Buster. Dorothy forbade it. Then Mary Frances asked her mother if she would accompany her to the Robertson home to "talk things over" with Mrs. Robertson and Buster. Dorothy would later testify that she agreed to the request although she never intended to go through with it; she was just attempting to stall until it became too late to make that visit. Mary Frances, in turn, called Buster and told him that she and her mother would be coming over soon. Mrs. Robertson and Buster waited at their home for the visit, but no one came. Finally, Mary Frances demanded that Dorothy take her to meet Buster and Hattie Robertson as she had promised. Dorothy refused. Mary Frances had had enough. She picked up the phone, called Buster, and told him to come get her.

Enraged and almost out of control, Dorothy again screeched that if Buster came over she would "blow his brains out!" With that, Mary Frances ran out of the Duke home into the night. Dorothy paused only long enough to grab the pistol and give pursuit, waving the pistol and shouting threats. Frank, however, overtook her and wrestled the pistol from her. Then, together, they got into the Collier automobile and set off in the direction in which Mary Frances had fled.

Dorothy later claimed that it was at this time that she saw fit to drop another bombshell on her husband. She had already told him of the sleeping-porch incident and that Buster and Mary Frances were married. Now she told her husband that Mary Frances had admitted to her that Buster had "seduced" her before they were married. She would later testify that Frank almost "went crazy," muttering, "What have they done to my darling little daughter?"

Meanwhile, Hattie Robertson and Buster left their home. At Buster's request, Hattie agreed to accompany him in the forlorn hope that they could "talk things over" with the Colliers. Having no car, they walked to the intersection of 17th and Bluff Streets, where they waited to catch a streetcar. While waiting at the intersection, Buster told his mother, "Momma, all I ever ask of anybody in this world is a chance to make good."[32] It was a request that was never granted; a chance never given.

While they were waiting for the streetcar, Frank and Dorothy happened by. They recognized Mrs. Robertson and Buster, and they stopped. Frank got out and confronted the Robertsons. The confrontation occurred at approximately 10:00 p.m. that Valentine's Day at the corner of 17th and Bluff Streets in Wichita Falls. It was witnessed by a bystander who was also waiting to catch the streetcar. His name was R. W. Windham, and he was a special police officer who was also a night watchman for the Panhandle Refining Company. Later, Windham, Frank Collier, Dorothy Collier, and Hattie Robertson would all testify about what happened next. Basically, they all told the same horrifying story.

Mrs. Robertson would later testify that Frank Collier got out of the car and said to her: "Mrs. Robertson what have you to say about Mary Frances?"

"Mr. Collier, I can say to you that she'll never be abused in my house," she replied.

Then, Hattie Robertson testified, Frank Collier grabbed her son's arm and said, "Buster, I want to talk to you." He was holding the pistol.

Buster cried, "Mother, oh mother, he's going to kill me!"

Frank Collier fired. Buster staggered and fell to the street in front of the car.

"Don't shoot my boy," Hattie screamed. "Don't kill my boy in cold-blooded murder!"

But Frank fired his .44-caliber Colt revolver at least twice more (possibly three times more) while Buster lay on the street—firing at such close range that powder marks were discovered on his clothes. All the shots hit Buster in the chest.

Hattie Robertson cradled her dying son in her arms. "Buster, Buster, speak to mother! Speak just one word to Mother," Hattie begged.

But it was too late. Buster could no longer speak.

According to Mrs. Robertson's testimony, Dorothy Collier, who by now was standing in front of the car, yelled to her husband: "Frank, back the car up so she can see he's dead."

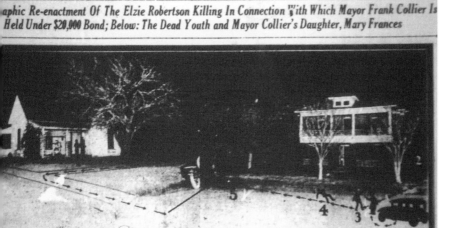

aphic Re-enactment Of The Elzie Robertson Killing In Connection With Which Mayor Frank Collier Is Held Under $20,000 Bond; Below: The Dead Youth and Mayor Collier's Daughter, Mary Frances

Sketch of Buster Robertson murder scene appearing in the February 16, 1925, *Wichita Falls Record News*. (Image courtesy of the *Wichita Falls Times Record News*.)

Meanwhile, the stunned Bob Windham had stared in horror while the whole tragic drama unreeled before him. Regaining his senses, he came over and took the pistol away from Frank, arrested him, and then called for an ambulance.

Buster was pronounced dead at the scene and taken to a funeral home. Dorothy Collier went into seclusion at her home. Mary Frances went home with the hysterical Hattie Robertson. Frank Collier went to jail. His bail was set at $20,000.

When the undertaker removed Buster's clothing, a silver locket slipped from the boy's body and fell to the floor of the funeral parlor. Buster had worn the locket on a string around his neck. Inside the locket was a tiny picture of a beautiful girl: Mary Frances Collier Robertson.[33] It was a sad and tragic ending to what was to have been a happy and romantic occasion: their first Valentine's Day together as husband and wife.

Next day's eight-column headlines on the front pages of both Wichita Falls newspapers screamed the story. The *Wichita Daily Times*: "Mayor Kills Elzie Robertson." The *Wichita Falls Record News*: "Colliers in Seclusion: Daughter Remains at Robertson Home."[34]

was $23.42 according to a statement by the state board of control. There are 17 eleemosynary institutions in the state.

vened.
When no one in Jamesport would give bond for the banker, he was placed in jail here.

ELZIE ROBERTSON SHOT AND KILLED

(Continued from Page One.)

the 78th district court which opens on the first Monday in March.

The petition recites that the couple had gone to Cotton county, Oklahoma, in June, 1934, procured a marriage license and were married. It was further stated in the petition, as grounds for annulment, that both of the contracting parties were minors and that neither had secured consent to enter the contract. It was stated in the complaint that they were each 17 years of age. It is said that since the filing of the suit Mary Francis Collier had reached the age of eighteen years.

According to members of the Robertson family, Mary Francis had called "Buster," as he was familiarly known, by telephone a short time prior to the shooting, asking him to come to her home at 904 Lamar street and take her to her home.

The young man asked his mother to accompany him and the two left the house together. They had proceeded only one block from their home when, according to Mr. Windham, the mayor met them and the shooting took place.

The mother in her hysterical condition at her home told that she begged the mayor not to shoot her son. She was unable to give any further information regarding the tragedy and kept calling for her boy.

Mayor's Daughter Reaches Scene

Members of the family stated that within a few minutes after the shooting, a call to the Collier home advised the young wife of the tragedy. According to people who resided in the community she arrived at the scene at about the same time that the ambulance drove up.

At the undertaking parlor it was found that three bullets had entered the body. One entered the left breast directly over the heart. A second entered the body a few inches above the first and passed through the body lodging underneath the skin just below the right arm pit. The third entered the body on the left side just below the ribs and lodged underneath the skin in the small of the back on the right side. Powder burns were noticeable on the boy's top coat where the bullets entered.

When the undertaker undressed the body at the parlors, a silver locket, supported by a string around his neck, fell to the floor. An examination of the locket revealed that it contained a miniature photograph of his young wife, Mary Francis.

The youth had been employed

Benefit DANCE

KEMP HOTEL

Friday, Feb. 20

Given under the auspices of the Business and Professional Women's Club.

TICKETS ON SALE AT TIPTON'S AND CENTRAL DRUG STORES

News article from February 15, 1925, *Wichita Daily Times,* reporting the murder of Buster Robertson. Ironically, the page two jump of the news article was run adjacent to an advertisement for a benefit dance at the Kemp Hotel that featured a sketch of two carefree couples embracing and gracefully gliding across the ballroom floor. (Image courtesy of the *Wichita Falls Times Record News.*)

Unintentionally, the *Wichita Daily Times* added an ironic and melancholy note to the story of the sudden end of the life of a lively youth who had gained some local notoriety as the best dancer in town. The *Times* jumped its front-page story to page two. The story was continued under this headline: "Elzie Robertson Shot and Killed." This appeared adjacent to a large and prominent advertisement: "Benefit Dance. Kemp Hotel. Friday, February 20. Given under the auspices of the Business and Professional Women's Club." In addition to the wording of the ad, it depicted silhouettes of two carefree couples embracing and gracefully gliding across the ballroom floor.[35]

Other news stories, notices, and advertisements appearing in the two local newspapers during the same time frame provide revealing insights into the life and times of 1925 Wichita Falls.

A front-page story in the same edition of the *Wichita Daily Times* and adjacent to the story of the killing of Buster Robertson was headlined: "Knife Cuts May Prove Fatal to Oil Field Worker." The story told about one oil field worker stabbing and critically wounding another during "a drunken brawl which climaxed a poker party" at a downtown rooming house. Another front-page story in the *Wichita Daily Times* of February 16, 1925, noted that the American Refining Company had raised the price it was paying for crude oil to $2.25 per barrel. Two days later, February 18, 1925, the *Wichita Falls Record News* reported that the public outrage over the high price of gasoline had triggered investigations in both the U.S. House and the U.S. Senate. The price of gasoline in preceding weeks had jumped from about sixteen cents per gallon to as high as twenty-one cents per gallon. Amidst much pompous posturing and finger-pointing, the distinguished solons exchanged heated accusations. One side attributed the increase to the law of supply and demand, pointing out that oil production had fallen off recently. The other, of course, blamed it all on "monopolistic" oil companies that were manipulating gasoline prices so they could pay their shareholders "unwarranted dividends."

An inside story of the February 16, 1925, edition of the *Wichita Daily Times* reported that seven hundred folks had assembled to hear Dr. Sartel Prentice deliver a nondenominational address warning that a spiritual reawakening was needed since people of that day had forgotten their moral responsibilities. He warned that "a religious renaissance was necessary to the saving of civilization." He cited as evidence the high divorce rate, a breakdown in morals, "opium traffic, liquor and other kindred evils."[36] The classified section underscored how important lodges were to 1925 Wichitans. Meeting notices were posted for eighteen separate lodges, mostly Masonic and Masonic related (such as Eastern Star and Rebecca Lodges for women, Rainbows for girls, and DeMolay for boys). The Knights of Pythias, Oddfellows, Elks, and American Legion lodges were also listed. Another inside story reported Sunday school attendance records of all the local churches. It proved that the Baptists were far ahead of the other denominations, although the Methodists ran a respectable second. Other churches listed included Catholic, Presbyterian, First Christian, Church of Christ, Lutheran, and Episcopal.

The following day's edition of the *Daily Times* reported that a law suit involving the estate of Mary Couts Burnett, widow of multimillionaire West Texas rancher and oil man Burk Burnett, had been settled. Under the terms of the settlement, most of her $5 million estate went to Texas Christian University in Fort Worth.[37]

In view of the wrecked dreams of the Colliers for their daughter's triumphant "coming out" entrance into the cream of Wichita Falls society, the *Daily Times*, in its society section, unintentionally, no doubt, sounded still another ironic and melancholy note. A light-hearted article entitled "The First Party Dress" was illustrated by a large sketch of a bejeweled society matron wistfully slipping a gorgeous silk dress (ruffles and bows galore) on her beautiful, curly-haired, innocent-faced, enchanted, early-teen daughter. One paragraph of the story gushed:

> Now she's suddenly grownup in a dress with billowing ruffle bows. A dress that was made for a party! A dress that stands for dances, and beaus, and corsage bouquets, and all the delicious things that make girlhood the light-hearted, magic time that it is.[38]

Elzie "Buster" Robertson was buried on Monday, February 16, 1925, in the Rosemont Cemetery in Wichita Falls. The epitaph carved on his

GIRLS I HAVE KNOWN   By Cynthia Grey

THE FIRST PARTY DRESS

In yet another ironic twist to the Buster Robertson murder story, the February 17, 1925, edition of the *Wichita Daily Times* ran a light-hearted society article describing a mother dressing her young daughter to attend her first party. The story, entitled "First Party Dress" was illustrated by this sketch. (Image courtesy of the *Wichita Falls Times Record News*.)

tombstone reads, "Mother's Love Never Dies." The *Wichita Falls Record News* coverage of the funeral and background of the principals involved was exhaustive. Mary Frances, who had remained at the Robertson home with Hattie, refused to take telephone calls from her mother. She and Hattie Robertson attended the funeral together. Hundreds overflowed the service at the First Methodist Church. Hattie collapsed, and the young widow became hysterical. The *Record News* observed that "the girl widow was pathetically beautiful" and described "her delicate skin, her blonde curls and her blue eyes that were weeping tears, the bitterness of which her schoolmates and friends could only guess between her sobs." She later told a reporter that she intended to remain with Mrs. Robertson and that she would attempt to "make her own way in the world" by "taking up painting for a living."[39]

Meanwhile, Frank Collier resigned his coveted post as mayor of the city of Wichita Falls with this statement: "I am in such a torn up mental condition and worry on account of recent events and family troubles that I am in no condition to attend to the important duties of mayor."[40]

The ex-mayor's troubles were just beginning. Less than two weeks after he killed Buster Robertson, a grand jury in the 30th Judicial District

Court of Wichita County indicted Frank Collier for murder. The State indicated that it would seek the death penalty and asked the district judge to deny bail for Collier. The prosecution was in the hands of a capable young district attorney named James V. Allred, age twenty-five. He had recently gained fame for standing up to the Ku Klux Klan—a gutsy call for any Texas politician in the early 1920s. After dying out in the 1870s, the Klan suddenly resurrected in the fall of 1920, and by 1922 it had enlisted nearly two hundred thousand dues-paying members in Texas. By 1925, the Klan counted about three million members nationwide and was active in all forty-eight states.[41] Allred's political courage later served him well, for he went on to serve two terms as governor of Texas from 1935 to 1939. Later in his career he was appointed as a federal district judge. Today he lies buried in the Riverside Cemetery in Wichita Falls.

Meanwhile, Frank Collier's attorney, Charles I. Francis, filed a writ of habeas corpus in an attempt to persuade the court to set bail for his client so he could be freed pending his trial. A hearing was set. But before it began another issue arose. Trial judge P. A. Martin ordered the newspapers not to print any of the evidence or testimony presented at the habeas corpus hearing. His stated reason for doing so had some logic behind it. Since the habeas corpus hearing would be a minitrial in itself, and thus sensational testimony would be aired, news coverage would undoubtedly report every word that would then be read and discussed by most Wichitans. Hence, when it later came time to select a jury for the actual trial, many potential jurors would very likely be "tainted" by having already formed opinions as to the guilt or innocence of the defendant. While there was much logic behind the court's order, it was obviously an unconstitutional restraint on the freedom of the press. Both of the Wichita Falls daily newspapers, in front-page editorials, protested the infringement upon their constitutional rights. In the end, however, even if there was some logic behind the unlawful attempt to muzzle the press, it served to arouse suspicions that the Wichita Falls "establishment" was exerting some influence on the court. After all, state judges are elected officials.

Judge Martin was certainly right about one thing; the habeas corpus hearing was sensational, and it certainly did make front-page headlines. The State's principal witnesses were Hattie Robertson and the eyewit-

James V. Allred of Wichita Falls was the district attorney who prosecuted Frank Collier and Dorothy Collier for the murder of Buster Robertson. Allred was later elected as governor of Texas. (Image courtesy of the *Wichita Falls Times Record News*.)

ness, R. W. Windham, who basically told the same account of the killing as previously stated.[42]

The killing of Buster Robertson was a stark and shocking tale. It supported the prosecution's contention that this was a death-penalty case, a clear-cut case of premeditated murder with malice aforethought. Therefore no bail should be granted to the defendant. But when the defense took the field, the focus was shifted from *what* happened and *how* it happened to *why* it happened, all in an effort to demonstrate that this wasn't a death penalty case after all. First, there was a nod toward an exonerating defense of temporary insanity. Along that line, Mrs. Collier took the stand. On cross-examination, District Attorney Allred asked her: "Why did your husband kill Buster Robertson?" Reply: "He wasn't at himself." She testified that she had told him that Buster had "seduced" Mary Frances before the marriage. Then, she said, her husband kept muttering, "My God, what have they done with my little girl?"

But the main thrust of the defense soon became clear. Instead of allowing the prosecution to try Frank Collier, the defense was determined to try Hattie Robertson. The basic contention was that Mrs. Robertson was an immoral woman, and her home was a virtual den of iniquity.

All this, the defense argued, explained Frank's motive for killing Buster, explained why his state of mind was inflamed by a "sudden passion" when he pulled the trigger. That, the defense contended, at least reduced the case from being a slam-dunk premeditated murder case (a death-penalty case), to one in which the lesser crime of manslaughter was a viable possibility. Thus, Frank Collier was entitled to have bail set. The court agreed, and soon Frank was released on a $25,000 bond. Meanwhile, Mary Frances had moved back in with her mother.

The murder trial of Frank Collier was set for Monday, March 16, 1925, in the 89th Judicial District Court of Wichita County, Texas, Judge P. A. Martin presiding. District Attorney James Allred headed the prosecution team, backed by assistant D.A. Earl Kuntz; Bernard Martin, special prosecutor hired for this trial; and Allred's brother, Ben P. Allred, also a special prosecutor. The latter had formerly been assistant to the U.S. district attorney of Northwest Texas. The defense team was led by Charles Francis, a close friend of Frank Collier since the days when Francis was batboy for the Wichita Falls Spudders and Frank was the team's star pitcher. Assisting Francis were two other Wichita Falls trial lawyers, W. F. Weeks and B. Y. Cummings.

Although the Collier murder trial commanded front-page headlines, there were other stories of national interest competing for front-page space. Down in Austin, one Texas legislator introduced a bill that told volumes about what was going on during those Prohibition days in America. Representative J. W. Stevenson proposed a four-dollar-per-gallon tax on "prescription whiskey," noting that during the past year Texas drug stores had sold some 80,000 gallons of booze, tax free, pursuant to prescriptions issued by thoughtful Texas doctors to favored patients—all for "medicinal purposes," of course. Representative Stevenson also called his colleagues' attention to the fact that thousands more gallons of the stuff was finding its way, tax free, into the hands of thirsty Texans by sales from "mail order houses, packing houses, commission houses and many other such lines of business."[43]

And, dateline Paris, France, a heated debate was underway in the national Chamber of Deputies over the issue of woman's suffrage. Proponents cited Texas Governor Miriam "Ma" Ferguson's role in support of their cause. The advocates circulated a resolution that claimed that Ma Ferguson had "accomplished what no man ever attempted before her regime. She has inaugurated open warfare against the Ku Klux Klan," and concluded that "the United States is better off since women were permitted to vote."[44]

Women may have been permitted to vote and hold political office in Texas, but they were not yet permitted to serve as jurors in criminal or civil trials. Judge Martin therefore summoned a special venire of three hundred men for the upcoming trial of Frank Collier. The twelve jurors finally selected provided an interesting comment on the demographics of the community. One was a merchant, two were farmers, two were oil field workers. Other occupations included carpenter, clerk, driller, shop foreman, and an oil lease broker. Reflecting the fact of how recently the county had been settled, as well as the recent influx of oil field workers, there were only two members of the jury who were native Wichitans.

The prosecution called the eyewitness, R. W. Windham, as its first witness, and he again described the killing of Buster Robertson by Frank Collier.[45] He testified that Collier shot the boy four times, including twice after Buster had fallen to the street. He told of hearing Mrs. Robertson scream, "Don't kill my boy in cold blood!" When Defense Attorney W. F. Weeks cross-examined Windham, he asked: "You don't know, from your own knowledge, whether any of the four bullets struck Buster or not, do you?" Windham responded: "I don't see how he could miss him. It looked like the gun was right against his breast." The State then called Arch Smith, the undertaker who had examined Buster's body and embalmed him. Smith said that Buster was about five feet four inches in height and weighed between 130 and 135 pounds. "He was well-proportioned for a boy of his age," Smith concluded.[46]

Then the prosecution caught the defense by surprise. District Attorney Allred announced that the State rested.

The defense expected the State to call Buster's mother, Mrs. Robertson, as a witness as the State had done during the habeas corpus hearing. Defense attorneys were obviously licking their chops, yearning for another opportunity to try Hattie Robertson instead of Frank Collier, intending to tear into Mrs. Robertson and thus expose her allegedly bad character and reputation as they had previously attempted to do. When the State unexpectedly rested, the defense attorneys howled in protest and demanded that the court require the State to call Mrs. Robertson as a witness. The judge overruled the defense motion, pointing out that the State had proved up a prima facie case and was required to do no more, further pointing out that there was nothing to prevent the defense from calling Mrs. Robertson as a witness. True enough, but to do so would have put the defense at a tactical disadvantage in two ways. First, by rules of evidence then in effect, the party who called a person as a witness in effect vouched for the credibility of that witness and then had to accept the truthfulness of her testimony, and secondly, the defense would have considerably greater latitude in questioning Mrs. Robertson if she were a prosecution witness. If the State called her as a witness and had her testify on direct, then the defense could take her on cross-examination and would therefore be allowed to ask "leading questions," something that the party calling the witness is not permitted to do.

With or without Mrs. Robertson as a cross-examination target, the defense was determined to launch an attack on the character and repu- tation not only of Mrs. Robertson but also of Buster. The defense first called S. J. McCrae, a former renter at Mrs. Robertson's rooming house. McCrea, who had to admit that he had been arrested for possession of narcotics, told the jury that he knew of two women of questionable character who had frequented the house while he was living there, and that one woman—a blonde—was "playing one of the men roomers" on the first floor. He also claimed he had once seen Buster come home drunk, and on another occasion he had given Buster a shot of mor- phine. Another roomer claimed that he once bought a bottle of whiskey from Mrs. Robertson. Others claimed that Mrs. Robertson sometimes called lewd women for the benefit of her tenants. The State countered by calling witnesses to prove that Mrs. Robertson supported herself and the seven children living with her by renting out rooms and tak- ing in sewing and laundry, with further assistance from the salary that Buster was making working at the refinery. The prosecution proved that Mrs. Robertson had never been arrested for selling bootleg whis- key or prostitution—or any other offense—and later in jury argument,

Allred wondered aloud why, if Mrs. Robertson really had been engaged in such illegal activities, she hadn't ever been arrested, and why wasn't her rooming house ever raided? He also pointed out that many of her roomers were oil field workers and hinted that very few roughnecks were renowned as teetotalers or devotees of a celibate lifestyle regardless of whose rooming house they called home.

Then the defense paraded a procession of prominent Wichitans before the jury, all of whom testified that prior to the killing of Buster, Frank Collier had a spotless reputation as a peaceful and law-abiding citizen—a fact that the prosecution never disputed. But the heavy hitters for the defense were the defendant himself and his wife. As in the habeas corpus hearing, the defense played two cards: temporary insanity for exonerating, and, failing that, then producing evidence of "aggravating circumstances" in order to avoid a murder conviction ("premeditated killing with malice aforethought") in favor of the lesser offense of manslaughter, plus, hopefully, persuading the jury to suspend any sentence and grant probation to the defendant.

Frank Collier testified that on that Valentine's Day evening he "went nearly crazy" and that he lost his mind and all self-control when his wife informed him for the first time that Mary Frances admitted that Buster had "seduced" her before their marriage. He told the jury that he did not even know if the gun was loaded and that he didn't know how many shots were fired. In fact, he claimed that he just didn't remember anything about what happened after he got out of his car that night. He denied that he and his wife were driving around in pursuit of Buster just before the shooting. They were out looking for Mary Frances, he testified, and just happened to run across Buster and his mother.

The defense counsel turned to the "mitigating circumstances" that led to the shooting. Collier claimed that at the time he persuaded Buster to go along with an annulment of the marriage, Buster admitted to him that he had "gambled and drank some and that he knew he wasn't fit to be Mary Frances's husband." According to Frank Collier, Buster told him that he had no father and that "an orphan didn't have a chance to make good." About his mother, Frank Collier contended that Buster told him that "his mother had to make money any way she could. That she was married when she was thirteen years old, and had a baby when she was fourteen. That she had raised ten children." Collier further claimed that Buster told him that he knew there were women around the house, "not the right kind of women, but that as long as his mother had to get money somehow, he guessed it was all right."

The ex-mayor testified that he and Mrs. Collier never approved of Mary Frances going with Buster and had devised several strategies to discourage it. First he believed that Mary Frances had "too much judgment to allow herself to fall in love with him" and that if left alone they would soon break up. But that didn't work. He reviewed the several strategies he and his wife had devised to break up the romance. None worked. On cross-examination Collier admitted that he had whipped Mary Frances two, maybe three, times for seeing Buster and that once he had slapped or hit Buster several times. He admitted that on another occasion he had threatened Buster with an automobile crank, though he claimed he never really intended to strike him.

Next, the defense called Dorothy Collier. She recounted the events that led up to the shooting, including the time she caught Buster in bed with Mary Frances on their sleeping porch and then took a shot at him as he dashed across their backyard in his underwear. Dorothy Collier told the jury that at the time her husband shot Buster he was "acting like a crazy man." On cross-examination, she admitted that just prior to the killing, Mary Frances had called Buster to come for her and that she told Mary Frances that if he came to the house she would "blow his brains out." Then when Mary Frances ran out of the house, she grabbed the pistol and ran after her, but Frank intercepted her and wrested the gun from her grasp.

During her testimony, an odd fact came to light concerning that pistol. Dorothy said it was a single-action .45-caliber Colt six-shooter that was a family heirloom,[47] and that it had been passed to her mother, Mrs. McCauley, upon the death of her brother, who, it turned out, was none other than the famous Texas Ranger Captain W. J. "Bill" McDonald, commander of Company B of the Frontier Battalion. Captain McDonald died in the 1918 influenza epidemic that swept the nation. Although Dorothy Collier (Captain McDonald's niece) said it was a .45-caliber pistol, an earlier *Wichita Daily Times* news story dateline February 15, 1925, reporting the killing of Buster Robertson said the lethal weapon was a .44-caliber single-action Colt revolver. If so, it was very probably the same .44-caliber single-action Colt six-shooter that McDonald used

Hattie Robertson, mother of Elzie
"Buster" Robertson. She witnessed
Frank Collier kill her son. Taken
from the February 18, 1925, edition
of the *Wichita Falls Record News*.
(Image courtesy of the *Wichita Falls
Times Record News*.)

when he killed Childress County, Texas, Sheriff John Pearce Matthews
in a Main Street gunfight in Quanah, Texas, in 1893.[48] Thus another
twist: the same gun that Captain McDonald used to kill the Childress
sheriff was probably the same one Frank Collier used to kill Buster
Robertson almost thirty-two years later.

After Mrs. Collier's testimony, the defense rested. The State then
called Hattie Robertson as its first rebuttal witness. The State thus
scored a tactical victory over the defense. The defense had hoped—
anticipated—that the State would call her during their case-in-chief so
the defense, during cross-examination, could pin her down on numer-
ous points they planned to exploit by subsequent defense witnesses.
However, by waiting until after the defense had called its witnesses,
who attacked Hattie Robertson's character and reputation and told of
alleged incidents involving alcohol and illicit sex, the State was then in
a position to put Hattie on the stand to refute those attacks and defend
her reputation. Plus, she had the last word before the jury.

When she was called as a rebuttal witness, Hattie Robertson was
brought into the courtroom on an ambulance cot, trembling and weeping uncontrollably. Expressionless, the Colliers stared at her while she
reiterated the story of how Frank killed her son while she was pleading with him not to shoot Buster "in cold blood," and how Dorothy
Collier then yelled for her husband to back up the car so that she (Mrs.
Robertson) could see that Buster was dead. Then, according to the *Daily*

Times reporter, Hattie Robertson "with vehemence and tearful earnestness," denied every derogatory accusation that defense witnesses had made, declaring that she did not even know the men who had testified to meeting women at her home. At one point during combative cross-examination by the defense, Hattie threw up her hands in exasperation and exclaimed, "My God, are they trying me or the murderer?"[49]

With that, testimony in the case finally ended. When both sides closed, a question that had tantalized all the spectators throughout the trial was finally answered. The burning question was, would Mary Frances testify? And, if so, would she be called by the State or the defense? And what dynamite testimony would she give? Apparently, both sides viewed her as a double-edged sword. Neither side wanted to risk hearing what she might tell the jury.

The story about the mayor of Wichita Falls and his wife killing their nineteen-year-old son-in-law was the most sensational news story in Texas from the date of the shooting on February 14, 1925, until the twenty-four-day trial of Frank Collier finally ended on March 26, 1925. Both the Associated Press and the United Press International put daily coverage on the wire nationwide. Needless to add, the Wichita Falls courtroom was packed daily, and some early birds arriving as early as 5:45 a.m. sold their seats for five dollars—a princely sum in 1925—to those who didn't get there until the courtroom had filled. Most of the spectators were women.[50] Even if they had had television soap operas back then, the unfolding Collier melodrama would undoubtedly have upstaged them all.

But the curtain was now about to rise on the dramatic climax of the trial: jury arguments. The jury would then have to decide (if they could) whether to find Frank Collier guilty of murder (penalty: five years to life, or death) or guilty of manslaughter (penalty: two to five years with the option of suspending the sentence and putting the defendant on probation) or not guilty. During the jury arguments it became apparent that the defense had given up any serious contention that Frank Collier was "temporarily insane" when he killed Buster and therefore should be exonerated. The defense focused on settling for a manslaughter conviction with, hopefully, probation.

To convict a defendant for murder, according to the court's instructions, the jury must believe that the homicide was premeditated and carried out with malice aforethought. Manslaughter, on the other hand, was defined as "voluntary homicide committed under the immediate influence of sudden passion arising from an adequate cause." The key words in that definition are "adequate cause" and "sudden passion." In that connection there was an old Texas statute—a relic of the Old South's "Honor Code"—that was still on the law books and upon which the defense relied. It provided that "insulting conduct by the deceased towards a female relative of the person doing the killing is deemed adequate cause to produce the sudden passion" referred to in the manslaughter statute. The "insulting conduct" upon which the defense apparently relied was Buster's alleged "seduction" of Mary Frances, conduct that Frank and Dorothy Collier no doubt deemed "insulting," although it was obvious that the recipient of such conduct considered it anything but insulting.[51] (That, in turn, raised an intriguing question of statutory interpretation: when the legislature inserted the words "insulting conduct" into that statute, did the lawmakers mean insulting to the female recipient or insulting to some offended male relative? The statutory language expressly provided "insulting conduct . . . *towards a female* relative." Still, it seems unlikely that the jury spent much time or intellectual effort parsing the law to ascertain its exact meaning.) In any event, it soon became apparent that the defense arguments were bottomed not on Texas statutory law, but rather on the Old South's Code of Honor (read: "the unwritten law"), even if the defense lawyers didn't specifically referred to it by that name.

Defense Attorney B. Y. Cummings leaned hard on the unwritten law in his argument. He hyperventilated:

> If you send this man to the penitentiary, every stripe that he wears will be a badge of honor for the part that he played in the defense of the virtue of womanhood.

> I'd rather have to plant my son, if I had one, underneath the sod than for my daughter to have to tell the next man that asks her to marry him about the skeleton that's in the family closet now.

It's been said that the boy is in his grave, but better him in his grave than a daughter in shame and disgrace without that priceless thing, virtue. Frank Collier tried to do the right and decent thing.[52]

Perhaps Buster should have arisen and thanked him. But prosecutor Ben Allred, when he argued for the State, had quite a different take on Frank Collier's motive: ". . . the real motive: Buster Robertson had not attained to the social position that this defendant had."[53]

Defense Attorney C. I. Francis, retorted:

There is a recognized instinct in man developed from time to protect his family . . . [and it] outweighs everything else. He believed that if he allowed Mary Frances to hang out at the Robertson home she would have become a prostitute. . . . He has not done other than that which he deemed necessary for the protection of his daughter's good name and home . . . to save his daughter from a life of shame.[54]

If, as Frank Collier and the defense contended, his daughter's virtue was already lost, then it is difficult to see—at least from a logical point of view—how it could have been restored by killing Buster. Nevertheless, logic be damned, it was the time-honored remedy prescribed by the Old South's Code of Honor and one of the most cherished of its unwritten laws.

Special Prosecutor Bernard Martin asserted his belief that there was no improper conduct between Buster and Mary Frances before their marriage and scored the defense for not calling Mary Frances and putting the truth before the jury. He also scored the defense for its "false and damnable attempts to assassinate a good woman's (Hattie Robertson's) character."

Martin then wondered aloud, "Isn't it a strange thing that the defendant hasn't brought a single peace officer to testify to the character of that home and mother?"[55] He went on to point out that Mrs. Robertson had never been convicted of any crime and that her boarding house had never been raided by peace officers. He told the jury that had Mrs. Robertson really been selling bootleg whiskey or running a house of ill repute then surely local officers would have known about it—and taken appropriate action. Furthermore, he called attention to the fact that Frank Collier was mayor of the city during the entire time and had "every local peace officer at his command." If such sinful, immoral, and illegal activities had been rampant at the Robertson house, as he now contends, then why hadn't he dispatched officers to raid the place and arrest the culprits?

Bernard Martin ended his jury argument by commenting that no righteous or honorable man would "shoot his son-in-law, and then in an attempt to get out of it, come into court and plead the virtue of his daughter and defame the character of his son-in-law's mother."

In his closing argument, Defense Attorney W. F. Weeks, having thrown in the towel insofar as an acquittal was concerned, told the jury this:

> I don't tell you that Frank Collier did not commit a crime. I don't contend that he is innocent of any wrong or crime. . . . I ask you for either a conviction for manslaughter with a suspended sentence or a conviction without suspending.[56]

In his closing, District Attorney Jimmy Allred was in no mood to cut the defendant any slack:

> They say the fact that Buster came from "No-Man's-Land" justified killing him, and yet Frank Collier has told you that he came from "No-Man's-Land" himself and that he delivered ice and sold newspapers to get along in the world.

Pointing to Frank Collier as he closed, Allred roared:

> What a travesty of justice letting the defendant off with a suspended sentence would be . . . ! You didn't give Buster Robertson any chance did you? What right have you to ask another chance for yourself after you killed him like a dog?"[57]

On March 26, 1925, the Collier jury, after deliberating for twenty-three hours, returned with its verdict: guilty of manslaughter. The jury assessed a three-year prison sentence. No probation.

The defense breathed a collective sigh of relief and counted it a victory. Although the defense went through the motions of an appeal, it was apparent that they only wanted to buy some jail-free time for Frank, who was allowed to remain free on bond during the appellate process. In fact, the defense didn't even bother to file an appellate brief upon behalf of Collier, no doubt fearing that the Court of Criminal Appeals might actually reverse the case and send it back for a retrial. In a brief statement affirming the conviction, the appellate court on January 13, 1926, made short work of it:

> No briefs are on file for appellant. The facts of the case need not be set out at length. They show a homicide for which there could arise no seeming justification, but whose circumstances a merciful jury would have accepted as reducing the grade of offense from murder to manslaughter.[58]

Although Frank Collier and his team were relieved that the appellate court affirmed the manslaughter conviction with its relatively light sentence, and although the appellate court viewed the jury's decision as "merciful," nevertheless Frank and the defense team wanted still more "mercy." They would soon seek it from another source.

Class played an important role in the Frank Collier murder trial, Nearly all of the bankers, prominent businessmen, wealthy oilmen, and other movers-and-shakers of the community supported Frank, and the defense called many of them as character witnesses for him. It can hardly be doubted that such an array of influential men who lived in the jurors' own community had appreciable influence on them, and most likely played some part in their decision to render a lenient verdict and sentence.

However, it would be a mistake to surmise that all Wichitans supported the Colliers. The sentiment was far from unanimous, and there may well have been about as many folks who sympathized with the Robertsons as there were "upper-class folks" who rallied to support the Colliers. While Frank Collier's trial was in progress, the *Wichita Falls*

Record News ran this headline on its front page: "Robertsons Will Get Fund for New Home: Over $1,000 Already Subscribed for Mother of Dead Buster." It was reported that the new home would cost approximately $4,000, and that money was coming in from everywhere: "25 cents from newsboys to as much as $50 from wealthy residents." The subscription petition recited:

> In view of the stricken condition of Mrs. Robertson at this time, she is unable to support her large family of small children. In this plight, we cannot escape the conviction that it is the duty of this community to at least provide a home for this poor woman in this hour of her desperate need and broken physical condition.[59]

The Texhoma Oil and Refining Company, where Buster worked when he was killed, soon added another $500 to the fund—no small sum in that day when crude oil sold for $2.25 a barrel. In the end, the trustees were able to buy a duplex for Mrs. Robertson in the 600 block of Van Buren Street in Wichita Falls. She was able to survive by renting out one side of the duplex plus doing sewing alterations and taking in washing.

Meanwhile, Dorothy Collier's murder trial was pending. Because of the immense publicity generated by the murder of Buster Robertson and the Frank Collier murder trial in Wichita Falls, the district court changed venue to the town of Haskell, county seat of Haskell County, Texas, a small village some 100 miles southwest of Wichita Falls. Judge Bruce Bryant, district judge of the 39th Judicial District of Haskell County, presided. Once again, Jimmy Allred would be the lead prosecution, assisted by the Haskell district attorney, Tom Davis, and the Haskell county attorney, Clyde Grissom. On account of health reasons, W. F. Weeks was dropped from the defense team, leaving Charles I. Francis and B. Y. Cummings, both from Wichita Falls, and W. H. Murchison of Haskell to represent Dorothy Collier. Trial was set to begin on May 25, 1925.[60]

The demographics of Haskell County were decidedly different from Wichita Falls. It was no oil boomtown; it was a rural farming community, much smaller in population than Wichita County. And unlike Wichita County, there were very few Haskell County citizens who could be characterized as wealthy, with next to no social elites in town.

Community demographics and the resulting difference that it made in the composition of the jury would influence the trial tactics of both the prosecution and the defense, and the outcome, of the Dorothy Collier murder trial. To begin with, the jury consisted solely of "common folks": ten small-acreage farmers, one drayman who was also chief of the Haskell fire department, and one barber. There were no "upper-class" jurors, a fact that did not bode well for the defense.

There was an even more important difference: in the Wichita Falls murder trial, the defendant was a man. Here, in Haskell, the defendant was a woman. The sexual double standard would prove to be a major factor in mapping out trial strategies. And the sex of the defendant would prove to be a double-edged sword for both sides.

In 1925, the fact that juries were all-male had a substantial influence on trial tactics. Probably most trial lawyers today believe that female jurors are typically more critical of female defendants and witnesses, less inclined to accept their version of events on face value. In that more plebeian Haskell jury, had there been some women (mothers, particularly) on the jury, Dorothy Collier's version of why it was necessary to kill another mother's son in order to protect her daughter's treasured social status in Wichita Falls would have been a hard sell—to put it mildly. Here, however, Dorothy would be facing an all-male jury, and it would consist of males reared south of the Mason-Dixon Line where, even in the post–World War I era, boy children were nurtured in the idealization of women and were taught to believe in women's inherent moral superiority. Both the prosecution and the defense would be playing in a ballpark far different from the one where modern legal contests are battled out.

Women were still pedestalized and believed less culpable, less accountable for their actions. Some Southern gentlemen even had difficulty believing that gentle Southern ladies were capable of evil intent. Indeed, back in seventeenth-century England, where it all began, one legal commentator explained: "The general rule is that all persons are responsible for their acts done in violation of the law; but to this rule there is an exception in favor of infants, insane persons, married women and irresponsible agents."[61] That such notions still had some purchase even in 1925 Texas is evidenced by a question put by prosecutor Allred to each prospective juror: "Will the fact that the defendant in this case is a woman influence you in any way in arriving at a verdict?"[62]

That attitude toward women was also responsible for another change in the prosecution's posture in this case. In the Frank Collier murder trial, the prosecution left the death penalty option open for jury consideration, but in the trial of Dorothy Collier the State announced at the outset that it would not seek the death penalty. It might have seemed acceptable, even proper, to demand that a jury hang Frank Collier, but to demand that a 1925 Southern jury hang Dorothy Collier for committing the same murder—well, that just risked casting the prosecution as an overbearing bully in the eyes of the jury.

The State opened by calling its star witness, Hattie Robertson. She made an effective witness. According to the *Record News* reporter, tears were observed in the eyes of at least two jurors and nearly all of the spectators, a large majority of whom were women. The climax of her testimony came when she described how, while Buster's body lay bleeding to death in her arms in front of the Collier automobile, Dorothy Collier ordered her husband to "back up the car, Frank, so his mother can see he's dead." The defense, wisely, declined to cross-examine Mrs. Robertson.

Then the State called the eyewitness, R. W. Windham, the special officer/night watchman, who repeated the testimony he gave during the Frank Collier trial, testimony that essentially corroborated Mrs. Robertson's account of the shooting. The defense declined to cross-examine Windham as well.

The prosecutors had one blockbuster witness waiting in the wings—a witness they had not called during the Frank Collier trial. The witness, Mrs. Frank Woods of Wichita Falls, was a confidant of Dorothy Collier. She was a most reluctant witness, obviously not wanting to testify against Dorothy. In fact, after only a few questions, the nervous young woman fainted and had to be carried from the courtroom. They weren't able to revive her, and she had to be removed to a private home, where doctors were called to attend her. The trial was postponed for two days while everyone speculated whether she would ever recover from her nervous breakdown.

Meanwhile, prosecutors got a court order from Judge Bryant prohibiting Frank and Dorothy Collier and all the defense attorneys from contacting Mrs. Woods. Finally, on the third day, she appeared to have recovered sufficiently to resume her testimony. She was brought into the courtroom on a cot, and over strenuous defense objections she was allowed to testify to two conversations she had with Dorothy—one before Buster was killed and one shortly after he was killed. In the first conversation, she quoted the defendant as saying, "I've had enough of Buster. If he don't leave her alone, I'm going to have Collier kill him or knock him in the head." Mrs. Woods said that Dorothy Collier also told her that "she would rather see Mary Frances in her coffin than married to Buster." After the killing, Mrs. Woods said that Dorothy told her that "had not Collier killed Robertson she would have." Dorothy ended her comments to the young woman with this devastating assertion: "We feel *we* were *justified*" in killing Buster.[63]

Ouch!

Mrs. Woods was then carried out of the courtroom on a cot. On that dramatic note the State rested its case.

It was now the defense team's turn—but to do what? The defense twisted on the horns of a perplexing dilemma. Would they proceed along the tactical lines they had pursued in the Frank Collier trial by attempting to try Hattie Robertson instead of Dorothy Collier; attempting to trash Hattie Robertson's character and reputation in an effort to persuade the jury that the Colliers were "justified" in killing Buster? Or, if not "justified," at least so inflamed by the threatened degradation of their princess by Buster and his mother that the most the jury should give her was a manslaughter conviction plus a suspended sentence? At that point, the defense was prepared to go down that same road again, as Dorothy Collier's team had subpoenaed a slew of witnesses used in the Frank Collier trial, all of whom had testified that Hattie Robertson had a bad reputation.

The "manslaughter" strategy had some advantages. It had worked in Wichita Falls. But then in Wichita Falls, the Colliers were prominent upper-class people and had the support of the influential and the powerful members of that community. In the small, rural, farming community of Haskell County there were few upper-class types (none of whom were jurors). Plus, once again, the Victorian double standard stereotype of the role of the sexes would impact trial strategy. The "manslaughter" strategy had more strength in the Frank Collier trial than it would have in the Dorothy Collier trial because of the sex of the defendant. A large part of the appeal to the jurors in Wichita Falls was the fact that Frank Collier, as a man, was compelled to do his duty (kill Buster) pursuant to the tenets of the old unwritten law's "honor defense" in order to "protect his home and his womenfolk." It would be harder to play that card with much effect in the trial of a woman; "protecting the home" just was not the perceived duty of a refined Southern lady. Then too, here in this community, before these jurors, it must have seemed to the defense team that this strategy just wouldn't play all that well. After all, in the end, it would be pitting one woman against another woman—the one, rather stoic and perhaps a bit haughty, who felt "justified" in killing the son of the other woman; the other, an obviously distraught mother who had witnessed the slaughter of her unarmed son right before her very eyes.

There was another trial strategy the defense could elect to take: forget manslaughter and a suspended sentence. Go for broke: murder or acquittal. It was a daring gamble, but it had advantages. First and foremost was the "Frank did it" defense. She didn't pull the trigger. She was just sitting in the car—a mere bystander—when Frank "went crazy" and shot poor Buster. Under that plan, it would not be neces- sary to call all those rather shabby witnesses to trash the character and reputation of poor, distraught Hattie Robertson and risk alienating the jury by attacking a cripple. It would also avoid allowing the State to put on a number of "rehabilitating" witnesses who would testify that Hattie was a good woman doing her very best to survive and feed six little children.

By adopting the "Frank-did-it" defense, Dorothy Collier's team hoped to limit the trial's emotional impact upon the jurors and instead steer the trial to a more cerebral plane; a careful and logical analysis of the facts as tested against the statutory definition of what consti- tutes a principal in a criminal offense. Also by adopting this strategy it would force the jury either to convict a woman of murder or acquit her, thereby avoiding the possibility of a compromise "manslaughter" ver- dict. No doubt the defense lawyers believed—hoped—that the jurors just couldn't bring themselves to brand Dorothy Collier (or any other woman) a murderer; believed that—worst case—at least one juror, who was so constituted, would cause a hung jury. After all, a mistrial is always a victory for the defense.

From a legal standpoint, the question boiled down to whether Dorothy Collier was a principal in the killing of Buster; that is, even if she hadn't actually pulled the trigger, still had she, by words and/or deeds, aided, abetted, directed, or encouraged her husband to kill Buster? Was she, in effect, a "partner" in the nefarious enterprise? The defense would argue that however much Dorothy Collier had hated Buster, and however much she even wished he were dead (after all, she had taken a potshot at him earlier), and even though she was glad that Frank had killed him, still, during the fatal confrontation at the intersection of 17th and Bluff Street that Valentine's Day evening, she had done nothing to encourage, abet, aid, or direct Frank in getting out of the car and shooting Buster. She did nothing other than sit in the car while Frank committed the crime. Sure, *afterwards* she might have called for Frank to back the car up so Hattie Robertson could see that Buster was dead, but that was *after* he had been killed—*after* the crime had been committed. Persuading the jury to ignore all that Dorothy did and said before and after the fatal showdown that night, but instead to focus solely on the law and on what happened at the time of the intersection confrontation—that and nothing else—would be a steep uphill battle for the defense lawyers. But it appeared, all things considered, to be their best shot at clearing Dorothy Collier.

For better or for worse, that was the strategy the defense adopted. As a result—so unlike the Frank Collier trial—not one word was uttered during the entire trial by either the State or the defense about the allegedly bad character of Hattie Robertson or any immoral activity at her home. However, the defense strategy suffered a severe setback when they called—or at least attempted to call—their first witness, Frank Collier. The defense team obviously needed him badly to tote the heaviest load in their "Frank-did-it" strategy. After all, since he had already been convicted, he could, with impunity, shoulder as much blame as possible and hopefully deflect any implication that Dorothy had played any part in his decision to shoot Buster or aided or assisted in the planning or the execution of the crime. Short of committing provable perjury, Frank was free to say just about anything that would be beneficial to Dorothy's cause. However, that plan was derailed by Judge Bryant, who sustained a prosecution objection to allowing Frank to testify. Judge Bryant ruled that Collier was incompetent to testify since he had been convicted of the felony offense of manslaughter. This was a major blow to the defense team. For the "Frank-did-it" defense to work, the Collier team sorely needed someone to tell their version to the jury, someone who would lay all the blame on Frank. Since Frank had been disqualified, that left only Dorothy. But putting Dorothy on the stand gave rise to some serious problems. First was the understandable concern about how well Dorothy would come across to the jury—especially her demeanor while testifying. While, as the *Record News* reporter noted, Hattie Robertson was an "effective" and sympathetic witness, it was doubtful that her counterpart, Dorothy Collier, would make a very effective witness or engender much sympathy. The same reporter told readers that while the trial proceeded (including Hattie Robertson's testimony), Dorothy seemed stoic and "unconcerned." That, plus her unrepentant attitude ("we felt justified"), did not bode well for an effective jury performance.

"Demeanor evidence" is often as important as, if not more important than, the actual words a witness speaks. A jury (or any audience, for that matter) judges the credibility of a witness by how he or she speaks—the inflection and emphasis on certain words, the mannerisms exhibited, the facial expressions, the eye contact (shifty-eyed or direct gaze), forthright or evasive replies, reluctance to answer certain questions, and so many other nonverbal communications. In the case of Dorothy Collier, the defense obviously felt that her "demeanor evidence" would not be good; felt that she would likely come off as rather evasive and calloused, especially when compared to Hattie Robertson's heart-tugging performance.

As bad as the "demeanor" problem was, putting Dorothy Collier on the stand would create an even more dangerous pitfall. She would be subjected to some potentially devastating cross-examination by the prosecution—particularly in light of Mrs. Woods's "we were justified" testimony. This testimony had not been presented in Frank Collier's trial in Wichita Falls. Here, however, if the defense called Dorothy to testify, the State, on cross, would force her either to admit she made that incriminating statement to Mrs. Woods or force her to call Mrs. Woods

a liar. In view of the heart-wrenching and emotionally devastating testimony of Mrs. Woods, Dorothy's self-serving denial would likely succeed only in branding herself as a liar in the eyes of the jury. If, on the
other hand, she admitted she said those damning words, then the "*we
were justified*" part would practically doom her to the role of principal
in the crime. Plus, the prosecution would no doubt zero in on the "we
were *justified*" part, and force Dorothy to explain at great length *why*
she and Frank felt "justified" in shooting an unarmed nineteen-year-old
boy to death—shooting him down like a dog on a public street right
in front of his mother.

The defense might elect not to put Dorothy Collier on the stand.
She had the constitutional right not to testify if she so elected, and
in that event the prosecution would be prohibited from commenting
on her failure to take the stand and protest her innocence. (Still, even
without any prompting from the prosecutor, a jury always wonders: "If
the defendant really is innocent, then why didn't he or she get on the
stand and tell us what really happened?") The Dorothy Collier defense,
therefore, faced a no-win dilemma. The question then became: Which
was the lesser of the two evils?

Eventually, an agreement was reached with the prosecution. The
defense would not call Dorothy to testify but would be allowed to read
a transcript of her testimony at Frank Collier's trial. The defense could
thereby avoid the anticipated bad "demeanor" evidence problem while
also shielding Dorothy Collier from searing cross-examination by the
State.

Why did the prosecution agree to allow the defense to read Dorothy's prior testimony from a transcript rather than forcing the defense
actually to put her on the stand? Since she was present and available to
testify, the State could have forced the defense either to put her on the
stand or forego her version of events altogether—an option the defense
couldn't afford. For the "Frank-did-it" defense to work, the defense had
to put Dorothy Collier's story before the jury one way or the other. So
why did the prosecution agree to cut this slack to the defense? Perhaps
the prosecutors felt their case was in such good shape at that point, they
didn't want to risk Dorothy's making a favorable impression on the jury
and didn't want to risk alienating the jury by aggressive (read: bullying)
cross-examination of a woman. Also, Hattie's testimony had been emotionally powerful and had gone unchallenged by the defense. Besides,

the version of events Dorothy testified to at Frank's trial was not all that damaging to the State. In any event, the defense team ended up not calling even one witness to the stand, instead contenting themselves with reading the transcript of Dorothy's prior testimony. Again, no one called Mary Frances to testify.

In rebuttal, the State, over defense objections, read a portion of the testimony Dorothy had given at Frank's habeas corpus hearing when, before his trial, he had sought to have bail set. The primary thrust of this testimony was Dorothy's admission that on the night of the shooting, she had made the threat to her daughter that "if Buster comes over here I'll blow his brains out," and that afterward she had fetched the pistol and run out of the house waving it around before Frank overtook her and jerked the revolver out of her hands.

That ended the testimony in one of the most peculiar murder trials in Texas history.

Judge Bryant then began preparing his instructions to the jury. Defense Attorney Charles Francis, Frank Collier's former batboy-turned-lawyer, requested that Judge Bryant add a paragraph to his jury instructions, a palliative in Dorothy Collier's favor that affords us a priceless window into the flavor of those times and its people. He wanted the judge to tell the jury: ". . . it is presumptive that a wife is always under the influence of her husband and is guided in some measure by his actions and wishes."[64]

Judge Bryant, however, refused to share that bit of nonstatutory folk wisdom with the jury. Even though that proposed jury instruction seems quaint indeed by today's standards, it does have a root in Victorian jurisprudence in England. As late as 1880, Justice Colin Blackburn warned one Kent County grand jury: "The law supposes that everything is the property of the husband and that the wife is under his control."[65]

Jury arguments ensued. The defense was limited to arguing the "Frank-did-it" defense upon the grounds stated above and to calling attention to how important an acquittal was not only to Dorothy Collier but also to her daughter, Mary Frances, whose father would soon be shipped off to prison.

District Attorney Allred, for the State, scoffed at the defense argument that Dorothy was just an innocent bystander, citing her hatred for Buster, her prior threats, and all her other acts and deeds (including shooting at Buster herself only a short time before Frank killed him), as well as her shrill, calloused direction to her husband to back up the car so Hattie Robertson could see that her son was dead. He also underscored Dorothy Collier's "we were justified" assertion. He summarized it all, contending that Dorothy was as much a principal to this crime as was her husband, and just as culpable—if not more so.

During the final argument, the courtroom was again packed, and again mostly with women. On the front row sat Hattie Robertson, crying, with her six small children huddled around her. The *Record News* reporter informed its readers that Allred's final plea was so impassioned that "it caused tears to fall from the eyes of even one of the most experienced lawyers in that courtroom." In reply to the defense argument that the jury's decision was of vital importance to the lives of the Colliers, Allred responded:

> Of course this case is important to the defendant. But it's important to Mrs. Robertson's children who sit over there and who sell newspapers on the street in order to make a living and help her.

Then, turning to Frank Collier, who was seated next to his wife in the courtroom, Allred thundered:

> I'll tell you where you made your mistake, Collier. You should have taken Buster to you even though you did not believe in him. That you'd give him a chance. You should have helped him make the best of what you thought a bad situation. But you didn't. You didn't give him a chance.

Closing, Allred commented on the demonstrated strength of the love Buster and Mary Frances had for one another:

> Nothing that was done seemed to be enough to keep them apart. And there was in the marriage vow which they took, "whatsoever God hath joined together let no man put asunder."[66]

On May 29, 1925, the jury retired to deliberate. Three hours later it returned with a verdict of guilty to which it affixed a ten-year prison sentence. Dorothy Collier, of course, appealed. Her attorneys contended that there was no evidence in the trial record to support the jury's conclusion that Dorothy was a principal in the killing of Buster Robertson. Actually, from the beginning, the defense's "Frank-did-it" strategy had been designed to a large extent with the appellate court in mind. With all the raw emotional strands in this case tugging at the heartstrings of the jury, it was difficult for the defense to persuade twelve laymen jurors to set aside all those emotional tugs and focus on the facts and the law and therefore to coolly analyze the case from a logical standpoint— that is, measure the facts against the statutory law. Under Texas law, was Dorothy Collier really a "principal" in the killing? It was a close legal question, and the defense stood a much better chance of success when that question was addressed to a panel of learned judges in the hushed, cerebral atmosphere of an appellate court rather than argued before a panel of farmers with all the usual bombast and hyperbole of trial lawyers in the circus-like arena of a courtroom. The Texas Court of Criminal Appeals wrestled with that issue, had difficulty with it, but in the end concluded that there was evidence that supported the jury's verdict and so, on November 3, 1926, affirmed her conviction.[67] Since the Court of Criminal Appeals is the highest appellate court in Texas that hears appeals of criminal cases, it would certainly have appeared that this was the end of the line for Dorothy Collier.

It wasn't. Dorothy Collier never served a day of that ten-year sentence. Even though she had exhausted her appeals through the Texas judicial system, there was always one last shot: a pardon from the Texas governor. That possibility would have seemed remote, particularly in view of the shocking nature of the crime. As everyone knows, pardons are only granted as an executive act of mercy, and usually only after the prisoner has served a significant portion of his or her sentence, has behaved well, and has exhibited remorse for the crime, as well as exhibited signs of rehabilitation. Dorothy Collier didn't fit any of those criteria. But she was one lucky woman. Lucky because another woman, Miriam A. "Ma" Ferguson, happened to be governor of the State of Texas. Ma Ferguson had been elected after her husband, James E. "Pa" Ferguson, had been impeached and removed from office by the Texas Legislature in 1917 for malfeasance. (Among other financial indiscretions, it turned out that Pa had enhanced his $4,000 governor's annual salary by accepting an anonymous $156,000 "donation" from bash-fully nameless brewers who, understandably, were mightily concerned over the rising sentiment in favor of prohibition.)[68] Pa responded to the indignity of removal by promoting the candidacy of his wife: "Two governors for the price of one," he crowed. To the astonishment of old-line politicians and political pundits, it worked. Ma won the 1924 gubernatorial race and, in the process, became the first woman elected governor of any state in the union.[69]

Between them, the Fergusons managed to confound, exasperate, and outrage traditional Texas politicians of the era for about a quarter of a century: Pa was governor from January 19, 1915, until removed on August 25, 1917; Ma was governor twice, first from January 20, 1925 to January 17, 1927, and then from January 17, 1933, to January 15, 1935. Their outrageously hambone antics were intentionally calculated to make a blatant appeal to the unwashed and the undereducated vot-ers, consisting primarily of the large rural farm population. Although both were intelligent—Ma was in fact a college-educated "Southern belle"—they deliberately played the role of the down-home country hayseeds. Ma, for instance, when on the campaign trail often wore shapeless flour-sack dresses, donned a bonnet, and posed for pictures in somebody's barnyard. To their credit, they did buck two popular trends of the day—the revival of the Ku Klux Klan and the push for prohibi-tion. (However, as noted above, their antiprohibition stance may have been due more to cash than to conscience.)

Both Pa and Ma were also notorious for yet another reason—their extremely liberal pardon policies, which kept the gates of the Texas prison system swinging open. For instance, during the years of 1925 and 1926, at a time when the population of Texas was less than a fifth of what it is today, Ma Ferguson granted executive clemency to 3,595 convicts.[70] The nationally famous humorist of that time, Will Rogers, once joked that the Fergusons "sent out pardons like Christmas cards." Rogers claimed, tongue-in-cheek, that one of those recipients wrote a thank-you note back to Pa Ferguson but called the governor's atten-tion to the fact that "I ain't been caught yet." Moreover, it was widely believed by capitol insiders in Austin at the time—and recent research tends to support the belief—that not all the many pardons granted by the Fergusons were motivated by their kind and merciful hearts. Cold,

Texas Governor Miriam Ferguson. Although a college-educated woman, Ma Ferguson played a "hayseed" role during her political campaigns for the benefit of the pre-
dominantly rural electorate. In this campaign photo she is posed with her daughter
and a Democrat donkey. Like many farm women of the time, she donned a bonnet,
which became a symbol of her political career. (It wasn't Ma's bonnet; she borrowed
it.) Governor Ma Ferguson rescued both Frank Collier and Dorothy Collier from jury
verdicts of guilty in the Buster Robertson murder trials by issuing prompt pardons.
(Image courtesy of the San Antonio Light Collection, the University of Texas, Institute of Texan Cultures at San Antonio.)

hard cash appears to have been a motivating factor in some cases.[71] In any event, for whatever motivating factor, and over the tearful protests of Hattie Robertson, on November 20, 1926—less than two months before Ma's term as governor expired and only seventeen days after the Court of Criminal Appeals had affirmed Dorothy Collier's conviction, and before Dorothy ever entered the gates of a Texas prison—Ma Ferguson granted Dorothy Collier ("that unfortunate woman," so sayeth Ma) a full and unconditional pardon.[72]

In recent years, critics of appellate judges have accused many of them of going beyond their proper role of *interpreting* laws, and instead simply *making up* laws to suit their own political views. In other words, critics say that contrary to our "separation of powers" system of government, the judicial branch has often usurped the role of the legislative branch. Governor Ferguson's pardon of Dorothy Collier has to rank as one of the most unique official documents in Texas history because it was a crystal clear case of the executive branch of government usurping the role of the judicial branch by, in fact, retrying a criminal case and not only overturning the jury's verdict but also reversing the ruling of the highest appellate court in the state. In one of the most lengthy pardons on record, Governor Ma proceeded to review the same evidence that the Court of Criminal Appeals reviewed in affirming Dorothy's conviction but came up with the exact opposite conclusion—that is, declaring that the evidence did *not* prove that Dorothy Collier aided or encouraged Frank Collier in the killing of Buster Robertson, and therefore was *not* a principal in the murder of Buster Robertson and therefore was *not* guilty of the offense of murdering Buster Robertson.

Ma prefaced her "legal opinion" by expressing incredulity that the State had "inflicted a verdict of murder on this unfortunate woman" and then proceeded to give a decidedly defendant-friendly interpretation to key evidence that the jury and the appellate court had found to be very damning to Dorothy Collier's cause. Example one, quoting Ma's pardon:

> The mother of the deceased testified that Mrs. Collier said just after her husband had shot her son, and while she was holding her boy in her arms, "Roll the car back Frank so she can see he is *dead*." This certainly is not any evidence of any conspiracy to hurt or kill any body [*sic*] and

was a suggestion of aid to have the light of the car to see the condition
of the *wounded* boy. [Emphasis added.]

Example two: Explaining Dorothy's testimony to the effect that
prior to the killing she had warned that if Elzie Robertson didn't leave
Mary Frances alone, she would have "Collier shoot him or kill him,"
Ma said:

It was not evidence that Mrs. Collier and Frank Collier had entered
into any agreement to kill the deceased, or had even discussed it.

Example three: Explaining away Dorothy's "we think we were justified" comment, Ma summarily dismissed it like this:

Putting the most acid construction on these remarks they cannot be
said to be any evidence or admission of agreement to kill anybody by
Mrs. Collier or Frank Collier.[73]

After thus finding Dorothy Collier not guilty, Governor Ferguson
went on to list in her pardon the names of more than 250 prominent
Wichitans who had petitioned her for the pardon. What were the tears
of Hattie Robertson when weighed against the power (and money?) of
all those "people who mattered"? In the end, the pardon was employed
as a means, not of *pardoning* Dorothy Collier, but of *exonerating* her.

Governor Ferguson was not done yet. On December 27, 1926—
slightly more than a month after she had pardoned/exonerated Dorothy
Collier and just at the midnight hour of her term as governor—Ma
Ferguson pardoned Frank Collier as well. At least she didn't undertake
to retry his case or contend that he was innocent—just nearly innocent.
The pardon, in part, reads: "While I do not mean to say that Collier was
free from blame, but I do not think he is a criminal. He acted under
great excitement and for the moment was not conscious or responsible
for what he did."[74]

Almost sounds like "not guilty" by reason of temporary insanity—a
verdict that, under the laws and constitution of the State of Texas, could
only have been made by the judicial branch. Governor Ma, in her pardon of Frank Collier, went on to list the names of approximately four

hundred residents of Wichita Falls who had signed a petition seeking Frank Collier's pardon, all of whom, the pardon explained, "want to forgive him." Hattie Robertson's name did not appear on the list.

It appears from the record that Frank Collier actually served less than one month of his three-year sentence.

An interesting side note: Governor Ma pardoned Dorothy Collier on November 21, 1926. On December 29, 1926, she pardoned Frank Collier. Dorothy Collier's pardon number is 19,868. Frank Collier's pardon number is 20,129—which meant that during the thirty-six-day interim between those two pardons, Governor Ma apparently cranked out 260 more pardons. If true, that figures out to be more than 7 pardons per day—even if Governor Ma worked on Sundays. The two Colliers' timing couldn't have been better!

Epilogue

As mentioned above, Hattie Robertson was given a duplex home in Wichita Falls thanks to a large number of sympathizers, the majority of whom contributed less than ten dollars each. She was thus able to survive and care for her children by renting out one side of the duplex plus taking in washing and making sewing alterations.

The Colliers resumed their life in Wichita Falls. Mary Frances reconciled with her parents and moved back into the family home. But things were never the same for any of them. Thanks to Ma Ferguson, Dorothy Collier never spent a day in prison; instead. she continued to live in the same home in Wichita Falls. But she was no longer the mayor's wife, and despite Ma Ferguson's attempt to erase the murder conviction and exonerate her, a taint remained. She would never again quite regain her former coveted status as one of the luminaries in the city's social elite. Dorothy "Dott" McCauley Collier died February 4, 1945.

Upon Frank's return from prison he was hired by the city to work as a manual laborer in its park department. Frank Collier stayed the course, and when he retired nineteen years later, in 1953, he was the park superintendent. Upon his retirement, Wichita Falls honored him with a "Frank Collier Night" at the city park. Shortly thereafter, on October 24, 1953, he died of a heart attack.[75]

Mary Frances continued to pursue her interest in art, and the Colliers sent her to the famous Pratt Institute in New York. Before she left, her mother—still running true to her heritage—gave Mary Frances these orders: "Don't take up smoking, and don't bring home a Yankee." Also running true to form, the headstrong Mary Frances promptly took up smoking, and then she married a Yankee, Robert Schultz of Wisconsin.[76] He was also an art student. After they returned to Texas, he worked for the Texas Highway Department until his retirement. They had one daughter, Jeanie Schultz Hill, of Hurst, Texas. Meanwhile, Mary Frances went on to become an accomplished painter who favored landscapes and still-life pictures. Her paintings were widely exhibited, and she won a number of awards. In addition, Mary Frances gave private art lessons, part of the time in Wichita Falls. She died October 12, 1983.

The 1925 slaying of Buster Robertson by the mayor and his wife and the subsequent murder trials amounted to the most sensational scandal in the history of Wichita Falls, and it certainly drew headlines all over the state and nation. However, as was so typical of the mindset of Southern folks of that era, the whole scandal was promptly hushed up and swept under the carpet by the entire Wichita Falls community. The local histories of Wichita Falls and Wichita County make no mention of the killing of Buster Robertson or the ensuing murder trials. One history gives a rather lengthy account of the life and career of Frank Collier, but it neatly sidesteps the scandal this way: "He resigned [as mayor] February 18, 1925, as the result of a personal matter." Later in the biographical sketch, the local historian abruptly resumes the account like this: "When Collier returned to Wichita Falls, he quietly took a lowly job with the city parks department."[77] The local histories make no mention of Hattie Robertson or her son, Buster Robertson.

And by tacit agreement of community members, nobody breathed a word of the scandal; not even to younger members of their own families.

Finally on July 31, 2005, some eighty years after the tragedy, a reporter for the *Wichita Falls Times Record News*, Trish Choate, broke the silence and astounded almost everybody with a thorough and well-written feature story detailing that 1925 "crime of passion." It even surprised Joe Brown, a lifelong resident of Wichita Falls who has been, and still is, a popular columnist for the *Times Record News*. Joe was born in 1934 and lived just around the corner from Hattie Robertson for years. In fact, as a youngster he often mowed Mrs. Robertson's yard. His dad instructed Joe not to charge Mrs. Robertson anything for the service, and he didn't. However, he recalled that "now and then she did slip me a couple of quarters." The amazing thing is that until Trish Choate's 2005 article, the veteran Wichita Falls reporter and columnist, Joe Brown, had never heard a word of the scandal. In his *Times Record News* column of August 10, 2005 (only ten days after Trish Choate's article), Joe Brown, under the headline "Untold Story," wrote: "Until two weeks ago, when I read the story . . . I had never even heard a hint about the young lovers' tragedy. You readers probably didn't either." He went on to opine:

> My parents and our neighbors never once talked about the events of
> 1925 in front of me, but remember that was a good 10 to 15 years
> before I was old enough to understand the difference between rich
> people and poor people.[78]

Reflecting on his boyhood days, Joe Brown recalled Hattie Robertson as a "heavy-set woman who drove a little car around town delivering dresses she had sewn for her customers."

The reader is left to reflect on what to make of it all; to wonder what in the world caused two of the city's leading citizens to become so emotionally unhinged that they launched such a bizarre, passion-driven bloody rampage that took the life of an innocent boy and tragically altered the lives of several others—including themselves? In retrospect, it seems clear that class was at the root of it all; more specifically, an overwhelming obsession with their social status in the community.

Although "class" was at the core of the tragedy and the motivations of the characters, it was a bit more complicated than simply dismissing it as a conflict between high-class and low-class. As in every examination of a "class," wherever or whenever studied, there are significant differences between members of any class. Both Colliers were "high-class" in the Wichita Falls society of 1925, but how each achieved that status, and how each viewed their respective stations in that society, and how vulnerable each felt when threatened with a loss of status, varied greatly.

To begin with, their respective paths to the top of Wichita Falls society were completely different. Seven-year-old Frank came with his single mother to Wichita Falls and began his career delivering groceries and ice and selling newspapers. Afterward he worked his way to the top of the ladder in Wichita Falls: a successful businessman, grand potentate of the Maskat Temple, and finally mayor of the city. It is ironic then that Frank Collier, whose early life so closely tracked that of Buster Robertson, seemed unwilling to give Buster a chance, even though Buster had a steady job at a refinery and was helping support his mother and younger siblings. From all accounts, prior to that fateful Valentine's Day, Frank Collier appeared to be a dedicated family man and a solid, sensible, and fair-minded citizen—the last person one would suspect of committing such a murder. What caused this seemingly level-headed, mature man to fly into such a murderous rage? Was a feared loss of social status his sole, or even primary, motivation?

Unlike Frank, Dorothy Collier was nourished from infancy on the antebellum South's menu of chivalry and rigid class distinctions. She inherited those notions of aristocracy from both sides of her family: both her father, Captain John Henry McCauley, and her maternal grandfather, Major Enoch McDonald, were Confederate heroes during the Civil War. Little wonder then that Dorothy, who grew to maturity in a family steeped in the Old South's traditions, should have come to believe that privilege, deference, and social superiority were all parts of her birthright. Perhaps it is not too much of a leap therefore to understand, at least from her perspective, why she viewed Buster, that determined suitor, as such a dangerous and unacceptable threat; why she felt they were "justified" in pursuing such a drastic solution in order to rescue the family from the shame of having their precious daughter marry way below their class. What would people think? After all, what other people thought of you, not who you really were, was at the very core of the Old South's Code of Honor. Frank, who had earned his way to an honored position, was less vulnerable to a family scandal involving an undesirable marriage than was Dorothy. Dorothy's perch atop Wichita Falls society was considerably more precarious, since it depended upon careful maintenance of the myth of her superiority to common folks, which, in turn, she believed had been gifted her by virtue of her aristocratic heritage.

That said, there was yet another reason why Dorothy might have justifiably felt so threatened by Mary Frances's marriage to Buster. Although by 1925 women had been accorded the right to vote, still it was basically a man's world, and women's opportunities were limited. Few could aspire to high-paying jobs or high-profile positions. Although Frank might have been hurt and keenly disappointed by Mary Frances and Buster's marrying and living together, he would still be the mayor, still have his business to operate, and still be accepted by his circle of friends. But where would that leave Dorothy? No job, no position, and, at least in her perception, a defrocked socialite—defrocked and ostracized.

Dorothy later claimed that her actions were all taken to protect headstrong Mary Frances from herself. However, her words and actions during the month before the killing cast doubt on that self-serving interpretation of her motive. One cannot help wondering, was Dorothy Collier determined to have Buster killed in order to save Mary Frances? Or did she want the boy killed to save herself—save herself from being disgraced and dethroned from her cherished social throne?

Clearly, maintenance of "class" and "keeping up appearances" were matters of life-or-death importance to Dorothy Collier. During the days leading up to the killing, it was Dorothy who kept waving a pistol around making repeated threats to kill Buster, who attempted to do just that when she fired off a round at the fleeing boy, and who kept inflaming Frank with accounts of Buster's "seduction" of Mary Frances. After the shooting, it was Dorothy who ordered Frank to shine their car lights on the dying boy for the benefit of his mother and who, never showing a hint of remorse, calmly explained to a friend why they were "justified" in murdering Buster.

One has to wonder if Frank Collier would have ever worked himself into such an uncontrollable rage that he felt justified in committing such a terrible crime unless egged on by a wife who was obsessed with retaining her exalted social status. Finally, one has to wonder how Frank, during the remaining twenty-eight years of his life, managed to deal with flashbacks of that blood-spattered, nightmarish spectacle of what happened so long ago on a Valentine's Day night at the intersection of 17th and Bluff.

And what of Mary Frances? There would never be another carefree, magical night of laughing and dancing with Buster in the ballroom of the Kemp Hotel. What would life have been like for her had the Colliers supported them and given Buster a chance? Who knows? Yet, the awful tragedy must have seared her tender soul. Years later, she taught private art lessons from her home in Wichita Falls. One of her art students was Myna Hicks Potts, who now lives in Chillicothe, Texas, some sixty-five miles or so northwest of Wichita Falls. In all the time they spent together, Mary Frances never spoke of Buster or the scandal that had taken his life. Mrs. Potts remembers Mary Frances as a "very talented artist" and always friendly and helpful. Yet, many times when Mrs. Potts arrived for her scheduled art lesson, Mary Frances "was unavailable." Mrs. Potts recalls Mary Frances as being "a very troubled soul."[79]

FIVE

The Cursed Fortune
PART ONE: FLOYD HOLMES AND WARREN WAGNER

he year was 1917, and big things were happening, momentous events that would alter the course of world history. Pledging to make the world safe for democracy, President Woodrow Wilson led the United States into World War I, and in Russia, the Bolsheviks were in the process of making that country safe for communists. Well, at least for some communists.

With such monumental headlines screaming around the globe, it was little wonder that hardly anybody paid much attention on that blistering hot July day to what Warren Wagner and his rag-tag crew of roughnecks and roustabouts were up to: dragging a primitive drilling rig onto a dusty site about a mile southwest of a drowsy and droughty West Texas village named Ranger. Then and there they spudded in the No. 1 McCleskey oil well and began, in the parlance of the oil patch, "makin' hole."[1]

It was, for sure, a pure wildcat venture—no producing well in sight for miles around, although a number of shallow and unproductive test holes had previously been drilled in the area. Geologists said it was a foolhardy waste of good money. And when they learned that Warren planned to drill to the ridiculous depth of 3,400 feet they gave him a resounding horse laugh.

Nevertheless, on July 2, Warren Wagner and his greasy gang cranked up their drilling contraption and commenced pounding a hole in the dirt way out there in the middle of a remote and desolate prairie.

Actually, Warren Wagner owned no interest in the well itself; he was only a contract driller of oil wells. A relatively small coal-mining company named Texas & Pacific Coal Company had purchased from a local farmer, John H. McCleskey, a mineral lease covering the McCleskey farm where the drilling was taking place. The company had mined coal for a number of years in the area, but its general manager, W. K. Gordon, smelled oil. Gordon was a persuasive and determined man, and despite negative advice from the oil experts, he finally persuaded the company president, Edgar Marsten, back in New York, to drill a deep test. Not only that, but somehow he talked Marsten into buying mineral leases covering about 300,000 acres in the area—all, however, at the modest cost of 25 cents per acre. Texas & Pacific Coal Company then contracted with Warren Wagner to drill the No. 1 McCleskey.

Inauspicious as its beginnings were, and insignificant as it seemed at the time, the No. 1 McCleskey was destined to become a major landmark in the United States petroleum industry, and it would transform a small coal-mining company into one of the most powerful corporations in the Southwest. And, either directly or indirectly, it would make a lot of oilmen black-gold rich—including Warren Wagner.

Meanwhile, Warren and his crew were hammering away twenty-four hours a day, seven days a week, with their old cable-tool rig. Unlike the efficient modern rotary bits with industrial diamond-studded teeth attached to the end of a heavy steel drill stem, the cable-tool rig relied upon a heavy six-foot-long bit tapered down to form a hatchet-like blade. A steel cable was attached to the top of the bit, and it was repeatedly pulled up the hole and then the cable was released so that the bit plunged downward until it slammed into rock at the bottom of the hole. This procedure was repeated until the bit became dull. Nowadays, when the rotary bit gets dull, the crew pulls the drill stem, screws on a new bit, goes back into the hole, and continues drilling. In 1917, however, the bit had to be pulled out of the hole and heated until it was red hot, at which time a burly "tool dresser" would pummel the blade with a sledgehammer until it was sharp once again. Thus, drilling had to be halted often to sharpen the bit and to clean drilling debris out of the hole.[2]

Warren Wagner continued this slow enterprise, thumping and pounding his way through layer after layer of rock, shale, and sand. Weeks passed; summer turned to fall. Back at the home office, President Marsten was becoming increasingly skeptical of the whole enterprise. But when they reached 3,200 feet, all hell broke loose. Millions of cubic feet of natural gas spewed out of its vast underground reservoir. Yet there was no victory celebration—there was absolutely no market for natural gas.

President Marsten was ready to throw in the towel. He wired general manager Gordon: "Think we have made a mistake. Better quit." But Gordon was no quitter. He was persistent, and he was persuasive. Gordon's conviction that oil was near never wavered. Finally, Marsten relented, but the drilling budget Marsten mandated was soon depleted. Gordon was forced to continue by surreptitiously "borrowing" funds from the company's commissary fund. Then, on October 17, 1917, more than three and a half months after drilling began and about the time that the Bolsheviks were storming the czar's Winter Palace in Petrograd, Warren Wagner and his crew reached a depth of 3,431 feet. One of the crew thought he heard a faint rumbling from far down in the bowels of the hole. Soon the faint rumble turned into an angry growl as it neared the surface. Then it turned into a mighty roar. Suddenly rocks and dirt erupted from the mouth of the well, followed seconds later by a spray of oil, which promptly blossomed into a gusher. One historian put it this way:

> Outlined against the blue-gray October sky, the first gusher at Ranger blew in. . . . [I]mmediately the flow increased—a beautiful sight with the late autumn sunshine glinting on the broad column of greenish gold—the color of dreams—that skyrocketed over the top of the 84-foot derrick.[3]

The McCleskey No. 1—the "Big Mac"—gusher when it blew in on October 17, 1917, near Ranger, Texas. (Image courtesy of Jeane Pruett, individually, and as President of the Ranger Historical Society.)

Only one person failed to see anything beautiful about that spectacle. The farmer's wife, Mrs. J. H. McCleskey, upon whose farm the discovery well was drilled, was furious at the sight of all that nasty black oil soiling and discoloring the feathers of her beautiful flock of White Leghorn chickens.

The No. 1 McCleskey ("the Big Mac" as they now called it) blew in, making 1,600 barrels of oil and 3.5 million cubic feet of gas every day. Oil was selling for about $4 per barrel; "Big Mac" was spewing out riches to the tune of about $6,400 per day in 1916 dollars, or the equivalent of $110,000 each and every day in 2008 money—all that at a time when a man could buy a new suit for $10.95 and a Stetson hat for $4.00. It was a discovery that "caused the whole oil fraternity of the U.S. to be 'tossed into the air' . . . and then dumped into the lap of Ranger."[4] The now-mighty Texas & Pacific Coal Company soon changed its name to the Texas & Pacific Coal *and Oil* Company.

The discovery of the No. 1 McCleskey triggered what became known as the Ranger oil boom. One commentator later called it "the most spectacular boom ever to have occurred within the United States."[5] The Ranger boom was of tremendous importance to the nation because of its timing. The United States, Great Britain, Italy, France, and Russia were in the midst of WWI with Germany and the Central Powers. Russia had supplied the Allies with oil since 1914, but when Russia withdrew from the conflict in 1917, it caused a critical petroleum shortage that threatened to halt Allied ships, planes, tanks, trucks, and locomotives. Just in the nick of time, the Ranger boom took up the slack and supplied the oil necessary to fuel the war effort; thus it became noted as "The Boom That Won the War."[6] A *Fort Worth Star-Telegram* reporter of that time, Boyce House, wrote two books on the Ranger oil boom. In one, entitled *Roaring Ranger*, he penned this breathless report:

> The World's Biggest Boom . . . The wildest, roaringest boom of
> them all—Ranger! . . . Truly, California in 1849, the Klondike, Butte,
> Spindletop—none of the other great riches, whether produced by gold,
> silver, copper or petroleum equaled Ranger.[7]

And the No. 1 McCleskey started it all. Before "Big Mac," small ranches and farms had been the primary source of income for the Ranger community, and cotton was the primary crop. But in the summer of 1917, the whole area was suffering from a prolonged drought. The few stunted cotton stalks that struggled to survive were devastated in the parched fields by an infestation of boll weevils.[8] To say that times were hard was a gross understatement. Strangely enough, however, shortly after Big Mac blew in, the Ranger community was blessed again. Breaking that two-year drought, heavy rains began to fall—and kept on falling on the thirsty land, soaking farms and turning the unpaved streets of Ranger into a quagmire.

Within little more than a year after Big Mac, the tiny hamlet of Ranger saw its population explode from a few hundred to more than thirty thousand. Commerce, especially the oil field supply sector, boomed. New banks took root overnight. The February 14, 1919, issue of the *Fort Worth Star-Telegram* noted that eleven days after it opened its doors, one bank had acquired deposits totaling $330,000, and each of two other new banks on either side of the street had already stuffed their safes with more than $15 million. The same issue of the *Star-Telegram* claimed that there were more millionaires in Ranger than in any other town of its size in the nation.

Fields of liquid gold. Downtown Ranger, Texas, at the height of the Ranger oil boom as depicted on a 1920 post card. (Public domain.)

In 1967, the Texas Historical Commission erected a marker entitled "Roaring Ranger" at the intersection of FM 717 and Main Street in Ranger. Describing the effect of the oil boom on the community, the plaque reads, in part:

> Ten daily trains brought in prospectors packed in the aisles or on
> tops of coaches. Ranger's dozen or so houses became a city of drillers,
> suppliers, oil company offices. Living quarters were so scarce that not
> only were beds of day-tour men occupied by the graveyard-tour men,
> but over-stuffed chairs were also rented for sleeping. Food was hard
> to get and prices were high. For two rainy years, Ranger was a sea of
> mud. A sled taxied people across streets, or a man in hip boots carried
> them piggyback. However, money was plentiful, and forces of vice
> moved in. After five murders occurred in one day, law officers arrested
> many criminals and expelled gamblers and vagrants. Ranger's success
> overshadowed its troubles. It is said to have yielded in a year twice the
> wealth of the best years in California and Klondike gold fields.[9]

Meanwhile, oil derricks popped up overnight like mushrooms in a dark forest. Oil leases that had been selling for 25 cents per acre before Big Mac now commanded premiums of $8,000 per acre, and one lucky fellow who had recently bought his farm, surface and minerals, for $4 per acre was able to retain ownership of the surface estate yet sell oil leases on portions of his farm for $30,000 each after a 10,000-barrel-per-day well blew in on a nearby tract.[10]

Back in 1901, when the mammoth discovery well, Spindletop, blew in near Beaumont, gushing 75,000 barrels of oil per day, nearby tracts of land that had been selling for $10 per acre suddenly skyrocketed in value. Some tracts brought as much as $900,000 per acre—and that in 1901 dollars. A woman garbage collector who had been feeding edible waste to her hogs was astounded when an oil speculator showed up one day and paid her $35,000 for her pig pen.[11]

Although Mrs. McCleskey had initially been incensed when all that mucky black stuff besmirched her beautiful White Leghorn hens, her attitude improved considerably after several months of receiving huge oil royalty checks. Whereas prior to Big Mac, Mrs. McCleskey spent her days feeding chickens, milking cows, and washing clothes by hand on the couple's little drought-stricken farm in Eastland County, two years later she found herself sitting on a $7 million bank account that was growing larger and larger by the minute. When a reporter showed up one day to ask her what she was going to do with all that money, she mulled over the question for a few minutes and replied, "First, I am going to Fort Worth and get a set of false teeth." Then, she added, she just might do a little traveling. "An agent has already persuaded me to go to San Antonio, and I am going to take my sister along."[12]

Unfortunately, Mr. McCleskey wouldn't be going with them. Sudden riches beyond belief had proved to be his undoing—it turned out that Mr. McCleskey just loved to eat peaches. Back when he was dirt-floor poor, he seldom had enough money to afford the luxury of a store-bought peach. However, when the money started rolling in, he abandoned the farm, moved to town, and began buying peaches—lots and lots of peaches. One day he stuffed so many down his gullet that it literally killed him—probably the only case in recorded medical history of death by overdose of peaches. Still, Mrs. McCleskey had nothing but kind words for her departed mate. She told the reporter that

John McCleskey and wife. A poor dirt farmer, McCleskey suddenly became "filthy rich" overnight when the No. 1 McCleskey gusher blew in on their farm one day in 1917. (Image courtesy of Jeane Pruitt, individually, and as President of the Ranger Historical Society.)

Mr. McCleskey had been "very shrewd in business. Why, once," she reported, "he sent a can of sardines back to the store when the price was advanced from 15 cents to 25 cents."[13]

Where did all that leave Warren Wagner, who had no interests in Big Mac and didn't own any oil leases in the area? Recall that Texas & Pacific, thanks to the prescience of W. K. Gordon, had leased nearly everything in sight (about 300,000 acres) before the McCleskey strike. However, Texas & Pacific hadn't locked down 100 percent of the surrounding acreage; the enterprising and aggressive Warren Wagner wasted no time in ferreting out an unleased tract—small, admittedly, but still unleased. In those days there were no state regulations prohibiting oilmen from drilling wherever they wished, no matter how close their location was to a neighbor's property line or to another oilman's well.[14] (In the drilling frenzy touched off by the Spindletop bonanza in 1901, at least 100 different operators jammed 214 derricks around the discovery well on postage-stamp size drilling sites so close together that the roughnecks could practically walk from one drilling platform to the next without ever touching the ground.)[15] The unleased tract that Warren Wagner discovered was the playground of a small rural school in the Merriman community south of Ranger near the village of Desdemona.

Soon Merriman school children, eyes agog, witnessed Warren Wagner and his grimy oil field crew construct on their playground a towering eighty-four-foot wooden derrick (that being about three times taller than any windmill those farm kids had ever seen). One can almost visualize those wide-eyed kids, noses pressed against the school's window panes, when the roughnecks fired up their monstrous, smoke-belching apparatus and began pounding and thumping away, perhaps at what used to be third base.

This time, Wagner was drilling the well for himself—less of course, the traditional one-eighth royalty due the landowner, which in this case was the Merriman school district. For thirty-seven days Wagner thumped and pounded away until he hit what he was looking for at 3,200 feet. The well blew in, flowing 5,000 barrels of oil per day. At the time, oil was bringing $4 a barrel, making each day's receipts total around $20,000—equivalent to $346,000 in 2008 dollars.

Although the school district received only a one-eighth royalty (compared to seven-eighths received by Wagner and his backers), the district suddenly became the wealthiest, per capita, school district in the world. Former Texas governor Oscar B. Colquitt declared in 1918 that the school's fund was sufficient to give every child in the district a high school education plus four years in college.[16] Meanwhile, Warren Wagner, son of a poor farmer, became a very, very rich man.

Warren Wagner was born in Bens Run, West Virginia, in 1883, the son of Thornton Wagner, a farmer. But farming was not in Warren's blood. He was excited about the infant oil industry. Shallow wells were being drilled in that area, and as a teenager he took whatever menial jobs could be found in the oil patch. He was particularly fascinated with the drilling process and drilling rigs. In 1901, Warren heard about the mammoth Spindletop discovery on the Texas coast, and the eighteen-year-old caught the next train south. For the next two decades he followed discovery after discovery—one oil patch to the next—all over Texas, New Mexico, California, and even into Mexico. Wagner finally managed to acquire his own drilling rig, and he soon achieved quite an enviable reputation drilling wells for various companies in the oil-rich north central Texas fields of Petrolia, Burkburnett, and Wichita Falls.

Warren Wagner was the drilling contractor on the mammoth No. 1 McCleskey discovery well, which touched off the Ranger, Texas, oil boom. Picture taken from May 9, 1921, edition of the *Fort Worth Star-Telegram*. (Public domain.)

Floyd and Alma Holmes. Floyd Holmes, a Nocona, Texas, farm boy, struck it rich in 1921 when he sold his interest in the oil-rich Electra, Texas, field near Wichita Falls for $3.5 million. In 1906 Floyd Holmes, age twenty-one, married pretty Alma Wegner, age seventeen. (Image courtesy of Downtown Medicine Mound Preservation Group, Medicine Mound, Texas, Myna Hicks Potts, president.)

He lived in Wichita Falls until 1914, when he settled in the small town of Strawn. It was while living there in 1917 that Texas & Pacific Coal awarded him the contract to drill the No. 1 McCleskey—a drilling triumph that, as we have seen, ultimately made Warren Wagner, at age thirty-four, rich and famous.[17]

A decade earlier, on January 23, 1907, in Shreveport, Louisiana, Warren married an attractive and strong-willed young lady named Norma Swift, a native of Nacogdoches, Texas. Life was not easy for Norma in those early years. For the first decade of her marriage, and even after she became a mother, she dutifully followed her hard-driving husband from one miserable oil field shack to the next. It was while they were living their hard-scrabble life in the Petrolia field that they met another young and struggling couple who dreamed big of striking it rich in the oil fields. In fact, they lived next door to that couple—Floyd Holmes and his wife, Alma Holmes. The two couples became intimate friends.

Floyd Holmes's background, character, "rags-to-riches" determination, luck, and career mirrored that of Warren Wagner in many significant ways—but, as we shall soon see, not in every way.

Floyd was born on December 15, 1885 (only two years after Warren Wagner's birth), in the north central Texas village of Nocona (named for a famous Comanche war chief, Peta Nocona). He was the son and grandson of Baptist ministers. His parents were the Reverend T. Jeff Holmes and Dora Deaton Holmes. Jeff Holmes was not only a minister but also an Indian fighter and a buffalo hunter who sold his hides in Fort Worth. Later in life, he settled down to a more bucolic and peaceable life: he became a farmer. Floyd was educated in Montague County in north central Texas. He worked on his father's farm until he was twenty-two years old. He had eight siblings, all of whom, unlike Floyd, were typical frontier children—basically hardworking, salt-of-the-earth folks, if somewhat limited in ambition and vision. Like Warren Wagner, Floyd Holmes was not about to rusticate his life away on some family farm in the middle of nowhere. Floyd was an extraordinarily handsome young fellow, and in 1906, at age twenty-one, he married a beautiful girl from the neighboring village of Saint Jo. Her name was Alma Wegener, the seventeen-year-old daughter of Ernest Wegener and Alice Reimers Wegener, the latter being a native of Germany.[18]

After some unsuccessful get-rich schemes, in 1910 Floyd and Alma moved to Petrolia, where he began buying and selling oil and gas leases. Three years later, he became a confidential (read: "secret") agent trading oil leases for Edward Swift of Chicago, a meat-packing magnate; in that capacity he traveled throughout Texas, Oklahoma, California, and Mexico. In the latter part of 1918, he formed, and became general manager of, Planet Petroleum Company. His partners were R. O. Dulaney and J. B. Googins, manager of Swift & Co., and a member of the wealthy Edward Swift family. The company had holdings in Texas, Louisiana, and Arkansas. During 1920 and 1921, the company's fortune skyrocketed when it developed the Electra oil pool just west of Wichita Falls and then in 1921 sold its interests to Empire Gas and Fuel Company for the whopping sum of $3.5 million in 1921 dollars—$37 million in 2008 money. That same year, Holmes organized the Comet Petroleum Company, incorporating it for $250,000 and becoming its president and general manager.[19]

Ranger is located only about eighty miles west and a dab south of Fort Worth. After the McCleskey and more big strikes in other West Texas towns such as Eastland, Cisco, Breckenridge, Burkburnett, Electra, and a dozen other hamlets, Fort Worth quickly became the gateway to the booming oil fields. Oilmen from every part of the globe headed for Fort Worth—"an army of oil operators," the *Fort Worth Record* called it.[20] In a feature article entitled "Rainbow's End," the *Saturday Evening Post* reported that Fort Worth had been invaded by "soldiers of fortune, pathfinders, trailblazers, scouts, big and little, attached and unattached . . . lease sharks, grafters and grabbers, operators, speculators, and gamblers"[21]—not to mention oil field supply salesmen, drilling contractors, freight haulers, and landowners seeking to peddle oil leases on their farms. A California film crew arrived to document the boom-time excitement and assured Fort Worth folks that the crowds on Main Street were thicker than could be found in "any city in the United States."[22]

By early 1919, newcomers swamped existing hotels. Sky-high rents were charged, even for cots in the hallways. Some out-of-towners were forced to sleep in chairs in hotel lobbies. Guests were limited to five-day stays. The twelve-story Westbrook Hotel at Third and Main Streets became the world's oil center. Day and night the lobby was in a turmoil of frenzied trading. Office facilities were inadequate, and fast-pitched trading spilled out of hotel lobbies onto adjacent sidewalks. A storefront at Fifth and Main Streets known as "Mack's Oil Board" became a curb market for oil stocks. Speculators, sales personnel, and stenographers packed the fifty by one hundred foot room, and a blackboard listing hot local stocks stretched all the way across the rear wall.[23] Hectic trading fueled such excitement that dreams of quick fortunes seemed but an eyeblink away from reality, and downtown Fort Worth was permeated with the intoxicating scent of easy money.[24]

One speculator bought an oil lease as he walked through the Westbrook's front door and then sold the same lease for a considerable profit before he could make his way to the opposite side of the lobby. Some hustlers who arrived with zero capital made up to $50,000 in a day.[25] The trick was to buy a lease, pay for it with a hot check, and then sell it so quickly that the funds could be deposited to cover the hot check before it hit the bank the next morning. Other oil patch frauds were perpetrated by self-proclaimed fortune tellers, who did a brisk business gazing into crystal balls and then advising suckers where new gushers were awaiting discovery. Better yet was the "boy with X-ray eyes," who, it was told, could see through the earth and find oil. Thousands of shares of stock in the oil company that owned the services of this talented lad were sold to the greedy and the gullible.[26] Another favored ploy some con men exploited with very profitable harvests was to "oversell" interests in a drilling prospect, touting it to investors as the next Spindletop. For instance, the con might sell 300 percent or 400 percent or more of total interests in the prospect. Then the promoter would purchase an oil lease at minimal cost in an area far from any known production with the expectation that the test would result in a dry hole. If so, then the promoter simply pocketed his sizable profit, shrugged, and explained: "Sorry, folks, maybe next time. The oil business is, after all, a risky business, you know." However, the manure really hit the fan if, unexpectedly, there really was oil at the bottom of the damned hole. Then what? How does one go about distributing 100 percent of the proceeds of oil production from a well so as to satisfy owners of 400 percent of that well? A snarl of angry lawsuits usually resulted, but in that day few hustlers were prosecuted. There seemed to be a sort of shrugged nonchalance in the air where oil investments were concerned: "All's fair in love and war—and in the oil patch. Buyer beware!" *Caveat emptor*, and a hearty laissez-faire to you too.[27]

Extravagance was the order of the newly rich, and the newly rich wannabes. The Westbrook's owners hired a noted sculptor to carve a twelve-foot marble statue that rivaled in glory the artistic triumphs of ancient Greece. The statue depicted a nude female figure of breathtaking beauty—and alluring appeal. (Well, there *was* this flimsy veil, but it really emphasized more than it concealed.) She was known as "the Golden Goddess," and her derriere was simply irresistible. Few men could resist giving that fantastic feminine feature a loving massage in passing. For superstitious wildcatters, it soon became an article of faith that rubbing the Golden Goddess's bottom was essential to staking a

In 1919, the Westbrook Hotel at Third and Main in Fort Worth became the world's oil-trading center. Its owners had a twelve-foot marble statue sculpted and named it the "Golden Goddess" to grace the lobby of their hotel. (Author's collection).

drill site where gusher-size results could be expected in the oil patch. No self-respecting oiler would dare spud a wildcat *without* bestowing the obligatory pat or two—or more.[28]

Meanwhile, oil gave a massive boost to the economy, and thousands of new residents flocked to Fort Worth. Refineries were built, and the town became a major hub of the petroleum industry—an industry that promised to expand exponentially each year as automobiles replaced horses. Downtown, skyscrapers sprouted like toadstools after a rain, and within four years Cowtown had become a city of skyscrapers. In 1922 alone, buildings worth $12 million were erected. Meanwhile, newly rich West Texans built mansions in upscale neighborhoods like Ryan Place, Park Hill, and Rivercrest.[29]

Quite naturally, therefore, it was to this oil heaven—this luxurious mecca on the prairie where presided the Golden Goddess—that newly rich oil folks like Warren and Norma Wagner and Floyd and Alma Holmes retreated to bask in the glow of their good fortune. No more freezing winters or stifling summers to be endured in those insect-infested tarpaper, gun-barrel shacks in the remote oil patches. Tin-can drinking cups and tin plates were replaced by crystal and china. Steaks and lobsters now—tinned sardines and crackers begone. It was all so . . . heady! So unbelievable! Paradise after purgatory.

But there was still more to Fort Worth in the 1920s—more than simply high-rolling oilers. The horrors of World War I were behind, and nobody foresaw the terrible poverty and hardships of the bleak Depression and drought years of the 1930s looming on the distant horizon, nor could they imagine the massive carnage of World War II during the following decade. Now, the nation was at peace and prospering. Now, the Roarin' Twenties were just gathering steam. It was the Jazz Age, and lifestyles were freer, easier, gayer. Flappers were seen wearing disgraceful dresses, dancing suggestive dances, and even smoking a cigarette[30] in public![31] Flasks, bathtub gin, and speakeasies outflanked Prohibition. Oldtimers, matrons, and preachers clucked away endlessly about such rampant, unabashed, and unrepentant outrages. But the sports and their flapper girlfriends simply refused to be "clucked" into submission; the party went on.

True enough, the Jazz Age did add spice and color to Fort Worth, but equally true is the fact that Cowtown had never been fully tamed from its wild and rowdy past. During the 1920s, Fort Worth had more than its share of colorful characters, and none more colorful than "Mr. Fort Worth," alias Amon Carter, owner of the *Fort Worth Star-Telegram*. Also known as "The Texan who played cowboy for America," Amon was an outrageous, flamboyant, irrepressible, fun-loving egomaniac. Wherever there was a parade, or a rodeo, or a prize fight, or anything else that drew a crowd, well, there was Amon—struttin', showboatin', and waving grandly to the crowd. During Prohibition years, Amon flaunted the liquor laws. He carried a whiskey-filled cane that he tippled from regularly. He was also an inveterate gambler and often hosted high-roller poker games attended by Fort Worth's elite. Still, Amon's favorite pastime was picking fights with those pompous prigs from neighboring Dallas, who had the unmitigated gall to seriously contend that their community amounted to something.[32]

"Wild and rowdy" Fort Worth's past truly had been, to understate it a bit. For years, frontier Texans had regularly pilgrimaged to Cow-

Amon Carter, the flamboyant owner of the *Fort Worth Star-Telegram*, was known as "The Texan Who Played Cowboy for America." (Image courtesy of *Fort Worth Star-Telegram*.)

town not only to market their cattle at its famous stockyards, but also to cut loose on a spree at the infamous Hell's Half Acre next door. In its time—and for a very long time—Hell's Half Acre was the stomping ground not only for parched, trail-weary cattlemen but also for outlaws (Butch Cassidy and the Sundance Kid come to mind), madams, and shady ladies, as well as a duke's mixture of gamblers, conmen, bartenders, loafers, and other unrepentant folks, all of whom were so loathed—and who so dearly loved to be loathed—by reformers, church ladies, and preachers. Speaking of which, this brings us to another Fort Worth denizen of the era who challenged Amon Carter for the title of being the most colorful and the most outrageous character in town—that candidate being the Reverend J. Frank Norris. Unsurpassed as a hellfire-and-brimstone fundamentalist crusader, for forty years J. Frank ranted and railed nonstop against all forms of sin known to God, man, and/ or J. Frank Norris. The relentless sin-scrubber not only rained down unshirted hell on the usual suspects (whores, gamblers, bootleggers, and boozers), but also on picture-show operators who exhibited movies on Sunday, purveyors of any other form of Sunday entertainment (except for himself), Catholics, Jews, other assorted heathens, and "modernists." He once paraded monkeys through a church service pronouncing them to be "Darwin's cousins." J. Frank finally got so outlandish that even the Texas Baptist Convention and the Southern Baptists as well as the Fort Worth Ministers Association had to expel him.[33]

During the Prohibition years of the 1920s, the Jacksboro Highway strip west of town became a rekindled version of Hell's Half Acre and home to dozens of illegal drinking, gambling, and brawling joints. The 1917 Fort Worth telephone directory listed 178 saloons but only sixteen churches, and during the same era gambling was so popular and entrenched in Cowtown society that even children received slot machines as birthday presents. "Panther City," as it was known early on, might have been shy of the high culture and sophistication of which Dallas so proudly boasted, but it was long on free-wheeling energy. Then too, there was more than a smidgen of earthy irreverence in the town's character. Freedom was always held in higher regard than conformity,[34] and although by the 1920s Panther City had become less of a cattle and horse-trading town, it still retained the distinctive "live and let live" attitude of its past.[35]

That, then, was the Fort Worth that welcomed Floyd Holmes and Warren Wagner and their wives shortly after the end of World War I.

Riding high on their amazing good fortune, Floyd and Alma had no trouble firmly entrenching themselves in the free-wheeling, Jazz Age high society of Fort Worth, and they loved every minute of it. One Holmes descendant recalls an incident when two of Floyd's "country" sisters took a notion to pay a sociable visit to their illustrious brother and his beautiful wife in Fort Worth. They didn't bother to tell Floyd and Alma they were coming, figuring no doubt, as was customary for country folks of that time, that the latch-string was always out and the doors always unlocked to welcome friends, neighbors, and kinfolk alike. Putting on their best "Sunday-go-to-meetin'" toggery (including a red wig worn by one sister), the two bumptious bumpkins departed the family farm at Saint Jo one day and caught the next train to Fort Worth. When they arrived unexpectedly that evening, Floyd and Alma were hosting a grand dinner party at their home for their society friends. Totally embarrassed by the sudden appearance of their klutzy country kin, Floyd immediately hustled both of his sisters upstairs and locked them in a bedroom. According to the descendant of one of the sisters, the pair "got pretty huffy" about being shunned by their "big shot" brother and became so enraged that they leaped out of a second-story window, walked to the bus station, and caught a ride home. They never had much to do with their "high-falutin' big shot" brother after that humiliation. In their shared opinion, and in the country-folk parlance of that day, Floyd was definitely "actin' way above his raisin'." Perhaps still in a huff over that slight, one of the shunned sisters later told a tale on Alma: she said that during one of their fancy parties, Alma got a bit tipsy and stumbled while descending the stairs with a champagne glass in hand. She fell. The glass shattered. A shard of glass pierced one eye, causing permanent loss of sight.[36]

Although Floyd Holmes, at age thirty-five, was already rich beyond his wildest dreams, the hard-driving hustler was not about to quit the oil patch. As mentioned earlier, in 1921 he formed another exploration company named the Comet Petroleum Company. He also organized the Mid-Continent Supply Company, a successful enterprise which supplied tools and equipment to other oil field operators. In 1922, he purchased the old Fort Worth Club building at Sixth and Main Streets, modestly renaming it the Holmes Building—later to be renamed the Mid-Continent Building.[37]

Although Warren and Norma Wagner were also well positioned to luxuriate in their mansion without further toil or risk, Warren, like Holmes, was not content to sit back and simply rake in monthly royalties from his oil production. He organized the Wagner Supply Company to furnish oil operators with drilling material, equipment, casing, and so on. He had branch stores in several towns, including Ranger, Gorman, Breckenridge, and other oil camp communities, but his headquarters was in Fort Worth. It proved to be a highly successful venture.[38]

Meanwhile, by 1921, Warren and Norma had two children, both boys—Carlos and Furlo, ages thirteen and eight. Floyd and Alma Holmes had one son, Woodrow Floyd Holmes, who, in 1921, was seven years old. Things just could not have been better for these two lucky couples. Or so it would have seemed to any casual observer.

But a reptile had slithered quietly into this Garden of Eden. That first became apparent to the public in 1920 when Norma sued Warren for divorce, accusing him of "cruel treatment," and demanding half of their $800,000 estate plus custody of the two boys. Then things got worse—a lot worse—not only for Warren and Norma, but also for Floyd and Alma.

About 4:30 on the afternoon of May 9, 1921, Warren Wagner was walking along a busy street in downtown Fort Worth when Floyd Holmes, in the presence of eyewitnesses, suddenly appeared, drew a pistol, and fired three shots. Warren was fatally wounded, but he didn't die immediately. He was taken to the hospital, where he survived for about three hours before expiring. Before he lost consciousness, Tarrant County assistant district attorney W. H. Tolbert had the opportunity to talk with him. He reported that Wagner said he was aware that he was dying. Tolbert would later report that Wagner also told him this: "He didn't give me a chance. . . . Holmes shot me through jealousy."[39]

Thus, it appeared for all the world that Warren Wagner and Floyd Holmes, by their own words (clear and beyond dispute) and deeds (openly performed), had just given the Tarrant County district attorney a bulletproof first-degree murder prosecution, gift-wrapped and presented on a silver platter—one that even a cub fresh out of law school could win, hands down.

But then Floyd Holmes hired Fort Worth attorneys W. P. "Wild Bill" McLean and his sidekick, Walter Scott. They specialized in winning unwinnable cases—especially when the case was sensational and the defendant was loaded. This was precisely that kind of case. And McLean and Scott had no intention of losing it.

For several decades after the turn of the century, W. P. "Wild Bill" McLean and his partner, Walter Scott, were almost unbeatable as criminal defense attorneys, winning a string of cases (mostly murder cases) that the prosecution believed were bulletproof. McLean and Scott were masterful advocates of the unwritten law, and their courtroom dramatics were better than anything on Broadway.

For example, Scott once managed to get a wife acquitted even though the evidence was clear that the woman had, with premeditation, killed her husband's paramour. She was only "protecting her home," Scott explained to a turn-of-the-century jury; and then, making an irresistible plea, he rose to theatrical heights when he reenacted the poor woman bravely defending her home. In his final jury argument Scott (still pretending to be the defendant wife), gathered the couple's several (imaginary) children about him and, in a doleful tenor, treated the jury to a heart-rending version of "Home Sweet Home."[40]

W. P. McLean was a member of a dynasty of prominent and successful Fort Worth lawyers consisting of his father (Judge William Pinckney McLean), a brother (Jefferson Davis McLean), two sons (W. P. Jr. and John), and a grandson (W. P. III). His father was a major in the Confederate army. After the Civil War, Judge McLean served as a member of the Texas Legislature, the U.S. Congress, the convention that adopted the Texas Constitution in 1876 (still in force today, though much amended), and the Texas Railroad Commission when it was first established, as well as judge of the Fifth Judicial District of Texas, and finally, as a private practitioner in Fort Worth from 1894 until his death in 1925.

But W. P. "Wild Bill" McLean was the star litigator of the family. He first distinguished himself even before he received his law license. While a law student at the University of Texas, he became the captain and quarterback of the school's first football team. After graduation, he served a short stint as a prosecutor, but soon found his true niche in the legal profession as a criminal defense lawyer. During the last thirty-five years of his legal career he successfully defended seventy-five clients charged with murder. The ever-colorful McLean earned the "Wild Bill" title by projecting a booming voice, a forceful demeanor, and brash trial tactics in the courtroom.[41]

McLean and Scott again and again demonstrated their courtroom mastery most often by reliance on blatant appeals to the unwritten law. Two related murder trials during the second decade of the twentieth century showcased the McLean and Scott magic. It started when Al Boyce, Jr., ran off with John Beal Sneed's wife. It ended when Sneed shot Boyce in the back. Then, not satisfied with that, he shot Boyce's unarmed father while he was sitting in a Fort Worth hotel lobby visiting with a friend. Both were killed instantly. Sneed admitted he was the shooter and didn't deny that he intended to kill both men. He didn't claim insanity, and there was no serious claim of self-defense. McLean and Scott rested their defense squarely on the unwritten law, which they euphemistically referred to as "protecting the home." Three excerpts from the final jury arguments tell it all:

Jordan Cummings for the State: "Regard for human life is the highest and the ultimate test of a country's civilization."

W. P. McLean for the defense: "Human life is not the highest consideration of our law, being less regarded by the law than domestic relations. . . . Every time a home is broken up, there ought to be a killing of all who assisted in it."

Walter Scott for the defense: "The best shots ever fired in Texas were the shots that took Al Boyce's life, and I hope every home destroyer in the land meets the same fate."[42]

Meanwhile, it soon became apparent that the Fort Worth district attorney's office believed that the prosecution of Floyd Holmes would be a stroll in the park. The State put on its entire case in two hours and called but five witnesses.[43] Still, the testimony of those five witnesses was unequivocal and potent: The shooting occurred in broad daylight on a crowded downtown street—Houston Street between Sixth and Seventh Streets. Two eyewitnesses at the scene of the incident saw it all and gave clear and consistent accounts. C. W. Harris and a newsboy, Luther Wilson, agreed as follows: Floyd Holmes was driving his car down Houston Street. When he got near them, he parked alongside the curb and got out of his car with a pistol. Then he concealed the pistol by holding it inside his coat. Holmes stood on the street side of his car for more than a minute, waiting. Then Wagner approached. He was walking with his head down, looking at the sidewalk. About the time Wagner walked past, Holmes came out from behind his car, stepped quickly onto the sidewalk behind Wagner, pulled the pistol from inside his coat, and fired three shots at the retreating victim. Then Holmes got in his car and drove away. It was undisputed that Wagner was not armed at the time.

Another bystander, G. F. Barnhill, testified that although he did not see the actual shooting, he heard the shots and when he looked in that direction he saw Holmes walk back to his car and drive away. Jim Hardcastle, chief deputy sheriff, testified next. He said he had a telephone call from Holmes shortly after the incident. Holmes told the startled deputy, "I'm the man who did the shooting. . . . [M]y name is Holmes. Don't worry about me. I'll be up in a few minutes." Sure enough, Holmes appeared at the sheriff's office about thirty minutes later, surrendered, and handed over his pistol, which still held the three empty shell casings. But he offered no explanation for the attack.

The State's last witness was Dr. G. F. Hyde, who had examined Wagner's body. He testified that Wagner was shot once from behind, the bullet entering an inch and a half from the spine, and then the second bullet hit him in the abdomen. He expressed the belief that the third shot missed.

With that the State rested without offering the jury any motive for the killing. Although the State is not required by law to prove a motive as a part of its case, most juries, particularly in murder cases, have difficulty convicting a defendant unless the State can explain why the accused killed his victim.

But what *was* the motive?

Money? It might have occurred to the jury that when one wealthy oilman killed another wealthy oilman, the motive was probably money. Perhaps it was an oil deal gone sour, or some kind of fraudulent drilling promotion? Or was it perhaps a woman? If so, then the first assumption probably would have been that Wagner was having an affair with Alma Holmes. But that would prove to be a false assumption.

On May 10, 1921 (the day after Wagner was killed), Assistant District Attorney W. H. Tolbert told the *Fort Worth Star-Telegram* that he had interviewed Warren Wagner at his bedside shortly before he died. That, according to Tolbert, was when Wagner told him, "He didn't give me a chance—Holmes shot me through jealousy." Tolbert further reported that Norma Wagner arrived at the hospital before Wagner died, but that Wagner refused to talk to her, saying, "I don't want to see you. You've done me dirty." According to Tolbert, Norma told him that Wagner had accused Holmes of "being too friendly" with her, and "that had caused the trouble which led up the fatal shooting." Curiously, at the time of the trial, the jury heard none of this, since the State chose not to call as a witness either Tolbert or Norma. The prosecution also chose not to inform the jury that there was a divorce action pending at the time of the killing; that Norma had sued Warren for divorce. And again, why? The State could have argued (supported by Tolbert's testimony had he been put on the stand) that Floyd Holmes was insanely jealous of Wagner. Perhaps Holmes was afraid that Norma and Warren would reconcile, and thus he would lose not only Norma but also a healthy infusion of cash from the Wagner divorce settlement. Yet the prosecution never advanced any of these possible scenarios to show an evil motive on the part of Floyd Holmes.

If the State was reluctant to offer the jury a plausible motive for the killing, McLean and Scott were not at all bashful in coming forward with a defense-friendly theory: the enraged Wagner had made public threats to kill Holmes because he believed those rumors about Holmes becoming "too friendly" with Norma. (Or, perhaps he *knew* Holmes had become "too friendly" with Norma.) Holmes, in turn, having heard Wagner's threats and believing them, knowing Wagner's violent nature and reputation, concluded that he was in imminent danger of being ambushed and killed by Wagner. Therefore, his only alternative was to launch a preemptive strike and kill Wagner in self-defense. There was, however, a legal problem to be overcome if McLean and Scott intended to hang Floyd's defense on a "preemptive strike" peg. But McLean and Scott believed they were up to that task.

The first defense witness very likely came as a surprise to the prosecution. The defense called Alma Holmes. By trial time, Floyd Holmes's "too friendly" relationship with Norma Wagner had been publicly aired in the *Fort Worth Star Telegram*,[44] and therefore her appearance as a friendly witness riding to the rescue of her allegedly unfaithful husband probably would have seemed unlikely. Yet, regardless of what the relationship between Floyd and Norma may have been, when the dust finally settled after the tragedy, Alma no doubt realized upon which side of the bread her butter was on. Plus, Alma probably figured that if there ever had been a romance between Floyd and Norma, by now it surely must have wilted and died. In any event, whatever prompted her to testify on behalf of her husband, Alma's testimony was to prove very beneficial to the defense. Alma testified that in April 1920, almost a year before the fatal shooting, she had received a letter from Wagner claiming to have evidence that there had been "improper conduct" between Floyd and Norma. (The letter, however, was never produced and introduced into evidence.) In the letter, she continued, Wagner tried to induce Alma to leave her husband. Later, she testified, Wagner called her on the telephone and reiterated the charges, adding that he discovered that his wife was carrying a picture of Holmes. Wagner ended by warning her that Holmes had better leave Fort Worth—that "this country is not big enough for both of us." Even later, according to Alma, Wagner stopped her on the street and again tried to persuade her to leave Floyd and again repeated his threats. She said that Floyd was aware of these threats and attempted to avoid meeting Wagner. Alma Holmes wound up by recalling that the two families had formerly lived in Petrolia, Texas, where they had been neighbors and intimate friends.

An even bigger surprise was in store for the jurors when the defense called J. B. McKissick, an oil well driller of Tulsa, Oklahoma, who had previously worked with Wagner in the oil fields in Maricopa, California. According to McKissick, he had a disagreement with Wagner after which Wagner shot him in the leg with a high-powered rifle. As a result, McKissick had to have his leg amputated. McKissick gave no explanation as to the cause of their trouble, and upon cross-examination by the State, he admitted that he had never sought to prosecute Wagner. When asked why he declined to prosecute, McKissick claimed he didn't because of "a lack of funds." However, he was unable to explain why a lack of funds prevented him from requesting prosecution from a state-paid prosecutor.

Another driller, E. B. English, took the stand next and gave testimony of questionable provenance. English said that he heard that Wagner had beaten another man so badly that he died. However, on cross-examination English could not recall the victim's name, could provide no substantiation of the incident, and could not remember who told him about it. It happened, he thought, in an oil field near Strawn, Texas. English, however, insisted that prior to the fatal shooting of Wagner he had told Floyd Holmes about the Strawn incident as well as the shooting of McKissick by Wagner. On further cross, English admitted he did not know whether either incident really happened.

The defense next called Wichita Falls oilman, banker, and rancher L. B. Hammond. Hammond told of more threats Wagner had made against Holmes. "Holmes is the cause of my troubles, and I am going to kill him," is the threat Hammond said he heard Wagner make a few weeks before the fatal shooting. He said Wagner made that threat in the Metropolitan Hotel in Fort Worth. A few minutes later, Hammond said he ran into Floyd Homes on the street. Hammond testified, "I stopped Holmes, who was going toward the Metropolitan, and told him not to go that way—that Wagner was there and that he intended to kill him." Holmes immediately turned and went back the way he had come, Hammond said.

A. M. Wilburn, another oilman, testified that he knew both Wagner and Holmes and that on Halloween night in October 1920 he met Wagner in the Westbrook Hotel, where Wagner made threats against Holmes. Referring to Holmes, Wagner said "that is the——I want. He is the cause of my troubles," according to Wilburn's testimony. McLean and Scott then called several prominent Fort Worth business and professional men, who testified as to the law-abiding character of Holmes—at least before May 9, 1921.

McLean and Scott saved their heavy hitter for last: the defendant, Floyd Holmes, took the stand. "I shot him because I thought he was about to shoot me" was the substance of his testimony.

Holmes began by reviewing his married life with Alma, then told that he first met Wagner while they were both involved in the Petrolia oil patch. At that time, Wagner rented a house from Holmes in Petrolia, and later they both were engaged in drilling in the Strawn oil field. Still later both families moved to Fort Worth. Holmes said that his wife showed him the April 20, 1920, letter Wagner had sent to her, and he told of hearing Wagner's threats on his life. He also testified that he had met Mrs. Wagner in a drugstore later and she warned him that he had better leave town if he valued his life. After that, he said, he began carrying a pistol.

Holmes gave his account of the killing. He admitted killing Wagner but contended that he had killed in self-defense. He said he feared for his life after repeatedly hearing of Wagner's threats to kill him, and that when he encountered Wagner on the street that fateful day he saw Wagner swing his hand toward his hip pocket, a movement he interpreted as an effort by Wagner to go for a weapon and carry out his threats to kill him. Therefore, Holmes continued, he had to shoot first to protect himself. This testimony was pivotal. From a *legal* standpoint, it came down to whether or not the jury believed that just before the killing, Warren Wagner had *seen* Floyd Holmes and *then* made *a movement toward his hip pocket*, which caused Holmes to believe that Wagner was attempting to draw a pistol and launch a lethal attack.[45]

As we have seen, for whatever reason, the prosecution chose not to favor the jury with Warren Wagner's dying statement to Tolbert to the effect that Holmes shot him "without giving [him] a chance." True, such testimony would have been hearsay, but it appears to have been clearly admissible under two well-established exceptions to the hearsay testimony prohibition.[46]

———————

There's no such thing as writing a "perfectly accurate" history, even if the history is limited to actual physical acts and words spoken. Accounts of eyewitnesses to a car wreck or to a killing that happened only yesterday often differ significantly even if the witnesses are all unbiased and attempting to accurately describe the incident. Then too, for diverse reasons, the accounts differ even more significantly with the passage of years.

As difficult as it is for historians to accurately describe the deeds and words of characters long since deceased, the difficulty is magnified when it comes to speculating on the mental processes of those characters that caused them to act and speak as they did. Plunging into the murky waters of ancient motivations is indeed a daunting task for even the best of historians. And yet, the motivations of key characters are often the most fascinating—and most important—part of the tale.

All of which is a prelude to speculating upon three key motivations in this murder case. First, why did the prosecution fail to call Deputy District Attorney Tolbert to the stand and thus inform the jury of Warren Wagner's dying declaration, a two-part statement—obviously unrehearsed and sincere—that went directly to the heart of the case? It directly and succinctly refuted two defense contentions. The first part of Wagner's statement ("He never gave me a chance") refuted Holmes's claim that self-defense was his motive by casting doubt on Holmes's contention that just prior to the shooting he had seen Wagner make some furtive "movement" in the direction of his hip pocket which Holmes said he interpreted as an effort by Wagner to draw a pistol and thus carry out his previous threats to kill him. The second part of Wagner's statement ("Holmes shot me through jealousy") would not only have refuted Holmes's self-defense assertion, but in addition would have provided the jury with a prosecution-friendly motive for the killing.

The prosecution's mistake in failing to put Wagner's dying statement in evidence was not only a serious error from the standpoint of logic, it was an even worse blunder from the standpoint of emotional appeal to the jury. When an emotionally distraught man who knows he is about to die blurts out some final words, the credibility of his statement is almost beyond doubt. Furthermore, from an emotional standpoint, it would seem that Wagner's dying statement, "he never gave me a chance," would far outweigh Holmes's self-serving assertion: "I thought maybe he was reaching for a pistol"—a pistol that was never there. Perhaps the prosecution's blunder can be chalked up to overconfidence in its case, having been born of inexperience and/or incompetence. Whichever, it was the kind of bush league mistake that a trial lawyer can't afford when playing against major leaguers like Wild Bill McLean and Walter Scott.

Another interesting question concerning trial tactics was raised by the failure of either the State or the defense to call Norma Wagner as a witness. On the day Wagner was killed, Norma told Deputy Prosecutor Tolbert that Wagner had accused Holmes of "becoming too friendly" with her and "that had caused the trouble which led up to the fatal shooting." Her statements were quoted in the next day's edition of the *Star-Telegram*, May 10, 1921. However, two days later, when a *Star-Telegram* reporter interviewed her, Norma's story had changed, significantly. She now contended that "I can imagine no reason for him killing my husband." She also contended that she had not seen Floyd Holmes in a year, nor had she heard Wagner even mention Holmes's name "lately." Norma also took the occasion to deny that the dying Wagner had refused to see her. To the contrary, Norma told the reporter that Warren had asked for her, but explained that by the time she arrived at the hospital, he was unconscious. She then went on to give the reporter a detailed account of a tearful reconciliation between herself and her husband, which, she claimed, had occurred on the day before he was killed. According to Norma, Warren acknowledged that *he* had been the cause of their trouble and that he wanted "to make restitution." She added, "I sat on his lap all the time . . . and he promised to do the right thing by me." With that, Norma continued, she had forgiven him and agreed to dismiss the pending divorce suit. (Norma chose not to disclose what sins Wagner had committed against her for which forgiveness was in order. For his part, the gentleman reporter chose not to pursue that indelicate line of questioning.) "He seemed so happy. . . . He repeated that he had found himself and that he was glad. . . . I am grateful that I had a frail part in bringing about the reconciliation," Norma modestly concluded.

Obviously moved by Norma Wagner's tearful account, the reporter wrote, "Mrs. Wagner is a slight woman, frail and delicate. Her hair is slightly gray, and her features care-marked." Then he added this observation:

> The Wagners have undergone many hardships together. From oil town to oil town she has gone with her ambitious husband, caring for the two boys and living the life of an oil operator's wife.

Apparently, the reporter also felt that it would have been insensitive to question Norma about the contradictory statements that she had made to the deputy prosecutor two days earlier. With such contradictory statements already known, it is not difficult to understand why neither the State nor the defense called Norma to the stand. Both sides probably felt that calling her as a witness would be like rolling a loose cannon on deck and then lighting the fuse—no telling which way she might fire. Plus, neither of the two versions she had previously given fit neatly into the game plan of either the defense or the State.

A third question about motives occurs to the contemporary historian. Whatever Holmes's true motive was in killing Wagner, *why did he do it in the way he did*? Despite Holmes's rather lame and late "hip-pocket movement" story, it clearly appears from the consistent testimony of the eyewitnesses and the forensic evidence that Floyd intentionally ambushed Wagner with intent to kill him. But why did he choose to kill Warren Wagner on a busy downtown Fort Worth street in the presence of a crowd of eyewitnesses? Why not hire some ruffian to kill Warren at a time when Floyd's presence was observed at some distant place, thus establishing a solid alibi? Or if he were going to kill Warren himself, why not hide on one of Wagner's remote oil leases and ambush him there with no witnesses present? Either scenario offered advantages. However, since Warren's threats were known by nearly everybody in the Fort Worth petroleum community, if Warren's bullet-riddled body turned up anywhere, Floyd would be the first suspect. Most likely, Floyd decided he not only had to kill Wagner before Wagner killed him, but he also decided that he had to do it in such a way that it would vindicate his honor in the process. Consequently, he had to kill Warren Wagner openly and take credit for it. True, to kill Wagner in this way created a difficult murder case to defend, but that may have been a consideration of secondary importance. Preservation of his pride and honor was of primary importance.

After all the testimony was concluded, District Judge George E. Hosey instructed the jury on the Texas law of self-defense. The jury was told that serious threats to kill, even if believed by the recipient, were insufficient, taken alone, to afford a defendant justification to kill the maker of the threats. There had to be more: namely, some act, movement, or word by the deceased that the defendant could reasonably have interpreted as an immediate intention on the part of the deceased to carry out his threat and kill the defendant then and there. Only then would the defendant be entitled to claim justification for killing his adversary on the grounds of self-defense.[47]

Was Holmes really telling the truth when, under oath, he claimed: "I shot him because I thought he was about to shoot me"? Or was that merely an obligatory nod in the direction of a legal justification, when the real defense was grounded on the unwritten law? In its final argument, the prosecution hammered home the undisputed fact that Wagner was unarmed when shot. Not only that, but both of the unbiased eyewitnesses testified that just prior to the shooting, they saw Wagner come walking down the street with his head down looking at the sidewalk. After he passed, they saw Holmes come out from behind the car and shoot Wagner in the back. Neither saw Wagner ever make any kind of movement that could be construed as an effort to reach for a nonexistent pistol. District Attorney Brown pointed out that the only person who testified that Wagner had made any kind of movement like that came from Holmes himself—hardly an unbiased witness. Meanwhile, the defense focused its firepower on testimony proving that Wagner was a violent and dangerous man and that he had been threatening to kill Holmes for several months. McLean and Scott had introduced plenty of evidence to support that conclusion. It also seemed obvious that Floyd Holmes did not take those threats lightly.

The lives, ambitions, and careers of Holmes and Wagner mirrored each other in many respects—but not in all. They were very different in one respect. Wagner's journey to riches via the oil patch was rough and physical and earned while dressed in a pair of greasy overalls. He was involved in the actual drilling of wells and the dealing with—and later the bossing of—roughnecks, drillers, tool pushers, and other very physical and violence-prone denizens of the early-twentieth-century oil fields. He was not the kind of man who could be easily intimidated. On the other hand, Floyd Holmes's journey to fortune in the oil fields was achieved with words and finesse and made while dressed in unsoiled suits. He was basically engaged in buying, selling, and trading oil leases and promoting drilling and development deals with landowners and other oil traders and investors. His was not a physically oriented career on the grimy side of the petroleum business. In short, when Floyd Holmes heard of the death threats Wagner was making, he rightly feared for his life. He probably suspected that to give Warren Wagner an even break in a fair fight would have been suicidal—or, at best, an against-the-odds risk he didn't care to take. Therefore, a preemptive strike may well have appeared to be his only realistic alternative.

In the end, the trial really came down to whether McLean and Scott could persuade the jury to ignore the man-made written laws of the State of Texas in favor of their "hip-pocket plea" of self-defense under the unwritten law. They had made that tactic stand up before in front of other juries. In fact, the "hip-pocket" ploy had become so common throughout the South and West that it had become a standard defense in the *lex non scripta* arsenal. When Judge Thomas J. Kernon gave his famous 1906 address to the American Bar Association on the subject of the unwritten law, he explained:

... the charge of murder or manslaughter is most frequently met by, what has come to be known, as the hip-pocket plea of self defense. [The defendant testifies] that the deceased reached for his hip pocket, as if to draw a pistol, when [he] managed to draw first and shoot the deceased in self-defense. The deceased is not in a position to deny the statement, and, although the killing is almost always murder or manslaughter under the law, the jury . . . promptly renders a verdict of "Not Guilty."[48]

Moreover, McLean and Scott had still more support from the unwritten law. Regardless of what the Texas legislators down in Austin had to say, Westerners, even in the late nineteenth century and into the early twentieth century, often preferred their own folk laws. One deeply ingrained provision was this: if a man was foolish enough to make public threats to kill another, well, he had just about signed his own death warrant, and the recipient of the threats was under no obligation to give his enemy the benefit of a fair fight.[49] He was entitled to make a preemptive strike while lying in ambush or by shooting his adversary in the back. Even if the deceased wasn't armed at the time, juries were most reluctant to convict the man who had been forced to vindicate his honor. One of the earliest commentators on frontier justice in the Old South had this to say about self-defense as defined by the unwritten law:

In criminal cases almost anything was made out to be [permissible grounds for] a self-defense killing: a threat, a quarrel, an insult . . . [and it didn't matter that the defendant killed his victim] from behind a corner or from behind a door—it was all self defense. In a time when killing Indians was a normal thing, the murder of whites did not seem so serious. In fact, horse-stealing, owing to frontier conditions, was much more often prosecuted and more seriously punished than murder . . . Though a man was murdered from behind his back, a jury of *his peers* usually acquitted the murderer.[50]

The fact remained, however, that the above passage referred to a time more than three-quarters of a century earlier when Indians still roamed the frontier. Over the years, the vitality of the unwritten law had gradually eroded before the slow march of civilization. Then too, the Wagner killing happened in 1921 at a time following World War I when a major shift had occurred in the way most Americans viewed— and had come to accept—the supremacy of statutory laws administered under court rules.[51] Nevertheless, the unwritten law mindset retained some potency. After 1920, the unwritten law might have been seriously challenged, but it was far from moribund, especially in places like old Fort Worth, where Western heritage and lifestyle were treasured.

The question remained, then: Could courtroom magicians McLean and Scott once again pull a rabbit out of a hip pocket even at this late date? It didn't take the jury very long to answer that question; it took only twenty-five minutes and one ballot for the jury to set Floyd Holmes free with a "not guilty" verdict.

Once again "Wild Bill" McLean and sidekick Walter Scott had won the unwinnable case.

In retrospect, there was supreme irony in this tragic drama. Two provisions of the unwritten law had collided to force the fatal confrontation. The common denominator of both of these two separate unwritten laws was the defense of honor. Provision number one made it obligatory for a man to exact some public and decisive—preferably lethal— revenge against any other man who had had sex (consensual or otherwise) with his wife. Thus, when the proud Warren Wagner came to believe, either rightly or wrongly, that his wife had had an affair with Floyd Holmes, he was not only enraged but, in his view, left with no alternative but to vindicate his honor by either killing Floyd personally or at least running him out of town. Floyd Holmes, on the other hand, had no desire to be slaughtered, and he couldn't afford to let Wagner run him out of town without forever after being publicly disgraced and humiliated, as well as being deprived of his lucrative business. Thus, provision number two of the unwritten law came into play: if a man publicly threatens to kill you, it then becomes necessary to kill him first in order to vindicate your honor and safeguard your life. Floyd Holmes and Warren Wagner were both trapped by separate dictates of the unwritten law in a no-win game—with tragic results.

After the Wagner murder trial, Floyd Holmes got back down to business—the oil business, naturally. As before, he proved to have the Midas touch. He continued to operate his exploration company, the Comet Petroleum Company, as well as his highly successful Mid-Continent Supply Company and the Mid-Continent Building in Fort Worth. Meanwhile, Floyd and Alma resumed their lavish lifestyle. In 1927, Holmes and his family took a vacation trip to Hawaii. He never made it back to Fort Worth. En route, returning to Texas, he stopped over in Los Angeles for a business conference. There he was stricken with meningitis, and on September 21, 1927, at age forty-one, he died, survived by his wife and their only child, a son, Woodrow Floyd "Woody" Holmes.[52]

Epilogue

After Warren Wagner's untimely death in 1921, his wife, Norma, was able to rise to the occasion and successfully managed Warren's thriving business, the Wagner Supply Company. In fact, she expanded the company to include nine West Texas supply houses in addition to the Fort Worth yards. The Wagner Supply Company became one of the largest oil field supply companies in Texas.

Alma Holmes was not so fortunate, however. She had little training or experience in business management, and she struggled to meet the challenge of the very complex and unexpected task that fate had foisted upon her. Alma enrolled in night courses at Pascal High School in Fort Worth, where she studied business administration.[53] Despite her efforts to overcome her inexperience, Alma was cursed by a turn of events that she could not have foreseen or prevented. First, Floyd died in the fall of 1927. In the fall of 1929, the stock market crashed and plunged the nation into a terrible depression—one that lasted more than a decade. On the heels of the Depression there followed a terrible drought that devastated the Midwest—and not only farm families. Last, and worst of all for Alma, oil prices dropped to ten cents a barrel.

It was at this dismal juncture that another player appeared on the Fort Worth scene—a young man, thirty-three year-old Kenneth William Davis, who had been a pilot in World War I. He arrived with a young

Following the death of Floyd Holmes in 1927, Kenneth W. Davis purchased controlling interest in the Mid-Continent Supply Company from Alma Holmes and later acquired total ownership. He expanded the company exponentially into a worldwide enterprise, the flagship of his fortune. (Image courtesy of *Fort Worth Star-Telegram* Photograph Collection, Special Collections, The University of Texas at Arlington Library, Arlington, Texas.)

After her husband's death, a despondent Alma Holmes leaped to her death from her tenth-floor apartment in the Forest Park Apartments in Fort Worth on January 12, 1942. (Author's collection.)

wife, a young son, a sixth-grade education, and little in the way of worldly riches. He did, however, have some practical education in the oil business, having been born and raised in the oil fields of Pennsylvania, the circa 1880s cradle of the oil industry.[54] Ken Davis might not have had much money in his pocket when he got to Fort Worth, but he was endowed with charm, a keen mind, much common sense, and an indomitable will to succeed. Plus, he was not bashful, and he was not lazy. He soon gained a reputation as a shrewd and sometimes ruthless, even tyrannical, businessman. Davis was not a tall man. In fact, he was short, dapper, feisty, and distinguished looking. Some compared him to the movie actor, James Cagney, a pompous, strutting, banty rooster. One file clerk later reflected that he strutted around looking the secretaries over. If he liked one, he'd have her brought up to the sixth floor to work with him personally. "He preferred blondes," she recalled.[55]

Perhaps it was his charm and his way with the ladies that led Alma Holmes to give Ken Davis a job with Mid-Continent Company soon after he detrained from Pennsylvania in 1929. A year later, with gritty determination and $5,000 in cash he had managed to scrape together, he bought a controlling interest in the struggling company. Alma Holmes retained a minority interest and a seat on the board of directors. Meanwhile, Ken's family grew. His firstborn was Ken, Jr.; then came Cullen, and finally, Bill.

Although Ken Davis made most of his fortune in the oil business, he wasn't a wildcatter. He disliked taking risks, and he knew that wildcatters usually drilled more dry holes than producers. The idea of pouring huge amounts of his cash into a hole in the ground that would probably end up being just that didn't appeal to Ken Davis. Much better to let others gamble on what was, or was not, at the bottom of the hole; he would make plenty safely, selling those wildcatters casing, pumps, tubing, and other supplies.

Meanwhile, Mid-Continent prospered, and the beautiful and prominent widow, Alma Holmes, and her business partner, Ken Davis, became close friends. Alma was active in Fort Worth church and social clubs and lived in a lavishly furnished tenth-floor suite in the fashionable Forest Park Apartments.

Once again, however, tragedy struck just when it seemed that things could hardly get any better. One Sunday evening in January

1942, Alma attended a service at the Broadway Baptist Church, where she had been a member twenty years, fifteen of which she taught a children's Sunday school class. After the service, she congratulated the pastor, the Reverand W. Douglas Hudgins, on his sermon and then chatted with friends. They said she seemed to be in good spirits.

Then Alma went home and leaped out of the window of her tenth-floor apartment. Before doing so, she had wrapped a towel around her head, then straightened out a wire clothes hanger and tied it securely around her waist to prevent her coat from flying up during her descent. She left no suicide note, not a word of explanation.[56]

At her funeral, Ken Davis served as one of her pallbearers. Years after the tragic event, two prominent Fort Worth citizens, a judge and a businesswoman, both of whom were well acquainted with Alma and Ken Davis, said it was her romantic involvement with Kenneth Davis that drove the elegant Alma Holmes to take that fatal leap.[57] At the time of her death, Alma was fifty-three; Ken Davis was forty-six.

Soon Mid-Continent Supply was owned exclusively by Ken Davis. By 1978, it was the crown jewel of the Davis family's international holdings, grouped under the name "Kendavis Industries," with annual sales exceeding one billion dollars. But the accumulation of wealth didn't end there; it just kept on growing and growing, and the Davis family got richer and richer.[58] At least for the Davis family, the sun shone brightly on its far-flung domain—nary a cloud in the clear blue sky, and the fields were bountiful unto harvest. But once again, just when it seemed that things could get no better for them, they didn't. They got worse, a lot worse, as a matter of fact. At least for one of the Davis family.

SIX

The Cursed Fortune
PART TWO: PRISCILLA AND CULLEN DAVIS

"If this were play'd upon a stage now,
I would condemn it as an improbable fiction."
WILLIAM SHAKESPEARE

That a curse followed Floyd Holmes's oil fortune seemed indisputable. A trail of blood followed that trail of oil, and whoever carried the purse got the curse as, over the years, one tragedy dogged the heels of the last. But whether by curse or by coincidence, what unreeled next scripted a story with a barrel of twists more unbelievable than any writer of fiction could have concocted. It was a tale of love and hate, of sex and greed, of deceit and death, and of sensational trials and incredible jury verdicts.

On the cold, drizzly evening of January 2, 1968, a well-dressed couple checked into Forth Worth's finest hotel. He was in his mid-thirties, lean, and reasonably handsome. She, on the other hand, was a stunner and a stepper. Short, shapely, and blonde, she knew how to flaunt her assets. Like, for instance, wearing that cute little miniskirt. And she hugged a big teddy bear.

The couple was married. Married all right—but not to one another. The man was rich—big time. The blonde's ancestry was what some would later describe as "poor white trash." But that didn't faze Priscilla. "Bold" and "brazen" and "saucy" fit her persona as snugly as the tight sweater that showcased her breathtaking feminine contours. She had an uplifted nose, a perky demeanor, and big, brown eyes. Her companion, the rich man, was Ken Davis's second son, Thomas Cullen Davis. Customarily, Cullen exuded an imperious air of indifference and invincibility born of much wealth long enjoyed and taken for granted—an air of indifference to the plight of lesser mortals and an air of invincibility to the slings and arrows of fate that inflicted wounds on those lesser mortals.

But this day, Cullen and Priscilla frolicked and cavorted without a care as they slammed the motel door shut behind them. The couple had barely shed their apparel, however, when a band of raiders kicked in their motel door. The not-so-merry band was led by Priscilla's husband, Jack Wilborn, and Cullen's wife, Sandra.

There followed a very loud and ugly scene, soon followed by two very ugly divorces. Then there was a marriage: Cullen Davis was thirty-four, and Priscilla was twenty-seven. It was Cullen's second marriage, Priscilla's third. He took Priscilla on a thirty-six-nation honeymoon. He also insisted that she have her breasts made larger—much larger.[1]

Cullen and Priscilla didn't live happily ever after. But at least in the beginning, everything was just swell.[2] Cullen enjoyed exhibiting his trophy wife at fancy doings about town and taking her on trips all over the rest of the globe: excursions to jet-set resorts and ski slopes—to the Riviera, Cannes, Nice, Monte Carlo, Rio, Morocco, Aspen, Vail, Las Vegas, just to name a few. It didn't take a wink for Priscilla to adjust to, and revel in, this new and lavish lifestyle; she was living life Neiman-Marcus large and loving every moment of it.

Fort Worth reactions to Cullen's new bride—Priscilla of the towering beehive hairdo, Priscilla of the black velvet dress with diamond-shaped cutouts around the midriff outlined in rhinestones, Priscilla of the miniskirt, walking around dragging a white mink coat behind her on the floor, Priscilla of the diamond necklace emblazoned with "Rich Bitch"—provoked comments ranging from the droll to the dreadful. But none were neutral, and nobody ignored her, and Priscilla lost not a moment's sleep worrying what they said about her. "Revolting," some society matrons sniffed. Others, perhaps not without some trace of envy: "She's gone from white trash to millionaire on a fake pair of tits."[3] And, "Started at the top." On the other hand, some, more charitably: "She's refreshing and delightfully unpredictable." Cullen's niece, Kay Davis, recalled that Priscilla often laughed with gusto at the dinner table, one of the few times that she had heard such laughter at her grandfather's mansion. "It just seemed like the house would echo with it . . . she would brighten up the whole room."[4] Others recalled her open-hearted spirit: "If she knew you were a pint low on blood, she'd give you a gallon."[5] Meanwhile, Priscilla's escapades were the talk of the town on the Fort Worth cocktail circuit and in the opulence of the town's most exclusive clubs. It wasn't as if the society matrons loved Priscilla, exactly. They just loved to hate her.

Although Cullen indulged his glamorous wife's taste for the luxurious lifestyle, the taciturn, moody, and temperamental millionaire did have a dark side. One night in 1971 when he came home and scolded Priscilla's oldest daughter, Dee, then age twelve, for failing to lock up the back door, she responded with sarcasm. Cullen responded by slamming her into a door and breaking her nose. Priscilla, hearing the commotion, ran into the room carrying a kitten. Cullen grabbed the kitten and slung it to the floor. It only stunned the kitty, so Cullen scooped it up and double-dunked it, this time fatally. Then, for good measure, he smashed a couple of chairs. Priscilla would later testify that Cullen periodically beat her.

The inevitable marital wreck occurred on July 30, 1974. Priscilla filed for divorce and obtained temporary possession of Cullen's pride and joy—his hilltop mansion. Plus, the trial judge, District Judge Joe Eidson, ordered Cullen to pay Priscilla temporary alimony to the tune of $3,500 per month—a tidy sum in 1974 dollars. But the money wasn't what really steamed Cullen. It was Judge Eidson's ejection of Cullen from his beloved $6 million castle overlooking the famous and exclusive Colonial Country Club. Worse, Priscilla was left to cavort

Cullen Davis, son of Kenneth W. Davis and husband of Priscilla Davis. (Image courtesy of *Fort Worth Star-Telegram* Photograph Collection, Special Collections, The University of Texas at Arlington Library, Arlington, Texas.)

Priscilla Davis, second wife of Cullen Davis. (Image courtesy of *Fort Worth Star-Telegram.*)

around in his private temple. And cavort she did. If Cullen had a dark side, Priscilla had a distinctly bawdy and naughty side to her character. And Priscilla never bothered to be discreet about anything. The divorce proceeding dragged on for two years while Cullen seethed and Priscilla played—openly. During the interim she had two live-in lovers—one a scruffy, bearded, happy-go-lucky, whiskey-drinking druggie named W. T. Rufner (who often invited his dope-smoking, motorcycle-riding buddies to hang out at the mansion), and then later, a "jolly giant" named Stan Farr. Farr, standing six feet nine inches and weighing in at 270 pounds, was a former Texas Christian University basketball player with a taste for casual nightlife and casual sex. After Rufner, Stan Farr moved into the mansion—and Priscilla's bed.

For two years, Priscilla and her carefree friends frolicked at the mansion on the hill. Then it got worse: Priscilla's attorney demanded another hearing on temporary orders. Priscilla wanted more money, and, thoroughly enjoying the status quo, she wanted the final divorce hearing postponed. (The divorce trial was set for a final hearing August

After separating from Cullen Davis, Priscilla took as her lover Stan Farr, a six-feet-nine-inch, 270-pound former college basketball star. Stan and Priscilla are shown here at the Colonial Country Club in Fort Worth. (Image courtesy of *Fort Worth Star-Telegram*.)

14, 1976.) At the close of the hearing on August 2, 1976, Judge Eidson ruled in favor of Priscilla. He raised the monthly alimony from $3,500 to $5,000 per month. That was bad enough, but much worse (from Cullen's perspective), Judge Eidson granted Priscilla's motion to postpone the divorce trial, thus leaving Priscilla and her party mates in sole possession of Cullen's castle. Priscilla celebrated; Cullen smoldered.

During the celebration that night with Stan Farr and their friends, Priscilla paused to reflect: "Maybe I won this battle, but it's not over yet. Cullen doesn't like losing. It's not the money, it's the battle. He wants to always be the victor."

Truer words . . .

That was a prophecy that would ripen into deeds very soon—like a little after midnight. Very strange things were about to be done before the next sun.

That night, an armed man dressed in black and wearing a woman's black wig broke into the mansion with murder in mind. When he arrived, only twelve-year-old Andrea Wilborn (Priscilla's daughter by Jack Wilborn) was there. The intruder shot and killed her. Later, Priscilla and Stan Farr arrived. The intruder shot both of them. Stan Farr died on the spot. About that time Beverly Bass, eighteen, and her boyfriend, Bubba Gavrel, arrived. (Beverly was a friend of Priscilla's older daughter, Dee, who, fortunately for her, was spending that night with another friend.) The intruder shot Bubba Gavrel. Although the wound was not fatal, it hit Bubba in the spine, thus permanently paralyzing him. In the mayhem, Beverly Bass managed to escape, screaming hysterically as she ran for her life. But not, however, before she got a close look at the assassin in the black wig. She had no doubt as to his identity. "Cullen did it!" she gasped when she finally calmed enough to restore coherence. When asked if she was certain, she exclaimed, "Yes, I saw his ugly fucking face."

Meanwhile, Priscilla, although shot in the chest, managed to stagger out of the mansion and reach the nearest neighbors. When they answered the frantic banging on their front door, there stood a bloody and hysterical Priscilla screaming, "Cullen is up there shooting everybody!" When she got to the hospital, she told a trauma nurse, "Cullen shot me!"

On the night of August 2, 1976, Bubba Gavrel, a guest at the Cullen Davis mansion then occupied by Priscilla Davis, was shot by a midnight intruder who Gavrel later claimed was Cullen Davis. The wound permanently paralyzed Gavrel. (Image courtesy of *Fort Worth Star-Telegram*.)

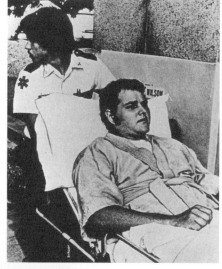

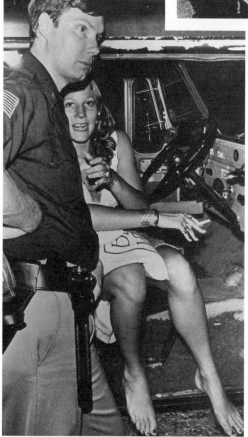

Beverly Bass, eighteen, was the friend of Priscilla's daughter, Dee. Beverly witnessed the midnight gunman when he shot her boyfriend, Bubba Gavrel. She ran and escaped. Later she identified the gunman as Cullen Davis. (Image courtesy of *Fort Worth Star-Telegram*.)

Cullen Davis was arrested later that night and charged with capital murder. Thus, it would have appeared that the prosecution had a lay-down hand: two independent and unequivocal eyewitness identifications of Cullen Davis as the shooter and the killer of Stan Farr and Andrea Wilborn—not to mention attempted murder charges stemming from the shooting of Priscilla and Bubba Gavrel. Motive? Well, what first occurs to the ordinary mind is that the divorce judge's ruling that afternoon was the straw that broke the camel's back. If the court wouldn't eject the insolent Priscilla and her sleazy playmates from his mansion, then he damn sure would!

The prosecution could have chosen to prosecute Cullen Davis initially under any one of four indictments: two attempted murder indictments (Priscilla Davis or Bubba Gavrel) and two murder indictments (Stan Farr or Andrea Wilborn). It came as no surprise that the State elected to prosecute Cullen first for the murder of Andrea Wilborn, an unarmed twelve-year-old girl whose only offense was attempting to sleep in her own bed in her own home. It also surprised few when the prosecution gave notice that it would seek the death penalty.

In Fort Worth more than half a century earlier, Floyd Holmes had quaked at the very real prospect of an impending noose fitting, or, if lucky, an extended view of prison bars from the wrong side out, in what appeared to be an unwinnable murder trial. However, Floyd Holmes had almost unlimited resources with which to finance his defense, including hiring "Wild Bill" McLean. Cullen, sharing a similar specter of doom, also had almost unlimited resources, and he too spared not the horses. He was determined to have the best defense that money could buy, and so he hired a Houston dynamo named Richard "Racehorse" Haynes, a master storyteller and a courtroom spellbinder who drank good Scotch whiskey, drove fast cars, raced motorcycles, and sailed the Gulf of Mexico aboard his forty-foot sloop. Armed with Cullen's checkbook, Haynes then proceeded to hire an expensive battery of experts who would do everything from assisting in jury selection to providing expert medical or scientific testimony supporting any desired conclusion. Media consultants were also hired in an effort to sway public opinion. Racehorse specialized in a "slash and burn" style of cross-examination of prosecution witnesses, and in this case he had the perfect target in his cross-hairs: Priscilla Davis. His overall trial strategy was to try Priscilla—that white-trash gold-digger—who flouted her scandalous affairs with sleazy whiskey-drinking, dope-smoking companions, thereby destroying her credibility as a witness while at the same time diverting the jury's attention away from evidence that Cullen had slaughtered an innocent child in a fit of rage and revenge. One junior member of Haynes's defense team, Steve Sumner, was assigned an important investigative task: dig up all the dirt he could on Priscilla, her lovers, and everybody else who had romped and rowdied at the mansion. Sumner jumped on the job like a starving dog on a juicy bone, and by the time the trial began, Haynes was able to boast that he knew Priscilla better than she knew herself. And not only that, Racehorse had a complete rogues gallery catalog of all the scuzzies and the scalawags who had partied with Priscilla, complete with a detailed description of all their various sins and crimes.

Before Cullen's trial ever began, the Fort Worth district attorney, Tim Curry, made a tactical blunder that was destined to cost the prosecution dearly. The DA announced that the State would petition the trial court to deny bail for Cullen in an effort to keep him in jail while the case was pending. That decision, in turn, necessitated a pretrial bond hearing.

In Texas, when a defendant murders more than one person during the same criminal transaction, or when the defendant murders someone during the commission of a felony such as burglary, then the district attorney may, as Tim Curry did here, elect to seek the death penalty.[6] Ordinarily, defendants in criminal cases are entitled to have a reasonable bail bond set so they may be freed during the pendency of the case. However, in death penalty cases, Texas law provides that the DA *may* (as Tim Curry did here) ask the trial court to deny bond "where proof [of guilt] is evident."[7] And therein lies the rub. In order to convince the trial court to deny bond, the prosecution at a pretrial bond hearing has the burden of producing witnesses, testimony, and other evidence to convince the judge that proof of guilt is evident. The defense meanwhile has no burden at this hearing. Therefore, while the prosecution is laying out its entire case, the defense can sit back and review all the testimony and evidence, probing for weaknesses in the State's case, conducting exhaustive cross-examination of all adverse witnesses—nailing them down on every detail of their testimony, hoping to catch them in some outright lies or inconsistencies or to discover soft spots—thus laying the groundwork for a devastating cross-examination blitz of key state witnesses when the case is finally called for a jury trial.

Plus, having a preview of the entire prosecution's case before trial, the defense has two other significant advantages. First, the defense can develop potent testimony or evidence to rebut the testimony of key state witnesses. Second, the defense is able to carefully analyze the prosecution's case at its leisure, find its weakest point, and then construct its own contradicting "theory of the case" (that is, "what *really* happened"). The defense also has the tempting opportunity to "shape" testimony of defense witnesses to advance its own theory of the case, "truth" sometimes coming in a poor second best in that race. Therefore, to permit the defense to preview the prosecution's entire case before trial is roughly equivalent to a poker player favoring his opponent by turning over all his hole cards before the betting begins. (Until the trial began, the defense didn't have to disclose *anything* to the prosecution.) To surrender this kind of tactical advantage to a brilliant attack-dog lawyer like Racehorse Haynes invites courtroom disaster—an invitation to stroll down ambush alley. Yet this is exactly what the Tarrant County district attorney elected to do when he laid all his cards on the table at a pretrial hearing in an effort to deny Cullen Davis bail.

Several factors undoubtedly played a part in the DA's decision to go for the death penalty and to deny bond to Cullen. First, it must be remembered that state prosecutors are political animals, elected officials whose careers are subject to the approval of their constituents. No doubt when news of the mansion massacre hit the headlines, there was much popular sentiment to "hang him high." Additionally, one suspects that the Fort Worth DA didn't want to appear to be soft on a wealthy "big shot." There also may have been yet another factor involved in the decision to try to keep Cullen in jail pending the murder trial. Cullen was enormously wealthy and had international connections, and, had he not been safely locked away, he could have easily caught a company jet and been long gone, and gone for good, by the time the trial was called. In that event, the DA would have been subject to public denouncement for allowing Cullen to escape his date with destiny in the courtroom. Overconfidence may have played yet another part in the DA's decision—an overriding belief that when you have a lay-down hand like the State had here (or thought it had), then what difference does it make if the opposition sees your hole card? After all, it did appear to be an open and shut case: three eyewitnesses who would testify that they recognized Cullen Davis as the shooter. And motive? Yes: Cullen had been enraged earlier that day when divorce judge Joe Eidson ruled in Priscilla's favor—raising her alimony, but worse, leaving her in possession of Cullen's mansion.

During the pretrial lull, Haynes launched a media attack targeting public opinion and, hopefully, prospective jurors. Haynes announced to reporters that the mansion shootings stemmed from a "society drug caper gone awry" and that he would expose the real killer at the trial, adding that it didn't surprise him that Priscilla was accusing Cullen. After all, their divorce was still pending, and big bucks were within Priscilla's greedy grasp if she could make that accusation stick.

On February 22, 1977, the trial commenced in Fort Worth but was aborted abruptly on account of a juror's misconduct. Then the defense got another break. The trial was transferred from Fort Worth to Amarillo, where it was presided over by District Judge George Dowlen. It was to prove a very favorable venue for Cullen Davis. For one thing, a rich and flamboyant rancher named Ray Hudson was on hand and ready to play an important role. Although he lived on an Arizona ranch, he had previously wheeled and dealed in the Texas Panhandle and had solid contacts there. Hudson also had a beautiful daughter, a divorcee named Karen Master, who lived in Fort Worth and who, since Cullen's separation from Priscilla, had become Cullen's live-in girlfriend. Thus, Hudson and daughter enlisted as active soldiers in Cullen's army.

At the trial, Racehorse Haynes planned to present a two-pronged attack. First, he would try Priscilla, not Cullen; second, he would offer an alibi for Cullen's whereabouts during the killings. The latter presented something of a problem for the defense, however. The defense could hardly afford to call Cullen himself as an alibi witness and subject him to the State's own relentless and potentially disastrous cross-examination. Cullen, as a defendant in a criminal trial, had a constitutional right to refuse to testify. He wisely exercised that right. That was where Karen Master came in. She would carry the alibi ball and dutifully testify that Cullen was in her bed when Andrea Wilborn was murdered.

After a lengthy jury selection process, the trial finally began. To prove motive, as well as to call the jury's attention to the enormous wealth of the defendant, the State led off by calling the divorce judge, Joe Eidson, who described the pending divorce including his pretrial ruling favoring Priscilla, which was announced on the eve of the murder.

The State called Priscilla Davis. Priscilla told this story: She and Stan Farr had gone out on the town celebrating the favorable pretrial decision by Judge Eidson. They came back about midnight. Only her daughter, Andrea Wilborn, was home when she and Stan entered the mansion. Stan went upstairs. Then she noticed a bloody handprint on the wall. (The blood was Andrea's blood; she had already been killed.) Priscilla screamed for Stan. The killer, dressed in black, wearing a woman's black wig and with his hands encased in a black garbage bag, confronted her. He said "hi." Then he shot her with a .38 pistol, the bullet striking her between her breasts just below the breast bone. He was about ten feet from her when he shot her. Despite the wig, she had no difficulty recognizing him. She screamed, "I've been shot! Cullen shot me! Stan, go back!" But Stan came down the stairs, and in the ensuing struggle, he was shot four times. He fell dead. Meanwhile, Priscilla ran out into the courtyard, but the intruder overtook her and dragged her back into the mansion while she was pleading with him to spare her. About that time, they heard someone else approaching. (It turned out that it was Beverly Bass and her boyfriend, Bubba Gavrel.) The man in black then turned his attention to dealing with the newcomers and left Priscilla lying on the breakfast room floor. (Both Beverly and Bubba would later testify that when they arrived, the man in black with the black wig confronted them. He shot Bubba, paralyzing him. But Beverly, who had been a track star in high school, broke away and made a successful dash for it, but not before, as she would later testify, she recognized the shooter as Cullen.) Meanwhile, Priscilla had managed to regain her feet and escape. As she was staggering across an open field to the nearest neighbor, she heard another shot—obviously the shot that wounded Bubba Gavrel. She pounded on the neighbor's door, and when it opened, that's when she screamed, "Cullen is up there shooting everybody."

Priscilla also told the jury of several instances during her marriage to Cullen when he had physically abused her. The prosecution closed out Priscilla's direct examination by asking her if, when she and Stan

Farr left the mansion earlier that fateful evening, her daughter Andrea Lee Wilborn was alive?

"Yes sir," she replied.

"Is that the last time you saw your daughter alive?"

Lips quivering, eyes clouding, her reply was barely audible: "Yes, sir."

Then the State turned her over to the tender mercies of Racehorse Haynes for cross-examination.

At this juncture of the trial, Judge Dowlen was called on to make the most important ruling in the case. The issue before him involved the latitude he would allow Racehorse Haynes in his cross-examination of Priscilla Davis. Racehorse, of course, wanted free rein to tear Priscilla limb from limb without limitation: "Try Priscilla, not Cullen!" It was critical to the defense to portray Priscilla as a greedy and licentious Jezebel who sponsored, and participated in, endless sex orgies as well as flagrant dope smoking. After all, conservative West Texans of that day in Amarillo typically viewed smoking a joint of marijuana as about as serious a criminal offense as their ancestors on the frontier had viewed stealing a horse.

However, there were two major legal obstacles standing in Haynes's path to the wholesale smearing of Priscilla. First, except in unusual circumstances, Texas law does not allow a cross-examiner to attack an adverse witness's credibility by inquiring about any acts of misconduct short of actual convictions for serious offenses.

Second, there is another rule of evidence coming under the heading of "relevance." Simply put, unless some prior act of misconduct on the part of the witness is *relevant* to some disputed issue in the case, the cross-examiner is not allowed to wave that dirty laundry before the jury. For example, assume that a Mr. Jones is mugged and beaten on a public street. In the subsequent trial, Mr. Jones identifies the defendant, Mr. Smith, as his attacker. Mr. Smith pleads not guilty, and his defense is mistaken identity. The sole issue before the jury therefore is the identity of the attacker. In such a case would the defense be allowed to prove that two years before the mugging Mr. Jones had had illicit sexual relations with a married woman who was not his wife? Or, that he was a trouble-maker in high school? Or that he is a lousy husband? Or that he once smoked a marijuana joint—even if he inhaled? Of course not. All that is not relevant to the sole disputed issue in the case:

identity of the mugger. The defense would not be permitted to clutter up the trial with such extraneous dirt in an effort to divert the jury's attention from the real issue of identity, or to unfairly prejudice the jury against the victim. In addition, as a practical matter, if cross-examiners were permitted to reveal every sin the witness ever committed from birth forward, trials would never end.

Therefore, since the sole disputed issue in the Cullen Davis trial was the identity of the man in black, the prosecution objected to allowing Haynes to drag Priscilla through the muck of any prior acts of misconduct that had no bearing on the identity of the killer. But Haynes argued that Priscilla's acts of misconduct (sex and drugs in the mansion after the separation of Priscilla and Cullen) did, in fact, have relevance to the identity to the man in black. The defense theory was that the mayhem that night was somehow drug-related—probably some drug deal gone sour.

"Show us," cried the prosecutors: show us that connection before you go about crucifying Priscilla. "How, specifically, can you connect any carryings-on of the party-goers at the mansion with the identity of the man in black?"

In that context, the usual (and correct) practice is for the judge (outside the presence of the jury) to require the cross-examiner to come forth with specifics: Tell me what specific acts of misconduct by the witness you intend to explore and how that testimony will bear on the issue of the identity of the killer. What is the connection? What witnesses will the defense call to substantiate the connection, and what will be the substance of their testimony? Unless the defense satisfies the judge that there really is a bona fide connection, the court should sustain the prosecution's objection and refuse to allow the defense to attack the witness by going into prior acts of misconduct. In the Cullen Davis case, however, Haynes and his associates gave Judge Dowlen only a vague assurance that the mansion shootings were somehow drug-related and that sometime later in the trial (after they had persecuted Priscilla on cross-examination) the defense, somehow, would eventually come forward with some unspecified evidence connecting Priscilla's misconduct with the issue of the identity of the man in black.

The risk inherent in not requiring the defense at this point in the trial to be specific about the supposed "connecting" evidence is apparent. If the court allows the defense to maul a witness such as Priscilla on cross, but then the defense fails to redeem its promise to come forward later in the trial with evidence that supports the alleged link between her misconduct and the identity of the killer, then what? Serious damage has already been done to the prosecution's case and the credibility of its witness. How does the judge un-ring that bell? The court could, of course, declare a mistrial, but that would result in a great waste of everybody's time, public money, and judicial resources. Or, the court could instruct the jury to disregard all that sordid evidence about the witnesses' misconduct. But that would really be no remedy at all. As old trial lawyers are apt to put it: "You can't throw a skunk in the jury box and then instruct the jury to disregard the odor."

Nevertheless, Judge Dowlen, unwisely, allowed the defense to get away with the "vague-assurance-of-coming-attractions" ploy, and so overruled the prosecution's objection and thereby pitched free rein to Racehorse Haynes, who gleefully anticipated making mincemeat of Priscilla on cross. The circus was about to begin. Somebody had remarked that Racehorse could cross-examine a fence post, nonstop, for forty-eight hours without ever stopping for breath, and he was about to prove that. He would hammer Priscilla unmercifully on cross-examination for thirteen straight days.

The prosecution realized that really bad things were about to happen to its case, and not only because Racehorse was a past master in the art of cross-examination. Two other factors forebode ill for the prosecutors. First, they knew that when Racehorse questioned her about sexual improprieties, drug use, or associations with low-life characters at the mansion, she would be less than candid and forthright; she would become evasive, or worse, just flat lie and deny. The prosecutors were unable to convince Priscilla that telling the truth, however embarrassing it might be, would be far better than appearing evasive in front of the jury, or even worse, allowing Racehorse to catch her in a lie. And therein lay yet another negative of which the prosecutors were painfully aware. There had been a number of unsavory freeloaders who had wandered in and out of the mansion while Priscilla reigned, some of whom had taken up residence there for brief periods of time.

Prosecutors knew that the defense investigators had made an exhaustive effort to uncover what had gone on in the mansion and who had done what and to whom, and that in doing so, the defense had taken some very interesting—and revealing—statements from some of the participants. The district attorney's men were soon to find out just what a thorough job defense investigator Steve Sumner had done. The jury was about to be treated to a parade of Priscilla's playmates, none of whom had impressive Sunday school attendance records. Worse yet, if, as the prosecutors anticipated, Racehorse nailed Priscilla to lies about her acts of misconduct, then most likely Haynes would later be able to trot out one or more of her playmates to expose her untruthfulness.

"Exhibit A" in that category was Priscilla's pre–Stan Farr lover, a cheerfully unrepentant rake and rogue named W. T. Rufner, who could also be accurately described as a brawling, whiskey-drinking, dope-smoking hard partier. (Before Priscilla, the cops had busted W.T. on a dope possession charge and placed him on probation.) Not only had W.T. been Priscilla's in-mansion lover for a spell during her separation from Cullen, but as it turned out, she had first had sex with W.T. even before Cullen and Priscilla separated—a fact that Priscilla, predictably, denied upon cross-examination. Later, Racehorse called W.T. to the stand and pried an admission from him that their sexual romps had begun before the separation.

The highlight of W. T. Rufner's appearance had not so much to do with his testimony as with a certain picture. It would become known as the "sock" photograph. It was a picture of Rufner and Priscilla. When Priscilla testified on cross, Racehorse showed her the picture, but Priscilla claimed she could not identify it. But the cocky and carefree W. T. Rufner, whose mind was forever unburdened by notions of trouble, worry, or guilt, had no problem recalling it. It depicted himself and Priscilla linked arm in arm in a most festive mood. Priscilla, holding a drink, was spilling out of her halter top and hiphuggers. Priscilla's handbag hung rakishly over W.T.'s right shoulder. Other than that, he was unencumbered by accessories—or garments. In fact, W.T. was stark naked except for a red-and-white striped Christmas stocking. The stocking was not on W.T.'s foot. It was worn over the most personal and intimate part of his anatomy, and the length of that sock made it appear that W.T. was a very big man indeed.

Later, but before the trial was over, the irrepressible W. T. Rufner showed up once again at the Amarillo courthouse, this time attempting to peddle an armful of new T-shirts for $100 a pop. The white

T-shirt featured a full-color, full-length depiction of W. T. Rufner in the altogether, adorned only by the now-famous red-and-white Christmas stocking—in place. Boldly emblazoned upon the shirt were these immortal words: "W. T. Socks It To 'Em."

Rufner wasn't the only nasty whom Racehorse paraded to the witness stand for the perusal by, and edification of, that Bible-belt jury in Amarillo. A number of others were called who tattled and told all about the very indiscreet carryings-on during Priscilla's tenure in Cullen's mansion. Finally, it all came to resemble a messy divorce case much more than it did a murder trial.

In the end, Racehorse and his defense team reneged on their promise to Judge Dowlen to connect up this tale of the extended mansion Mardi Gras debauchment with any motive for murder by anybody other than Cullen. True, there was ample evidence that Priscilla and her friends had *used* drugs during their parties, but there was no evidence of any drug dealing or of any "drug deals gone sour" as the defense had represented there would be. Racehorse also reneged on his pretrial promise to unveil "the real killer."

The prosecution tried to get its train back on track with the testimony of Beverly Bass and Bubba Gavrel. Beverly testified without equivocation that she recognized the shooter and that it was Cullen. The defense would later make the rather weak argument that after Priscilla suffered a life-threatening wound in the chest, and after Beverly witnessed Bubba being severely wounded, and while the shooter was still roaming around in the immediate area, they—Priscilla and Beverly—somehow got together, held a conference, and calmly arrived at a joint decision not to identify the real killer, but instead to blame it all on Cullen Davis. Only then did they separate, run off in different directions, each hysterically screaming "Cullen did it."

When the defense finally got through raking the State's witnesses over the coals, Racehorse called Cullen's girlfriend, Karen Master, to the stand to provide an alibi. She testified that on the night of the shootings she woke up at 12:40 a.m. and discovered that Cullen was snuggled up in bed beside her asleep. However, shortly after the mansion shootings, Karen had testified before the Fort Worth Grand Jury and told a different tale. During her Grand Jury testimony she failed to mention that when she awoke shortly after midnight Cullen was in bed with

The irrepressible W. T. Rufner, a dope-smoking party animal, was another of Priscilla's boyfriends after she and Cullen separated. (Image courtesy of *Fort Worth Star-Telegram*.)

her. (In fact, she had previously told investigators that she had taken a sleeping pill earlier in the evening and hadn't seen Cullen for hours.) When confronted with this omission by the lead prosecutor, Joe Shannon, at the trial, Karen shrugged and explained that this detail must have simply slipped her mind. Besides, she didn't think it was really all that important at the time.

In his final argument, Joe Shannon attempted to refocus the jury's attention on the real issue before them: regardless of Priscilla's misbehavior and loose lifestyle, "it did not give anybody the right to go in there to slay a twelve-year-old-girl." Shannon also pointed out that, despite all of Racehorse's battering of Priscilla, he still hadn't "made a single dent in Priscilla Davis's story about what happened inside that house in the early morning hours of August third." Finally, and most impervious to logical attack by the defense, was the fact that both Priscilla and Beverly, immediately after the shootings, had run off in different directions almost simultaneously and hysterically blurted out the same story to innocent bystanders: "Cullen did it." When people are traumatized by such horrible life-threatening experiences, Shannon explained, "they tell the truth"—they have neither the time nor the presence of mind to calmly concoct and then coordinate their lies with others, whether self-serving or otherwise.

The prosecutors closed their case on that note, still confident that logic and reason would carry the day. Even the defense attorneys suffered a sense of foreboding gloom when the jury began its deliberations. Both camps were wrong. Much to the dismay of the State and to the exhilaration of the defense, on November 17, 1977, at the end of a judicial marathon that had lasted almost five months, the jury returned a "not guilty" verdict.

Upon hearing the news, a tearful Priscilla Davis had this to say: "Cullen always thought he was invincible. Now he knows it." Once again her words would prove to be more prophetic than even she realized at the time.

In retrospect, several factors figured in the unexpected victory of the defense. Certainly the "leave-no-stone-unturned" pre-trial investigation of Steve Sumner for the defense was one; and, of course, the masterful trial performance—especially on cross-examination—of Racehorse Haynes was another. But there were three other major factors: (1) the prosecution's blunder in insisting on denying bond to Cullen, which necessitated a pre-trial bond hearing that, in turn, had the effect of handing over the prosecution's entire playbook to the defense with plenty of time to prepare counter maneuvers; (2) Judge Dowlen's decision to allow Racehorse virtually unlimited latitude not only to demolish Priscilla and her credibility but also to parade all of Priscilla's most unappealing playmates before the jury; and (3) Priscilla's own character flaws—not only her immoral lifestyle, but also her proclivity to evade or deny unpleasant truths.

Mike Cochran, a Fort Worth–based Associated Press reporter, covered this and the other Cullen Davis trials and wrote the definitive book exploring in depth all of Cullen's adventures and misadventures. In his book, *Texas vs. Davis*, Cochran recorded the following penetrating analysis of the Amarillo verdict:

> I blamed Priscilla more than the prosecutors. Rightly or wrongly, prosecutors were trying a murder case, not conducting an exercise in emotional psychology. And Priscilla made their jobs infinitely more difficult. They spent too much time trying to protect Priscilla from

herself. I suspect she couldn't help it. But the jury acquitted Cullen because it didn't like or didn't believe Priscilla; probably both. If she had told the jury, "Look, I am what I am. I've slept around, I've associated with dopers, I'm a lousy candidate for Mother of the Year. But what the hell right does that give Cullen to kill my 12-year-old daughter?" If she'd just leveled with the jurors from the outset, maybe they'd have believed her when it counted. But they convicted her just as surely as they acquitted Cullen.[8]

That all said, and all true enough, still there may have been yet a bit more to this judicial fiasco, none of which would appear in the official transcripts of what happened in the courtroom. First, even though the "Wild West" had receded into history years earlier, and even though statutory law had officially ousted the unwritten law, still some undercurrents of the unwritten folk law may well have lingered at least in the subconscious of 1977 West Texans. Indeed, until 1973, when the Texas Legislature repealed an 1856 statutory relic of frontier times, it was still entirely legal for a husband to dispatch his wife's lover—but only if the husband caught the pair *in flagrante delicto* and then fired the fatal shot before the miscreants "separated."[9] And, although women had been granted the right to vote upon ratification of the Nineteenth Amendment in 1920, still it wasn't until 1955 that Texas permitted women to serve on juries. As late as 1961, three states (Mississippi, Alabama, and South Carolina) continued to exclude women from jury service. Even as late as 1994, United States Supreme Court Justice Blackmun found it necessary to review the reasoning behind the exclusion. Justice Blackmun noted that the prohibition of women on juries was derived from English common law; and then, quoting from an earlier case, set out the reasoning:

The civil law, as well as nature herself, has always recognized a wide difference in the respective spheres and destinies of man and woman. Man is, or should be, woman's protector and defender. The natural and proper timidity and delicacy which belongs to the female sex evidently unfits it for many occupations of civil life. . . . The paramount destiny and mission of woman are to fulfill the noble and benign offices of wife and mother. This is the law of the Creator.[10]

Blackmun commented that this attitude of "romantic paternalism put women, not on a pedestal, but in a cage." (In a sense, women might well have applauded rambunctious Priscilla for debunking—once and for all—the myth that there exists a "natural and proper timidity and delicacy which belongs to the female sex.")

When Judge Dowlen allowed Racehorse to run unchecked for days on end, hammering away on Priscilla, her lovers, and other trashy associates, thus exposing their flagrant debauchery and their recreational use of drugs, he pitched Racehorse the slack he needed to transform the legal trial of a man who was accused of brutally murdering an innocent twelve-year-old child into a social trial of Priscilla, who was accused of the crime of immorality—thereby turning the whole proceeding into a morality play, one which left a most unsavory taste in the mouth of a socially conservative, 1970s Bible Belt jury. Although Cullen Davis himself might not have been exactly the picture of dear old Uncle Wiggly, he was, nevertheless, a husband. And he had been forcibly ejected by Priscilla and the divorce judge from his home—his castle—for more than two years while his gold-digging, immoral wife brazenly committed adultery, over and over again, and rubbed his nose in it—publicly. Had Cullen Davis killed Stan Farr, his wife's notorious lover, only four years earlier, he could have done so in front of a crowd and bragged openly about vindicating his honor, since the old 1856 Texas statute granting aggrieved husbands free shooting rights wasn't repealed until 1973. Moreover, both Cullen and the members of the jury had reached maturity in a society that still condoned such killings—either by virtue of statute or, failing that, by virtue of the unwritten law. In the end, it is difficult to believe that some lingering subliminal echoes of the old unwritten law and its underpinning, the Code of Honor, didn't play a significant part in the jury's final decision. The courtroom drama of the Cullen Davis trial, as it unfolded over five long months, serves as a reminder that there is nothing quite like a crime of passion, when featured as the centerpiece of a sensational murder trial, to illuminate the social history and present mores of any given society.

Something else that doesn't appear in the official records of the trial may well have played an even more important part in the outcome. What happened after the trial offers a clue; it emitted a very unpleasant odor that, in retrospect, stunk up the entire judicial episode. Immediately after the verdict, a jubilant Cullen Davis, his girlfriend, Karen Master; Karen's dad, Ray Hudson; Racehorse Haynes; and all the other defense team and a host of supporters all loaded up and headed straight for Amarillo's popular, upscale oasis, Rhett Butler's, for a victory celebration. At one point, well into the party and after more than a few toasts to the triumph, Ray Hudson was in an expansive mood. He shared this insight with a reporter:

> Them prosecutors . . . they didn't have a chance, brother. Those cock-suckers never realized it was put together that way. There wasn't nothing left unturned. It was all covered. . . . I knew when a juror sneezed or farted. I had the finger on the pulse. We had that son-of-a-bitch won before the jury ever sat down.[11]

Much later, as we shall document, Ray Hudson would make an even more startling—and incriminating—comment about the Amarillo trial.

Meanwhile, after the Amarillo verdict, a reporter remarked to Cullen, "You know, Cullen, the prosecutors were convinced up to the end that the verdict would be guilty. Cullen just smiled and replied, "Yeah, but *they* didn't know the jury's first vote was ten-two for acquittal. *I did.*"[12] Cullen, however, declined to explain just how he came to know that.

The night of the victory celebration, yet another remarkable thing happened. Judge George Dowlen showed up at Rhett Butler's and hoisted a few. Then he took a seat next to Cullen and joined the festivities—not exactly what one would expect from a dispassionate and impartial trial judge in a horrendous murder trial; not something that added much dignity to the court. Three jurors also joined the celebration, as did one of the court bailiffs, D'Ann Hill, who tearfully hugged Cullen and told him how thankful she was that he had been acquitted. The Cullen entourage then began speculation on which Hollywood stars would portray the real-life characters in the movie version of the Cullen Davis story. Cullen modestly favored Al Pacino to play his role.

No one bothered to raise a cup in memory of the brief life and tragic demise of Andrea Wilborn.

The following day, Cullen graciously hosted a cordial victory luncheon to honor the jurors. Then two days after the verdict (and before leaving town), Amarillo millionaire Stanley Marsh 3 threw a bash for Cullen, Karen, and all the rest of their followers and hangers-on. "Stanley 3" (normal people would have referred to themselves as "Stanley Marsh III") had been viewed for decades as Amarillo's foremost eccentric, hands down. Not only an eccentric, but also an iconoclast. For openers, Stanley 3 never hesitated to voice his very liberal political and social opinions in this very conservative community. But that was the least of it. His far-out sense of humor was exceeded only by his bizarre taste in art—at least "art" as Stanley 3 defined it. It may safely be posited that his taste lay on the far fringe of *avant garde*. Perhaps his most famous artistic achievement came when he bought a fleet of used Cadillac cars—those circa 1950s barges with elongated tail fins. Stanley 3 had them hauled out to a farm he owned on the western outskirts of Amarillo along Interstate 40 (old Highway 66), and, in an open field, buried them, all in a row and all nose down and deep—with the rear ends, fins skyward, sticking out of the earth at the same angle. Thus travelers on I-40 were treated to a view of Stanley 3 "art." He fondly referred to it as his "Cadillac Ranch."

Therefore, inviting Cullen et al. to his digs (which he called "Toad Hall") undoubtedly appealed to Stanley 3's sense of the outlandish and the outrageous. At the party, he focused his attention on Cullen, but Cullen seemed to be in a more subdued mood than he had exhibited at his victory celebration. Nevertheless, Stanley 3 pursued. He wanted to discuss Priscilla. Cullen predicted that Priscilla would soon end up working in an all-night doughnut stand in Waco. When Stanley 3 asked Cullen why he married her in the first place if she was such a hussy and a harlot, Cullen deflected the inquiry by commenting that Priscilla had changed for the better after they were married, but that when Fort Worth society refused to accept her, she "went back to her old ways." Stanley 3 then, to keep the conversation flowing, suggested that perhaps a tiger just couldn't be expected to change its spots. Cullen immediately corrected him, pointing out that tigers don't have spots—they have stripes.[13]

Cullen also seemed uninterested in discussing art and unimpressed with Stanley 3's artistic tastes, even when Stanley directed his attention to the backyard of Toad Hall, where the large letters "A-R-T" were silhouetted against a harvest moon. He also showed very limited interest in a pair of Chinese hairless dogs that Stanley 3 had caused to be tattooed with wings and flames.

In the end, Stanley 3 became disenchanted with Cullen. Cullen didn't exhibit much wit or even a smidgen of Stanley 3's outrageous sense of humor, and his taste in art, if any, was in Stanley 3's estimation, pedestrian at best. Cullen had proven to be a disappointing dud. After the partygoers departed, a reporter asked Stanley what his opinion of Cullen was then. To make sense of Stanley 3's reply to that query, the reader must first be informed that Stanley 3 had a pet pig named Minnesota Fats, the pig being named in honor of a very fat and earthy world champion billiard player of that era.

"Let me put it this way," Stanley 3 replied. "I don't think Minnesota Fats [the pig, not the pool shooter] would have enjoyed drinking with Cullen." Then he added: "Fats was just a pig, but he had standards. Blood will tell, I always say."[14]

But perhaps Cullen was just having an off day. The next morning he and Karen were smiling broadly when a TV news crew photographed them boarding Cullen's Learjet. He told the news folks that he would be back at his desk at Mid-Continent Supply in Fort Worth on Monday morning, and then he and Karen were off for a Thanksgiving skiing expedition in Colorado.

Stanley 3, meanwhile, was planning a new artistic triumph: he planned to have the five-hundred-acre field of wheat he owned mowed into the shape of a giant hand—the *Great American Farmhand*, he would call it.

The defeated and disheartened district attorney's office, meanwhile, having lost its strongest case, glumly retreated to Fort Worth. They were in no hurry to try Cullen for the murder of Stan Farr or the attempted murders of Priscilla and Bubba Gavrel. In fact, it appeared unlikely the prosecutors would ever get around to those cases unless some new and really incriminating evidence surfaced. And so, one would have thought that, at least from Cullen Davis's perspective, "all's well that ends well." And that was that.

One would have thought . . .

Cullen II

On August 2, 1978, less than a year after the Amarillo jury cleared Cullen for the murder of Andrea Wilborn, and two years to the day after the mansion massacre, one of Cullen's low-society, pool-shooting buddies, David McCrory, arranged to meet FBI agent Ron Jannings at a McDonald's restaurant in Fort Worth. The tale he told was so incredible the FBI man was, to put it mildly, skeptical. Cullen Davis, McCrory told the FBI agent, had a "hit list" of people he wanted exterminated and had approached him to find a reliable hit man. Although skeptical, Jannings notified an assistant U.S. attorney plus other FBI agents and a Texas Ranger. The team put a wire on McCrory and tailed him to his rendezvous with Cullen. What they heard stunned even the veteran officers. Cullen, so they heard, did indeed have a hit list, and quite a list it was: Priscilla, of course, plus Beverly Bass, the maimed Bubba Gavrel, and his father, Gus Gavrel. (Cullen apparently feared Bubba and his father might file a multimillion-dollar civil suit against him.) But Cullen's number one on the hit list parade was even more unbelievable. It was Judge Joe Eidson, the divorce court judge who had so infuriated Cullen by ordering an increase in temporary alimony for Priscilla, postponing the final divorce hearing, and most of all, leaving Priscilla in sole possession of Cullen's castle while the divorce was pending. But that still wasn't enough to satisfy Cullen. For good measure, he added the judge's wife to his hit list: "Do the judge and then his wife . . . ," Cullen was quoted as saying on the tape. In addition, Cullen wanted McCrory to furnish him a .22-caliber pistol with a silencer. Twenty-five thousand dollars was the price put on Eidson's head. (Apparently that was meant to take care of Mrs. Eidson also.)

By now the officers were convinced that this was no hoax. The Fort Worth district attorney's office was notified, and together they concocted a plan to nail Cullen Davis securely to the crime of conspiracy to commit the murder of Judge Eidson. Judge Eidson was notified, and he agreed to participate in a Cullen trap. Judge Eidson put on a ketchup-stained shirt and posed as a corpse in the trunk of a car. Pictures were taken, and McCrory, again wired, was sent to present Cullen with evidence (including Judge Eidson's identification cards) that the Eidson hit had taken place and was successful. A part of the resulting tape recording went like this:

> McCrory: "I got Judge Eidson for you."
> Cullen: "Good."
> McCrory: "I'll get the rest of them dead for you. You want a bunch of people dead. Right?"
> Cullen: "All right."

McCrory then gave him the .22-caliber pistol with silencer, and Cullen (although he later denied it) gave McCrory $25,000 cash for the hit.[15]

Shortly thereafter, Cullen Davis found himself once again caged in the Fort Worth jail, charged with conspiracy to murder Judge Eidson. Newspaper headlines trumpeted the news. *The Fort Worth Star-Telegram*: "Cullen Davis Back in Jail; Plot to Kill Judge Charged." *The Dallas Morning News*: "Davis Held in Murder-for-Hire Scheme." Another Fort Worth district judge, Judge Gordon Gray, when he read the story beneath those headlines, exclaimed: "They've got that guilty son-of-a-bitch this time!"

The federal and state officers as well as the Fort Worth prosecutors agreed. This time, surely, with McCrory's testimony backed up by a team of experienced and credible officers, and all that backed up by those damning tapes, surely there was no wiggle room, even for Racehorse Haynes and his wrecking crew. But Cullen Davis, once again digging deep into the oil fortune that had originated with Floyd Holmes, didn't economize. He brought on the best that money could buy. This time, instead of Amarillo, the trial was transferred to Houston, where Cullen would answer an indictment charging him with conspiracy to kill Judge Eidson. Houston Judge Wallace "Pete" Moore would preside.

Once again, the Fort Worth district attorney did the defense a huge favor by insisting that Cullen be denied bail pending the trial. Although this criminal charge didn't carry a death penalty possibility, nevertheless another Texas statute permitted a judge to deny bond to Cullen. If a defendant, while out of jail on bond for a felony offense, allegedly commits yet another felony, then bond can be denied. (Bear in mind that Cullen still faced the outstanding felony indictments for killing

Stan Farr and wounding Priscilla and Gavrel and had been out on bond for those offenses at the time he was alleged to have conspired to kill Eidson.)

The bond hearing yielded a treasure trove of discovery for the defense. They got to listen to (and obtain copies of) all the State's tape recordings, see all the videos, photographs, and other physical evidence, plus put key witnesses under oath and nail them down to their stories. Racehorse kept the State's key witness, David McCrory, on the stand for four days, grilling him on dates, times, content of conversations, phone calls—artfully setting him up for the kill when trial time rolled around.

In the end, the defense knew everything about the State's case; the State knew virtually nothing about the defense Racehorse Haynes was crafting. Plus, by virtue of Haynes's meticulous cross-examination of McCrory, he found a way to drag Priscilla back into this case. During the bond hearing, McCrory testified that before taking his story of Cullen's hit list to the FBI, he had first told his friend Pat Burleson, a karate instructor, about Cullen's solicitation of a hitman. Burleson, in turn, put McCrory in contact with the FBI agent, Ron Jannings, and then got out of the way. Or so he thought. But once Haynes heard about Burleson, he subpoenaed him. During his testimony, Burleson said that he had met separately with both McCrory and Priscilla several times just prior to Cullen's arrest. While there was nothing to suggest that there was anything clandestine or sinister about these meetings (other than a friendly sexual romp or two between Burleson and Priscilla), it was all Racehorse needed to construct a defense. According to Racehorse's version of events, McCrory, Priscilla, and Burleson had conspired to frame Cullen. Now Haynes could tar McCrory with the same brush he had used so effectively—and would use effectively again—to tar Priscilla with. And poor Burleson, well, he would just have to take his share of the tarring too.

Following the bond hearing, Haynes's defense team, now armed with its adversary's detailed game plan, began its meticulous preparations to ambush the prosecution and explain away the inexplicable. Cullen's girlfriend, Karen Master, would again play a key role in the defense. However, her father, Ray Hudson, would not make the trip to Houston. By now he had become completely disillusioned with Cullen Davis. He grumbled, "I coulda gone to jail for what I did last time, and I ain't gonna push my luck no more." Nobody except Hudson and Cullen knew precisely what it was that he had done in Amarillo. But, according to Associated Press reporter Mike Cochran, who covered both trials (and wrote the definitive book *Texas vs. Davis*), Cullen paid Hudson $45,000 for his services, and, in 1978, when taxes fell due, Cullen peeled off another $19,000 for Hudson to appease the Internal Revenue Service. Reporter Cochran tells it that one of Cullen's accountants had the temerity to ask Hudson how that $45,000 was spent, to which Hudson snapped: "You dumb shit, that's the last thing in the world you want to know. I could have got 20 years." He later added, "[Cullen] don't give a shit for anyone. My life is a hell of a lot better without Cullen Davis. . . . I still ask myself sometimes why I did anything for that cocksucker."[16] Being excessively mealymouthed was never one of Ray Hudson's shortcomings.

Hudson may have defected, but Cullen still had Karen—as well as Racehorse and company, and a big bankroll to fund the defense when they all rolled into Houston.

After the State had placed all its evidence before the jury, including the damning tape recordings and a photograph of the posed "corpse" of Judge Eidson in the trunk of a car, plus all the testimony of the investigating officers, the prosecution, now headed by a new prosecutor, Jack Strickland, rested its case.

The defense called Priscilla as its first witness, ostensibly to prove that Priscilla was the prime mover behind a conspiracy (with McCrory and Burleson and possibly others) to hire a hitman to kill Cullen, or maybe just to extort money from Cullen, or maybe just to frame Cullen for conspiring to kill Judge Eidson. Take your choice. Of course, Racehorse had another unstated agenda: he wanted to replay the character assassination of Priscilla before the Houston jury as he had done so effectively in Amarillo. But, to his credit, Judge Moore was not about to allow Haynes to berate Priscilla for thirteen days; not about to listen to endless irrelevant accounts of sex, drugs, and wild parties at the mansion. Much to Haynes's chagrin, Judge Moore shut him down.

Racehorse, Cullen, and Karen now faced the daunting task of explaining away those damnable, and damning, tapes, as well as the $25,000 that Cullen gave McCrory at the time McCrory told him that the hitman had "got Judge Eidson for you." Not to mention the matter of the .22-caliber pistol with the illegal silencer delivered by McCrory to Cullen.

As it turned out, Karen and Cullen—with a little help from friend Haynes—had an explanation for all that. Karen went first and set the stage. After all, she had recently had considerable experience in explaining things that seemed improbable. According to Karen, some two months before Cullen's arrest she had received a very alarming telephone call from David McCrory: "Karen, I have some information that I think you should know. I know for a fact that Priscilla Davis and Gus Gavrel, Sr., have a contract out on Cullen's life." (Later, on cross-examination, Karen acknowledged that in her prior grand jury testimony, she had neglected to mention anything about McCrory's cryptic warning. As she had previously done in Amarillo, telling things during trial that she had somehow forgotten to mention in earlier grand jury testimony was simply shrugged off as an innocent oversight.)

Karen then told of an even more curious phone call. This one, she said, occurred on August 10, 1978—just ten days before Cullen's arrest, *and just before the McCrory tapes.* The call was for Cullen, but she answered it. She said the caller identified himself as an FBI agent named Acree. She then handed the phone to Cullen.

Now it was Cullen's turn to take up the tale. And the more Cullen's tale unfolded, the curiouser and curiouser it got.

Yes, McCrory had called him in June as Karen said, warning him that Priscilla and Gus Gavrel were about to put a contract out on him. And then in August, a man who identified himself as FBI agent Acree called him and warned him that he was the intended victim of an extortion plot by McCrory. Cullen had never met FBI agent Acree, but he took the caller's word as to his identity and the authenticity of the message. Cullen asked the caller what he should do about it, and the caller told Cullen to simply "play along" with McCrory and "follow his suggestions and do whatever he says." Then the caller said that he would "be back in touch with you." However, he never did get back in touch.

It seemed not to have occurred to Cullen that there was anything unusual about this procedure—strange indeed that a supposed FBI agent he had never met would not personally interview him and present some credentials, or take his statement, or investigate the prior relationship between himself and McCrory, or wire him up to record any subsequent conversations with McCrory. The next day, according to Cullen, he did meet with McCrory. At that meeting McCrory reiterated the story about Priscilla supposedly having hired a hitman to kill him. In fact, again according to Cullen, McCrory claimed he had actually met with Priscilla's hitman. However, McCrory said that they could "turn the tables on Priscilla" by offering to pay the hitman more money than Priscilla was offering. But, of course, McCrory went on, he was going to need proof that Cullen was willing to cooperate with the hitman and up the ante. It was at that point, Cullen contended, that he consented to make a tape-recorded conversation with McCrory that would convince Priscilla's killer or killers that he was serious, that he would beat her offer. At the same time, the tape would serve as insurance that the killer would not turn on him and McCrory. This conversation between Cullen and McCrory was supposedly recorded by Cullen, but somehow he lost the recording and couldn't produce it at the time of trial. But their next conversation was recorded.

That was the recording the FBI had wired McCrory for in order to nail Cullen, and that was the tape-recording the prosecutors played for the jury. According to Cullen, however, he knew that the conversation was being recorded, but as per FBI agent Acree's instructions, he was just "playing along" with McCrory and agreeing to whatever he said—all in order to help the FBI agent Acree entrap McCrory in his extortion scheme—simple as that.

Later, the prosecution produced the real FBI agent, Jim Acree, in open court, where he denied ever speaking to Cullen or Karen either on the telephone or otherwise. Cullen and Karen were then forced to admit that the real agent Acree certainly didn't *sound* anything like the phantom FBI agent who had called them. (McCrory, of course, denied he ever warned either Cullen or Karen that Priscilla was planning a hit on Cullen either by phone or in person, or that he had ever heard of such a plot.) Stranger yet, neither Cullen nor Karen ever got around to telling the story of their supposed cooperation with the FBI in order to entrap McCrory or Priscilla until the Houston trial. One might have reasonably presumed that the moment Cullen was arrested for conspiring to kill the judge, he would have immediately screamed his head off for his FBI contact, Jim Acree, to come and rescue him by explaining how Cullen had simply been "playing along" with McCrory on the instructions of the FBI. Also, this crucial call from the phantom FBI man must have slipped Karen's mind when she testified before the grand jury shortly after Cullen's arrest. She didn't get around to remembering it until she testified at the trial in Houston. Further, Karen disremembered that initial warning call from McCrory when she testified before the grand jury. Just didn't seem appropriate to unduly burden the grand jury with such unimportant stuff like that.

What about the .22 pistol equipped with the illegal silencer that McCrory had given him? Cullen's explanation: He never asked McCrory for one in the first place. McCrory just showed it to him that day and offered it as a present, and, although he hadn't requested it and really didn't want it, he reluctantly allowed McCrory to press that gift upon him. Again, just "playing along" with McCrory as per FBI instructions.

What about the $25,000 that Cullen gave McCrory? Cullen's explanation: Actually it was McCrory's money. McCrory had previously won it in Las Vegas, and since he didn't have a handy place to stash it, he asked Cullen to hold it for him, and Cullen agreed to do so. McCrory then asked Cullen to give it back and, of course, like a good and trusted friend, he simply returned it to McCrory without question—at the time the tape was recording.

During one point in the trial, Judge Moore castigated Racehorse on account of a "borderline breach of ethics" in his zealous defense of Cullen Davis. Associated Press reporter Mike Cochran, in relating the incident, made this prescient observation:

> . . . it raised a disturbing point. . . . One could justifiably wonder to
> what lengths he might go to win the case. And was it for Cullen's free-
> dom or Racehorse's own ego he was now battling?[17]

To pursue further that line of inquiry, consider the preposterous tale that Karen and Cullen came up with to explain Cullen's way out of the damning FBI recordings of the crucial conversation between McCrory and Cullen. Now, for the very first time at this late date, Karen and Cullen claimed that Cullen really knew all along that he was being taped, but he was "just playing along" with McCrory pursuant to telephone instructions from some phantom FBI agent he had never met, seen, or heard from before or after. That this tortured and illogical tale was false seems probable. If it was false, then the question arises: who invented the lie? Cullen? Karen? Or Racehorse? But all that is only speculation; we will never know what really went on behind closed doors in the defense team's strategy sessions. Still, it returns us to Mike Cochran's original question (prompted by Judge Moore's castigation of Racehorse Haynes), to-wit: to what length would Racehorse go to win? Under our adversarial system of criminal justice, every defendant, however despicable and/or guilty he or she may be, is entitled to a vigorous advocate who leaves no stone unturned in representing his or her client. Yet there are ethical and legal boundaries.

In his final jury argument, Jack Strickland called Cullen's tale "the most contrived, foolish, flagrantly ridiculous story ever perpetrated on the ears of 12 innocent jurors." Trouble was, as ridiculous as it was, four jurors must have bought it. Hung jury. Mistrial. Back to Fort Worth.

Before the retrial, however, there was the matter of that long-delayed divorce action. Priscilla demanded $50 million plus attorneys' fees. The new divorce judge cut that request considerably, and awarded Priscilla $3.475 million plus some trinkets. Cullen finally regained possession of his precious mansion.

Retrial of the criminal conspiracy case began on July 9, 1979. Fort Worth District Judge Gordon Gray presided, and much to the consternation of the district attorney's office, Judge Gray refused to change venue. On account of Cullen's great wealth and the position of the Davis family in Fort Worth as well as all the publicity in Fort Worth about the killings, the prior trials, and the prosecutorial misfires, Fort Worth was the last place the State prosecutors wanted to retry the case. But Judge Gray, perhaps allowing himself to become more personally involved in a pending trial in his own court than a judge should be, denied a change of venue. And so, Fort Worth it was.

Early on, Judge Gray warned Racehorse Haynes that it would not be open season on Priscilla in his court, and that before he could question her, or any of her companions, about any misconduct, Haynes would have to demonstrate to the judge (outside the presence of the jury) the relevance and materiality of the query.

That settled, the trial began, and it was basically a replay of the Houston trial. Cullen contended that the prosecution's tape-recording was just a "sham" he surreptitiously participated in only on the phantom FBI man's instructions to "play along" with McCrory. There was, however, a slight shift in the defense strategy. To further attack the authenticity of the tapes, the defense brought in a semanticist, a professor of linguistics at Georgetown University. Dr. Roger Shuy testified he had analyzed the taped conversation and in his opinion it was clear that McCrory had "dominated, manipulated and controlled the ebb and flow" of the taped conversations between Cullen and McCrory. According to Dr. Shuy, Cullen was just a "passive patsy" who simply went along with whatever McCrory said.

In final jury arguments, Racehorse Haynes was eloquent. He somehow adroitly portrayed America's rich (such as Cullen) as America's oppressed. Then he returned to his basic "ABC" theme: Anybody But Cullen. He recounted the alleged "conspiratorial meetings" between Priscilla, McCrory, and Pat Burleson (the karate instructor) during the four critical days in August, and recalled how the devious McCrory had made a "passive patsy" out of poor gullible Cullen, who believed he was following FBI instructions.

Jack Strickland's reply for the State was also brilliant as he pilloried Cullen for the ridiculous and nonsensical "just-playing-along" story. Nearly everybody felt certain that this time Cullen would go down. Even one of Haynes's junior attorneys muttered, "Jack nailed our ass to the wall."

But not quite.

When the jury returned with a "not guilty" verdict, prosecutors, not to mention the press and courtroom spectators, were as stunned as if somebody had hit them squarely between the eyes with a baseball bat. After receiving the jury's verdict, the presiding judge, Judge Gordon Gray (the same judge who, when the case broke, exulted, "They've got the guilty son-of-a-bitch this time"), shook his head in disbelief as he descended from the bench. He had a one-word comment: "Fuck!"

Jurors later attempted to explain the seemingly inexplicable. When they listened to the incriminating tape recordings, they had detected a mysterious "clicking" sound and thus had concluded that the tapes had been *fabricated by law enforcement*. Therefore, they believed Cullen's self-serving testimony and disbelieved the testimony of McCrory, as well as the testimony of all the FBI agents, the state officers, and all the other prosecution witnesses. Obviously, the jury must have concluded that these witnesses were all lying—committing perjury—just to nail the unjustly persecuted Cullen Davis. For prosecutors and lawmen, the bitter irony of the jury's head-scratching deduction was that neither Racehorse Haynes nor any of his defense team had even mentioned this "mysterious clicking" on the tape during the trial or argued that this proved the recordings were doctored.

In fact, the jurors bragged about "solving" the case all by themselves, picking up a key clue (that "mysterious clicking") that all the mentally challenged professional detectives had overlooked. They out-sleuthed the sleuths, out-copped the cops. Better, they must have concluded, to play detective and "solve" the case than to play juror and weigh the evidence presented. The outcome gave a whole new meaning to the term "runaway jury." One juror, who bragged that her verdict was a triumph of justice, even claimed that everybody connected with the prosecution was simply persecuting poor Cullen on account of greed. All of them—not only Priscilla and McCrory, but also everybody else on the prosecution side, including the FBI, the Rangers, the investigators and even the district attorney's office, Jack Strickland included—were just in it for the money!

How and why did the jury arrive at such an incredible verdict? Upon reflection the jurors' explanation seems weak and implausible at best—it has a distinctly disingenuous ring to it. And the outspoken jurors seemed a bit too eager to justify a verdict that bucked a tide of overwhelming evidence, a bit too eager to grasp at straws to rationalize a decision that even they must have realized was suspect. Experienced trial lawyers sometimes comment that jurors "find what they want to find, whether real or imagined." True enough, but that leaves an even larger question unanswered: why? Was it something that happened during the trial, or before? Was it something that happened in the courtroom or outside the courtroom? Did it have anything to do with class? Or axes to grind with law enforcement? Did it have to do with extensive media coverage of Cullen's acquittal in Amarillo, followed by the hung jury in Houston? In the collective mind of the jury, had Cullen somehow managed to acquire the image of the victim of a greedy, gold-digging slut of a wife and the whipping-boy of overreaching, career-focused prosecutors? Did it have anything to do with the increasing number of Cullen "groupies" who crowded into the courtroom each day cheering their hero? Those questions were left unanswered.

After the bashing, the disheartened Tarrant County district attorney threw in the towel and dismissed the other criminal cases pending against Cullen—indictments for the murder of Stan Farr and for the assault with intent to murder Priscilla Davis and Bubba Gavrel.

The day after the Fort Worth jury acquitted Cullen, *Dallas Times Herald* reporter Bryan Woolley opined, "It will be a long while before Tarrant or any other county will dare try another as rich a man [*sic*] for murder." And then, under the headline "Texas Gothic Horror Story Ends at Last," Woolley put a wrap on the matter, bidding farewell to Priscilla and Cullen. "Trials for murder and for divorce and for hiring to murder. Child custody suits. Sex. Dope. Creeps and weirdoes coming and going to the mansion, to the courthouse, selling T-shirts. . . . Cross, double-cross, triple-cross. Plot, counter-plot, counter-counter plot. . . . Had it been sold as fiction, the public would have rejected it as preposterous, overblown . . . too lathered with blood, lust and corruption for even the most insatiable addicts of Texas Gothic." And so, Woolley sighed, suddenly it was all over.[18]

He should have known better.

The Aftermath

David McCrory testified that Cullen Davis gave him $25,000 cash to pay a hitman to exterminate Judge Eidson. At the trial, McCrory so testified and disclaimed ownership of the $25,000. At the same trial, Cullen disclaimed any ownership of those funds. After the trial, the $25,000 ended up in the custody of the trial court. The question then arose: who owned that $25,000? After considering it for a while, McCrory thought that if nobody was going to claim it, well then, "Why not me?" A wise counselor, however, advised McCrory to let it rest. "At the trial you testified under oath that the $25,000 was not yours. If you now

claim it, you might well subject yourself to being indicted for perjury."
McCrory decided to let well enough alone.

———

After Cullen and Priscilla were divorced, Cullen married Karen Master. Later, on May 4, 1980, Cullen and Karen Davis walked the aisle of the First Baptist Church of Euless (a Fort Worth suburb). The next day's *Dallas Morning News* headline read, "Cullen Stands Up for Jesus Christ."[19]

That headline met with widespread interest, but decidedly mixed reviews.

Cullen's niece, Kay Davis: "It could have been worse. Cullen might have joined the Moonies."

Jack Strickland: "Killers for Christ," and recalling the title of a popular World War II song, added, "Praise the Lord and Pass the Ammunition."

Not to be outdone, W. T. Rufner, still as unrepentant and unabashed as ever, gave his take on the matter: "Now that Cullen and God are together, I'm beginning to wonder about God."

Confession and Avoidance

Although Cullen Davis had escaped the clutches of the criminal justice system, he still faced potential multimillion-dollar liability in the civil courts stemming from the wounding of Priscilla Davis and Bubba Gavrel and the killing of Andrea Wilborn and Stan Farr. Financially, things got a lot worse for Cullen when, in the oil bust of the mid-1980s, the price of oil plunged from thirty-five dollars per barrel to less than ten dollars per barrel. In 1985, Kendavis creditors dragged the company into a Dallas bankruptcy court demanding repayment of hundreds of millions of dollars in loans. In 1986, due in large part to Cullen's dwindling fortune, he was reportedly able to settle the multimillion-dollar suit Bubba Gavrel filed against him for less than half a million. But that still left pending the civil suits filed by the heirs of Stan Farr and by Jack Wilborn and Priscilla.

Meanwhile, in their charismatic Assembly of God church, Cullen and Karen were making much loud ado about their born-again spiritual fervor, publicly denouncing devils and demons as well as liquor, tobacco, worldly music, old girlfriends, pictures of old girlfriends, stolen goods, and pagan art. In one histrionic fit, Cullen decided that all his oriental art collection was just too satanic (citing the biblical condemnation—Deuteronomy 7:25—against worshipping "graven carved images" of pagan gods), and so Cullen and his pastor reportedly proceeded to smash about a million dollars' worth of jade, gold, and silver art objects. Then he threw the splintered remains into Lake Worth.

That may have been a bit bizarre, but nothing to top what Cullen did next. One Sunday evening in 1986, Jack Wilborn and his wife, Betty, were attending services at their church in a Dallas suburb when they suddenly became aware other members of the congregation were whispering and looking toward them. There next to them stood none other than Cullen Davis. After the service Cullen reportedly said, "Jack, could you forgive me for what I did? I want you to know I'm so sorry for all the pain I've caused you."

Although shocked almost to the point of speechlessness, Jack later said that he replied, "Cullen, I forgave you a long time ago."[20]

Then, in the presence of the tearful and awestruck congregation, the two men embraced. And wept.

Word of Cullen's confession soon leaked out. When Jack Strickland heard about it, his reaction was considerably less than teary-eyed: "It doesn't do anything to put back the pieces of the various lives he ruined. . . . All it really does, I suppose, is make Cullen feel better. It's kind of like John Wilkes Booth sending a condolence card to Mrs. Lincoln." Eventually, Associated Press reporter and Cullen Davis chronicler Mike Cochran caught wind of it. He contacted Jack Wilborn and confirmed the story. The reporter then called Cullen for comment. At least he tried to call Cullen for comment, but Cullen refused to return his calls. Finally, the reporter called Cullen's attorney, Steve Sumner, and told him that he was going to run the story but would give Cullen an opportunity to comment if he wished. Ten minutes later, Sumner called the reporter and confirmed that there had been such an encounter between Cullen and Wilborn, but insisted that Cullen had gone there not to seek Wilborn's forgiveness, but instead *to forgive Wilborn*.

The stunned reporter, momentarily taken aback, finally asked the logical question; "Forgive Wilborn *for what?*" "Well," the lawyer relied, "for hiring photographers and private detectives to gather evidence against him and Priscilla in that long-ago divorce suit" between Wilborn and Priscilla.[21]

When Wilborn heard this revised version, he also was stunned. He dismissed it as "silly," "ridiculous," and "incredible." After the church confession, Jack Wilborn said he believed that Cullen was sincere, and so had been debating whether to proceed with the multimillion-dollar civil suit he had filed against Cullen. But when he heard Cullen's "ridiculous" revision, his mind was made up. He and Priscilla consolidated their wrongful death suits, both stemming from Andrea's slaying. The same jury would also hear Priscilla's suit for personal injury.

The State's longest-running legal drama was thus revived for one more chapter. Trial date was set for the spring of 1987.

The judge presiding was Claude Williams. At the outset, he told the lawyers that the only issue in dispute was the identity of the shooter, and he would not tolerate any inquiries into Priscilla's misdeeds without prior approval from the bench upon showing of relevance and materiality. This trial would focus on the life and death of Andrea Wilborn.

Cullen hired Steve Sumner to represent him. Priscilla and Jack were represented by a team of attorneys that included Bob Gibbins, a widely respected trial lawyer from Austin. Prospects for victory in this arena must have appeared dismal to Sumner. He was up against a powerhouse opponent. Cullen couldn't refuse to testify now. This time the plaintiffs had a preview of what Cullen's testimony would be. No Priscilla-circus diversion would be tolerated. No T-shirt peddling W. T. Rufner disrupting the proceedings. Plus, now there was Cullen's "confession" for him to explain away. And, unlike a criminal prosecution where unanimous consent of the jurors is required to convict, in a civil suit, a ten-to-two vote or better will carry the day for the plaintiff.

Still Sumner did have one trump card: Karen Master Davis, little Miss Mary Poppins herself. And, another idea occurred to him. Since the deck seemed to be stacked against him (including being outnumbered by high profile trial lawyers and facing a judge who appeared to be hostile to his cause), Sumner decided he might as well play the "underdog" card. Cullen, after all, had been forced into bankruptcy, and he had been dragged through the criminal courts though always acquitted—all of which had been widely publicized in Fort Worth.

Sumner's strategy therefore would be to pick a jury that might be sympathetic to the underdog. As such, he wanted as many minority jurors as possible—especially those who might resent authority and authority figures and those who might be disinclined to trust police testimony. Bottom line was that when the jury was seated, one-half of the jurors were minorities.

Nevertheless, the trial seemed to go well for the plaintiffs. Priscilla behaved on the stand, and Beverly Bass contributed damning testimony. Bob Gibbins also called Russell Vorpagel as an expert witness. Vorpagel was a former FBI criminal profile specialist, who testified that as a result of his analysis, Cullen was "selfish, egotistical, chauvinistic, emotionally unstable, insecure, domineering, paranoid and not prone to consider the results of his actions." He concluded that Cullen "fit the profile of the mansion killer to a 'T'."[22]

Karen countered by telling the jury what a compassionate and loving person Cullen was, and that he could never have done such a cruel thing. This explanation was in addition to the usual alibi that explained Cullen's whereabouts when Andrea was murdered.

Still, that left the little matter of Cullen's tearful confession, which needed a lot of explaining. Perhaps realizing that his first revised version (that he had gone to Wilborn's church to forgive Wilborn) was just too far-fetched for belief, upon further reflection he now came up with a second revised version on the encounter. Turns out he really had gone to Jack's church to seek forgiveness from Wilborn after all—but not for killing Jack's daughter. He informed the jury that God had told him to go to Wilborn and ask Wilborn to forgive him for his role in causing Wilborn's divorce from Priscilla. He realized Wilborn might have suffered a touch of mental anguish when he caught Cullen in bed with his wife. Seeking forgiveness was, after all, the Christian thing to do.

During each of Cullen's trials, beginning at Amarillo, a growing number of fawning "groupies" appeared in the courtroom to show support for Cullen, never missing an opportunity to touch or talk to him. Treats ranging from pastries to pickles, from flowers to chef's salads, were regularly bestowed on Cullen and his lawyers. Photographs and autographs were obtained. Groupies pushed, shoved, and bloodied one another in a struggle for choice seats. The judge occasionally had to subdue their cheerleading outbursts and once had to rebuke them for verbal abuse of David McCrory. One groupie distinguished herself by sticking her fingers in her ears anytime there was testimony unfavorable to Cullen. One afternoon when several groupies groped for Cullen, an investigator dryly remarked, "They're sicker than he is." After Cullen's spiritual conversion, the groupie-count swelled considerably when members of his church appeared in the audience. During breaks in the proceedings, Cullen was all smiles as he posed for his daily round of photographs with his Bible-wielding supporters. A *Dallas Morning News* photographer snapped a picture of a groupie snapping a picture of another groupie hugging Cullen. One member of the sect gave Cullen a button saying "I Love Jesus." No W. T. Rufner circus this time; it was becoming a revival.

One evening during the previous criminal trial (the retrial of Cullen for conspiring to kill Judge Eidson), Cullen invited some of his defense team to go out for drinks at a Fort Worth disco restaurant. When they arrived, all tables were taken, but before their first drinks were served at the bar, a number of customers offered Cullen and associates seats at their tables, and two young women dragged Cullen, unresisting, to their table. One man came over and said to Cullen, "I know you're being railroaded, and that's a goddamn shame." He went on to explain that although he realized he was a "nobody," he would be honored to have Cullen in his home. Before the party was over, almost everyone there had come by to offer Cullen drinks, words of support, and invitations. One who witnessed all this groveling later shrugged in disbelief as he related the episode to several friends. He said, "I'm not sure what all that meant, if anything, but I've never seen anything like it. It's a toss up as to who's crazier, Cullen or the weirdos he attracts."

In situations like the Cullen Davis trials, where proof of guilt seems more than just overwhelming, frustrated prosecutors also often scratch their heads and wonder "what it all means." What is it about demented killers or other violent criminals that brings these weirdos out of the cracks in the woodwork and compels them to enlist as courtroom group-ies—or worse, compels them to try to get on jury panels that try these killers? Is it simply because there is a whole forest full of "nobodies" out there who desperately want to become "somebody" even if it entails associating with anybody who is in the public spotlight, regardless of how despicable that person may be—simply to bask in the refracted glory-glow, however dim, fleeting, or tainted it may be?

There may be something more, too. The collective American psyche seems to accommodate a curious dichotomy when it comes to hero-worshipping of both lawmen and outlaws. Americans—most, anyway—applaud the steely-eyed and fearless frontier heroes such as Wyatt Earp and Wild Bill Hickok who confront and conquer nasty vil-lains who threaten the community's peace and order. At the same time, there co-exists, in many at least, an instinctive American spirit of indi-vidualism and dissent as well as a distrust of the possessors of power, which cheers (even if not vocally) the bold, brazen, and charismatic rebel bandit who flouts the establishment and all its constricting rules and who is determined, whatever the cost, to "do it my way"—think Butch Cassidy, the Sundance Kid, Billy the Kid, Jesse James, and even Bonnie and Clyde.

Whatever the root causes of inane groupism may be, for honest though ill-paid law officers and prosecutors who sacrifice and struggle to protect the public and vindicate the rights of crime victims and their families, there is absolutely nothing as frustrating as being obliged to deal with—or even be defeated by—such brainless and unappreciative crackpots. (On the other hand, there is nothing more despicable than corrupt, or even overreaching, lawmen or prosecutors who lie or take shortcuts with the law in order to massage their egos or advance their careers. The foregoing comment, however, is not made to suggest that such was the case in the Cullen Davis trials.)

Finally, once again a jury retired to ponder the question: "Was Cullen Davis the killer in black?" This time it was the $16.5 million question. However, the answer would be more symbolic than real, because in less than two weeks, Cullen Davis would file personal bankruptcy claiming he had debts amounting to $865 million and property valued at $1.8 million. Cullen would eventually settle out of court with the children of Stan Farr for $250,000, although the possibility of their collecting any of that was remote.

Was Cullen the killer in black? Would the inquiry be finally, officially, resolved?

Sadly, the answer to that question would not be forthcoming from this jury. It deadlocked, eight to four in favor of the plaintiffs. The four holdouts were black. Sumner had gambled and won on the belief that minority jurors would support the defense in this kind of civil case. The four jurors apparently formed their belief early on and, apparently, without considering the evidence. They refused to reveal to their fellow jurors how or why they formed their opinions, or even discuss the evidence, and they resisted any effort to resolve the impasse. The resulting mistrial was a victory for the defendant.

Cullen was, as ever, magnanimous in victory. "I give credit to the Lord Jesus Christ for the outcome."

Priscilla: "I will go to my grave knowing that Cullen Davis killed my child."

One of the plaintiff lawyers, Hal Monk, his face flushed and his voice trembling with anger, said what many felt but were reluctant to put into words. He said: "Four of the jurors either lied when they took the oath that they would follow the court's instructions, or they were too stupid to follow the court's instructions."

Or, was it perhaps . . . money?

Jury foreman Kenneth Pool fled the courtroom in tears. He finally regained his composure and returned with an unbelievable account of what went on in the jury chambers. In a note to the judge he accused the four holdouts of jury misconduct. He explained: "Not once but twice they ignored Judge William's instructions and likewise spurned all efforts to break the deadlock. . . . They would not explain how they arrived at their opinions. . . . They went in with closed minds. They wanted Cullen innocent."

But the evidence convinced jury foreman Pool of Cullen's guilt. "There is no doubt in my mind that he shot those people. It tears me apart. It really tears me apart."

"Cullen," he cried, "got by with murder."[23]

Epilogue

The civil case would never be retried.

Priscilla Davis died of breast cancer on February 19, 2001, in Dallas, Texas, at age 59.[24]

The sad saga of Floyd Holmes's oil fortune seems finally to have ended in a Dallas bankruptcy court. The fortune may be gone, but is the curse?

Cullen is still out there.

Epilogue II

The Floyd Holmes's oil fortune is gone, and maybe the curse that followed it died. Priscilla died. But the Cullen Davis story simply refuses to die.

Mike Cochran, who covered the Cullen Davis trials and then wrote the authoritative book on the subject, thought he had heard and seen just about everything during his forty years plus as a reporter for the *Associated Press* and the *Fort Worth Star-Telegram*. But one day, some twenty-four years after the mansion massacre, he got a phone call that stunned even this veteran newshound. It came out of the blue from Ray Hudson, father of Karen Davis, Cullen's alibi-testifying wife. It will be recalled that Ray Hudson played an important behind-the-scenes role for the defense team during Cullen's 1977 murder trial in Amarillo. He later refused to join the defense team during Cullen's conspiracy-to-murder trial in Houston, broadly hinting that what he had done on Cullen's behalf in Amarillo, if disclosed, would likely cost him some prison time. However, regardless of whatever kind of skullduggery he had committed in Amarillo twenty-four years ago, Hudson was now immune from prosecution by virtue of the statute of limitations.

By the year 2000, Hudson might have been safely beyond the clutches of the legal system, but he was now worried about punishment from a higher authority. "I want to get right with God," Hudson blurted out to the astonished Mike Cochran. Confession of his wrongs, he believed, was a fundamental step in seeking spiritual forgiveness. "I have to get it off my chest for my sake . . . It's making me uncomfortable . . . wondering about that little girl [and] what part I had to do with helping someone get off that blew her away."[25]

What had he done? According to Hudson, he had been the bagman who paid off certain people for favors and information during the trial. For instance, he had paid a talented artist $300 per sketch to draw flattering pictures of members of the jury, which were slipped surreptitiously to them during the trial—courtesy of Cullen Davis. He had gleaned valuable information from a waitress who worked at the hotel where jury members were sequestered, and he had also shared cocktails and obtained valuable inside information on jury conversations from Wylie Alexander, the court bailiff who was in charge of attending to the needs of the jury during the trial. (Whether he actually paid the cocktail waitress and the bailiff, he didn't reveal.) In any event, prying jury secrets out of a court official and passing them to a defendant in a criminal trial was a serious case of corruption of justice. But that was small potatoes compared to Hudson's next revelation: he said that he had bribed the chief investigator for the prosecution's team—paid him $25,000 during the five-month trial to supply daily intelligence bulletins on the State's plans and strategies. The investigator, Morris Howeth, a former chief investigator under District Attorney Tim Curry, sat in on nightly strategy sessions with prosecutors, and then, according to Hudson, contacted him and revealed what the State planned to do in court the next day.

When reporter Cochran followed up on the allegations, Racehorse Haynes and the other defense lawyers denied it. The accused investigator, Morris Howeth, also denied it, although he declined an offer to submit to a polygraph test.

But in another unbelievable twist in a case already overloaded with unbelievable twists, Cullen Davis, when told of Hudson's account, confirmed it. "Well," Cullen allowed, "the cat's out of the bag now." He said that Hudson made the payments to Howeth and submitted them to him as a part of his (Hudson's) expenses. Asked if he believed such payments might be unscrupulous, Davis shrugged it off: "I didn't give that any thought."

And what about his lawyers?

"I don't recall that they ever objected," Davis said.

Later, when *Star-Telegram* columnist Dave Lieber interviewed Cullen in June 2002 as a follow-up to Cochran's story, Cullen Davis again confirmed Hudson's story. "It happened," Cullen smiled. "My attitude is, it's just one of those things that happened. Here I was charged with stuff I didn't do, and I'm going to get help from anybody who will give it. Wouldn't you?"

Stay tuned—for Lord only knows what next.[26]

Afterthoughts

SOME REFLECTIONS ON FRONTIER
LAW, WRITTEN AND UNWRITTEN

Waning of the Unwritten Law

aken together, our stories tell of the waning of the unwritten law and of the waxing of the statutory law as the nineteenth century turned into the twentieth century and the frontier culture of the American South and West matured. For instance, in the first story, Colonel John Hallum escaped conviction in an 1897 attempted murder trial that seemed to be a slam-dunk for the prosecution by boldly ordering the jury to ignore all those "puny mandates" of the Texas Legislature and free him by obeying a "higher authority": the unwritten law.

As the years passed, defense attorneys in murder cases became more circumspect when they relied on the unwritten law to free their clients. In court, they euphemistically referred to it by such code phrases as "protecting the home" or "defending his sacred honor." And, during the same trial, however preposterous it might have sounded, the defense attorney labored mightily to torture the facts of the case to fit some statutory mold such as self-defense or temporary insanity, all in an effort to provide the jury with a legal peg upon which to hang the emotionally desired "not guilty" verdict. In the last story, a 1977 murder trial, there were definite echoes of the unwritten law, though it was more of an underlying factor in the defense strategy and not referred to even by a euphemism. Also interesting was how, in two of the stories, clever defense attorneys adroitly employed the strong arm of the unwritten law to free female killers.

The unwritten law did have certain advantages over written law. The written law confined lawyers and courts to a letter-of-the-law straitjacket, while the amorphous contours of the unwritten law permitted popular justice to be tailored to fit each factual situation as it arose. Then too, the unwritten law was more flexible in another sense: it could change and evolve with the times without having to resort to the cumbrous, time consuming, and often unsatisfactory process of legislative reform. Those then were the advantages of the unwritten law in a frontier society; the disadvantages and their yawning potential for miscarriages of justice need not be reiterated. Let us then explore the evolution of the unwritten law by assuming several different hypothetical scenarios.

Jury arguments have concluded in a murder trial, and the case has just gone to the jury. Testimony revealed the following: The defendant had discovered that his wife had been having an affair with their pastor. The defendant armed himself and patiently waited for several days until the unsuspecting preacher came within his gunsights. Then, without warning, he shot and killed the parson. The victim was unarmed. Several credible eyewitnesses described the ambush to the jury.

Another murder trial. These are the facts presented to the jury: A young, unmarried woman had consensual sex with a married man and became pregnant. The man promised to divorce his wife and marry her; but after the baby was born, he reneged on his promise. Several days later, the spurned mistress caught the man unarmed and shot him in the back as he ran away from her. He died. She immediately called the sheriff to the scene and admitted that she killed her lover.

Yet a third murder trial. The murder victim suspected that the defendant was having an affair with his wife, and he made several threats that he intended to kill the defendant. These threats were communicated to the defendant. Instead of relating the threats to law enforcement or going to court and obtaining a restraining order, the defendant decided to take the law into his own hands and launch a preemptive strike against the victim. He did so, catching the unarmed victim unaware as he walked down a city street, his head down and his hands in his pockets. Two bystanders told the jury what happened.

In none of these three murder trials was there a viable statutory justification for the homicides. What would be the likely jury verdict in each of these three cases? In trying to predict the result, first assume that the trials were held in Texas or any of the southern states before an all-male jury in 1895.

Would the result likely have been the same had the trials been held in New York or a New England state?

Would the result likely have been the same in any of these different venues had the trial been held in 1915? Or even in 1925 after the significant change in American culture following World War I?

What if the trials had been held in 1975 or 2000? (Note, by this later date, juries would have been composed of men *and* women.)

Obviously, "the unwritten laws" we have explored would have been asserted by defense attorneys—at least in the western and southern states—even if they didn't call them by name. Even in the last half of the twentieth century, the honor defense, though weakened, was still a significant factor in the decisions of juries—at least in Texas and the South.

Waxing of the Written Law

The stories told in this book document how the unwritten law readily excused violent self-help redressment of individual wrongs, real or perceived, even when a killing resulted. If and when the survivor was subsequently hauled into court to answer for the bloody deed, he—or she—more often than not literally got away with murder. The unwritten law has gone far beyond the realm of statutory law in justifying homicides. True though that is, the written laws of the frontier themselves were astonishingly lenient in favor of violent offenders when compared, not only to criminal laws of modern America, but also to the common law of England as it existed even before the frontier west. An extensive discussion of the violence sanctioned by those frontier criminal statutes is beyond the scope of this discussion. However, a few of those defendant-friendly statutes may be cited by way of example.

We have already explored the 1856 Texas statute that was part of the Texas Penal Code until repealed in 1973, which extended generous shooting privileges to an aggrieved husband who caught his wife's lover in his gun sight, and the companion statute that only mildly condemned any male family member who dispatched somebody who had been ill-mannered enough to direct "insulting words or conduct" in the direction of "a female relative."

Another example: under the English common law of self-defense, a person attacked, even if threatened by imminent death or serious bodily injury, was required to retreat as far as safety would permit before responding with a lethal counter-attack. It was commonly referred to as the duty to retreat "until your back is against the wall" doctrine of self-defense. But under early Texas law, there was no statutory duty to retreat when so attacked. The Texas rule was known as the "no duty to retreat" or the "stand your ground" doctrine of self-defense—a philosophy much more congenial to a frontier Westerner's way of thinking.[1]

Under the English common law, the preservation of human life was deemed more important than the protection of one's property. Consequently, under the English common law, one was never justified in killing another merely in defense of property—not so in Texas. Killing in defense of property was justified in a number of different contexts, such as preventing robbery, arson, burglary and theft at night.[2] In the latter case, the privilege of blowing away a nocturnal thief continued even if the culprit had abandoned the purloined property—but only if he was still within gunshot range. In 1891, a fellow named Whitten was given a pass for shooting a horse thief even after the fellow had thrown down the reins and run for his life. The court explained the law this way:

> It makes no difference whether the party has abandoned the property and is fleeing from the place of the theft; if he be shot while he is still within reach of gunshot, the homicide is justifiable.[3]

In 1885, Mr. Lilly shot a neighbor during a squabble over who owned several pigs. The appellate court explained that the homicide was justified since Lilly had resorted to all other reasonable means to prevent the theft of the pigs that he contended he owned.[4]

By its liberal policy with respect to excuses for taking human life, and the aid and comfort extended to those who were quick to resort to violence, the 1856 penal code demonstrated how cheap human life was regarded. There were, however, some practical reasons that caused the 1856 Texas Legislature to enact criminal statutes that tolerated plenty of self-help justice, including a lenient justifiable homicide policy. In the first place, 1856 Texas was still sparsely populated, the western half hardly at all except for a few roving bands of Indians. Even as late as the 1890s, many of those who migrated to Texas were criminals who came to Texas because lawmen were few and far between, and a goodly portion of those who did wear badges were themselves thinly disguised outlaws. Local authorities, even when conscientious, were poorly equipped to cope with such a large and bold lawless element.[5] Courts, even when they were established, were usually a long horseback ride away, and the judicial system was rudimentary and often ineffective.[6]

It was also a time when hardscrabble settlers who struggled to keep food on their tables considered livestock thefts to be the most serious criminal offense, taking precedence in the public mind over murder. Hence, when there arose a dispute over a man's pigs or a dispute over the boundary of his land, taking the matter to a distant civil court for resolution was not often a realistic option. The frontier legislature therefore permitted self-help justice at a time when lawmen, courts, and lawyers were frequently unavailable, or if available, were either corrupt or ineffective.

While the 1856 penal code may have been tailored to suit the needs of a raw frontier, it far outlived its time. By mid-twentieth century, Texas legal scholars began to complain that the legally sanctioned killing of another human being should be regarded as justifiable only when human life was at stake and then only as a last resort.[7] In a 1959 law review article, Professor William M. Ravkind noted that much of the 1856 penal code, including the provisions addressing justifiable homicide, was still in effect even though a century had passed and the frontier had disappeared. He concluded his article as follows:

A study of jurisprudence will show that the law governing society
tends to keep in step with the development of the society itself. . . . The
provisions of the [1856] penal code concerning justifiable homicide . . .
do not reflect the tempo of our modern-day society, but rather are
representative of the code of the "old west." . . . The legislature [should]
reconsider the laws which shelter the violent elements of our society
and which were outdated several decades ago.[8]

Professor Ravkind's observations raise a most interesting point
about the relationship between society and the law. When the Texas
Legislature enacted the penal code of 1856, that law was well ahead of
a society which still approved of self-help violence under the unwritten law as well as lynch mob justice. However, as Ravkind noted, by
1959 society was well ahead of the 1856 penal code, which was still in
effect and would remain in effect until repealed in 1973. The law had
remained static while society had advanced, and somewhere between
1856 and 1959, society had overtaken and forged ahead of the law.

The "Pedestalization" of
Women in Frontier Courts

In recent years, some Texas women historians have made an interesting point comparing the role and status of women in the Old South's
elitist antebellum society with that of women on the Texas frontier
both before and after the Civil War. Despite harsh frontier conditions,
Anglo-Texan males, they argue, nevertheless still clung to Southern
idealizations of women gleaned from provincial history, literature, and
folklore. In this connection, they have pointed out that Texas lawmakers were more realistic and took a more pragmatic approach at least
in some civil domestic relations matters involving issues such as common law marriages, bigamy, illicit cohabitation, bastardy, as well as
endorsing more lenient defenses in divorce actions. Also, until well
after the Civil War, Texas lawmakers accommodated the sexual needs
of frontier males in a situation where women were in short supply:
no law was passed criminalizing prostitution. These historians go on
to challenge as unrealistic the "proverbial pedestalization" of frontier
Texas women portraying them as "submissive, domestic, pious, refined,

and in need of masculine protection," concluding that the birthplace of the unrealistically idealized image of Anglo-Texas frontier women was "in the mind of Anglo-Texas men."[9] Or, as another commentator put it, "woman's virtue is man's greatest invention."[10]

These points are well taken. There can be no doubt but that the typical woman who endured and survived the hardships, the dangers, and the primitive living conditions on the Texas frontier was a far different creature than the dainty, refined, and dependent Southern belles of antebellum times,[11] or that Texas statutes of that era did, in some areas, take into account the surrounding circumstances of that very different society.

However, this book and the stories recounted focus on the unwritten laws and the honor defense in criminal cases—murder cases primarily—where illicit sexual conduct triggered the violence. While it may well be true that the birthplace of Southern idealizations of women—including pioneer Texas women—"was in the minds of Anglo-Texas males," two facts must be borne in mind. First, until well past the mid-twentieth-century mark, the juries who tried all Texas court cases were composed entirely of those Anglo-Texas males; and second, a vast majority of those males were schooled from childhood in the Old South traditions of the pedestalization of women, Victorian sexual taboos, and the propriety and necessity of violent self-redressment of any insult to a man's honor. Consequently, even if the premises upon which the unwritten laws (including the honor defense) were constructed proved to be the unrealistic idealization of women, the unwritten laws were nevertheless very real during that era in the minds of Southern males as well as those living in Texas and the western states and played an important role in murder trials involving illicit sexual conduct or involving insults, real or perceived, to a man's honor.

Parting Shots

Even in this more enlightened day, juries do not always render verdicts in accordance with existing written laws. Causes vary—racial prejudice immediately comes to mind. Prominent examples are the O. J. Simpson and Rodney King cases in California. But there were other causes. Another California jury refused to convict a man for theft involving a relatively small amount of property even though evidence of his guilt was overwhelming. Reason: under California's "Three Strikes and You're Out Law," a conviction would have resulted in an automatic life sentence for a petty thief, since the defendant had two prior criminal convictions.

Two fairly recent Dallas cases also provide intriguing topics for criminal justice ruminations. Until the early 1990s, Dallas police and prosecutors considered sports betting and bookmaking charges to be automatic convictions. But then states, including Texas, created lotteries—in effect creating their own gambling monopolies—and high-stakes poker games became popular on television and the Internet. Suddenly, juries began to balk at convicting local gambling offenses.

Another Dallas case was heard by a six-person jury since it involved a misdemeanor criminal offense, to-wit: lewd dancing. A topless dancer was the defendant. The evidence was clear, undisputed, and very inculpatory: the defendant had indeed cavorted a lot closer and more suggestively to patrons of the topless club than the law allowed. The jury retired to consider its verdict, and the first vote was five to one in favor of a guilty verdict, the lone dissenter being a white, middle-aged man. He railed against police and prosecutors for wasting a lot of time and taxpayer money prosecuting "victimless crimes." Ultimately, this made sense to the other five jurors: "not guilty."[12]

While the O. J. Simpson and the Rodney King verdicts may be dismissed in an overview of judicial history as inevitable misfires that are bound to occur in even the best of criminal justice systems operated by human beings, the jury verdicts in the "Three Strikes" California case as well as in the two Dallas cases cited are not as easily explained or dismissed. In both the King and Simpson cases, it appears that racial prejudice was the key to the "not guilty" verdicts, but it doesn't appear that either jury rejected the underlying criminal statute (murder) in reaching its decision. In the other three "not guilty" verdicts, however, this was not the case; the juries clearly rejected and intentionally refused to honor the applicable criminal statutes.

Tom Charron, director of the National District Attorneys Advocacy Center, a training school for prosecutors, commented: "Today's jurors are not used to being told what to do. They take their personal beliefs into the jury room." (What a familiar ring that comment has. Could any

1895 advocate of "the unwritten law" have put it any better?) Charron concluded: "The rest of us need to learn to adapt to this new world."[13]

Are we coming full circle to the point where we were in the heyday of the unwritten law? In other words, if the written law doesn't suit, can we then feel free to ignore it and make up our own law? And, while we're at it, are we then free to disregard the oath to render verdicts in accordance with the law and to obey the court's instructions?

In the stories told herein, juries often ignored existing criminal statutes in favor of self-addressment of individual wrongs under the unwritten law. Even though the written laws of the frontier were lenient when it came to sanctions against assault and justifiable homicide, they paled considerably when compared to the self-help violence condoned by the Old South's Code of Honor or the frontier's "Code of the West." Likewise, lynching was condoned when a community's sense of morality was outraged, whether triggered by racial intolerance or otherwise. In the 1890s, a number of grisly mob-led lynchings in Texas fueled loud protests from enlightened citizens, groups, and even from some leading Texas daily newspapers. The Texas Legislature finally responded in 1897 by enacting some anti-lynching legislation. (This is in addition to the murder statutes already on the books.) Yet no convictions resulted under the new law. Legislators in far-off Austin might have dared to risk voting for anti-lynching laws, but local sheriffs, prosecutors, and judges knew better. They were not about to commit political suicide by arresting or prosecuting constituents when a lynching took place in their own backyards, because they were well aware that overwhelming popular sentiment supported that brand of swift, direct, and unappealable "justice."[14]

It was obvious that during this era the statutory criminal law was ahead of society and struggling to drag it forward. However, it would take decades for the slow march of civilization to produce the sea change in communal values necessary for society to catch up with the law.

All that having been said, let's take another look at the "not guilty" verdicts rendered by juries in the California "Three Strikes" case and the two recent Dallas cases. Do they present yet another question for legal and social historians to consider? Unlike the unwritten law and the lynching cases, wherein statutory law was ahead of society, do these cases indicate that society is once again ahead of our criminal law, dragging it forward in society's wake?

A last thought for scholars of different disciplines who may wish to probe the legal dynamics of social change: we know that changes in the mores of a society lead, at least eventually, to changes in its criminal laws; but do changes in criminal laws sometimes lead not only to changes in the conduct of individuals, but also to changes in the mores of that society? And, if so, to what extent? For instance, even though the Texas anti-lynching statute of 1897 did not produce any immediate results, did it nevertheless play a part in advancing our society's maturity?

Nobody can seriously contend that a study of any criminal justice system, here or elsewhere, can accurately be described as an exact science. Nor can either culture or the law be considered static. The legal process is very much a part of the history of any state, and the context of time and place plays a critical role.[15] Finally, as we have witnessed by the stories told, there is nothing quite like a crime of passion played out during the courtroom drama of a sensational murder trial to illuminate the social history and the contemporary mores of any given culture. Such cases teach us much about the complex relationship between law and society.

NOTES

Foreword

1. Robert M. Ireland, "Insanity and the Unwritten Law," *American Journal of Legal History* 32 (April 1988): 157–72. Ireland, "The Libertine Must Die: Sexual Dishonor and the Unwritten Law in the Nineteenth-Century United States," *Journal of Social History* 23 (Fall 1989): 27–44.

2. Robert M. Ireland, "Frenzied and Fallen Females: Women and Sexual Dishonor in the Nineteenth-Century United States," *Journal of Women's History* 3 (Winter 1992): 95–117.

3. Ibid., 99.

4. Ibid.

5. Ibid.

6. Ibid., 101–105. Also, see Louise Lander, *Images of Bleeding: Menstruation as Ideology* (New York: Orlando Press, 1988). Lander surveys three centuries of male ideologies and attempts to dismantle those traditional male concepts and to replace them with female-centered understandings. The objective was to make menstruation a "nonissue." Ibid., 187. On more general issues, see Harlow M. Huckabee, *Lawyers, Psychiatrists and Criminal Law* (Springfield, IL: Charles C. Thomas Publisher, 1980). Also see Pauline M. Prior, "Murder and Madness: Gender and the Insanity Defense in Nineteenth-Century Ireland," *New Hibernia Review* 9 (Winter 2005): 19–36.

7. Richard Glyn Jones, ed., *The Mammoth Book of Women Who Kill* (New York: Carroll & Graff Publishers, 2002). This volume contains a short bibliography and short tales of women who commit murder.

8. Stephen Robertson, "Seduction, Sexual Violence, and Marriage in New York City, 1886–1955," *Law and History Review* 24, no. 2 (Summer 2006):

331–73. Also see Eric H. Monkkonen, *Murder in New York City* (Berkeley: University of California Press, 2001).

9. Jeffrey S. Adler, *First in Violence, Deepest in Dirt: Homicide in Chicago, 1875–1920* (Cambridge: Harvard University Press, 2006): 109–19.

10. Ibid., 112.

11. Christopher Waldrep, "Law and Society: Structuring Legal Revolutions, 1870–1920," *Journal of the Gilded Age and Progressive Era* 5, no. 4 (October 2006): 319, 320.

12. Clare V. McKanna, Jr., *Homicide, Race, and Justice in the American West, 1880–1920* (Tucson: University of Arizona Press, 2001).

13. McKanna, *The Trial of Indian Joe: Race and Justice in the Nineteenth-Century West* (Lincoln: University of Nebraska Press, 2003). McKanna, *Race and Homicide in Nineteenth-Century California* (Reno: University of Nevada Press, 2002). McKanna, *Apache Murder Trials in the Nineteenth Century* (Lubbock: Texas Tech University Press, 2005). Also, see Lynwood Carranco and Estle Beard, *Genocide and Vendetta: The Round Valley Wars of Northern California* (Norman: University of Oklahoma Press, 1981).

14. Kevin J. Mullen, *Dangerous Strangers: Minority Newcomers and Criminal Violence in the Urban West, 1850–2000* (New York: Palgrave Macmillan, 2005).

15. Edward J. Escobar, *Race, Police, and the Making of a Political Identity: Mexican Americans and the Los Angeles Police Department, 1900–1945* (Berkeley: University of California Press, 1999). Eduardo Obregon Pagan, *Murder at the Sleepy Lagoon: Zoot Suits, Race, & Riot in Wartime L.A.* (Chapel Hill: University of North Carolina Press, 2003).

16. Adler, *First in Violence*, 112.

17. Lawrence M. Friedman and Robert V. Percival, *The Roots of Justice: Crime and Punishment in Alameda County, California, 1870–1910* (Chapel Hill: University of North Carolina Press, 1981).

18. Ibid., 183.

19. Ibid., 265.

20. Gordon Morris Bakken, *Practicing Law in Frontier California* (Lincoln: University of Nebraska Press, 1991): 99–137.

Introduction

1. Article 1220, *Texas Penal Code* (1925). This statute appears to first have been enacted in 1856 as Art. 562 and brought forward in succeeding Texas Penal Codes as Art. 567 (1879 Code), Art. 672 (1895 Code), Art. 1102 (1911 Code), and then Art. 1220 in the 1925 Code. This Texas statute had ancient roots. According to the recognized authority on early English law, William

Blackstone, the killing on the spot by a husband of a man discovered in the act of adultery with his wife was allowed by the laws of Solon, as likewise by the Roman civil law (if the adulterer was found in the husband's own house), and also among the ancient Goths. William Blackstone, *Commentaries on the Laws of England*, 4 vols. (London: 1765–69): vol. 4, 181. See also William M. Ravkind, "Justifiable Homicide in Texas," *Southwestern Law Journal* 13, no. 2 (1959): 509–511. Also, Mark M. Carroll, "Families, Sex and the Law in Frontier Texas" (doctoral dissertation, Houston, Texas: University of Houston, 1996): 401–402.

2. *Price v. State*, 18 Tex.App. 474 (1885). See also *Tarrant v. State*, 25 S.W. 2d 836 (Tex.Ct.Crim.App. 1930); *Williams v. State*, 165 S.W. 583 (Tex. Ct.Crim.App. 1914); *Oliver v. State*, 159 S.W. 235 (Tex.Ct.Crim.App. 1913); *Gregory v. State*, 94 S.W. 1041 (Tex.Ct.Crim.App. 1906).

3. *Burger v. State*, 231 S.E. 2d 769 (Ga.Sup.Ct. 1977).

4. *Reed v. State*, 59 S.W. 2d 122 (Tex.Ct.Crim.App. 1933). Also see C. S. Potts, "Is the Husband's Act in Killing Wife Taken in Act of Adultery Justifiable Homicide in Texas?" *Texas Law Review* 2, no. 1 (1923): 111.

5. *Sensobaugh v. State*, 244 S.W. 379 (Tex.Ct.Crim.App. 1922). Also see Paul Kens, "Don't Mess Around in Texas: Adultery and Justifiable Homicide in the Lone Star State," *Law in the Western United States*, edited by Gordon Morris Bakken (Norman: University of Oklahoma Press, 2000): 114–17.

6. Art. 597, *Texas Penal Code* (1925).

7. *R. v. Brown*, 24 Q.B. 357d (1890).

8. Lawrence Friedman, *Crime and Punishment in American History* (New York: Basic Books, 1993): 34.

9. Carolyn A. Conley, *The Unwritten Law: Criminal Justice in Victorian Kent* (New York: Oxford University Press, 1991): 187.

10. Jeffrey Miller, *Ardor in the Court! Sex and the Law* (Toronto: ECW Press, 2002): xiii, 2.

11. William Blackstone, *Commentaries on the Laws of England*, facsimile of first edition of 1765–1769 (Chicago: University of Chicago, 1979): 191–92.

12. *Maddy's Case*, 2 Keb 829, 1 Vent. 158 (1671); *sub nom* Manning, T. Ryan, 212.

13. Sec. 35–315, *N.M. Stat. Ann.* (Courtright, 1929); William Stumberg, "Defense of Person and Property under the Texas Criminal Law," *Texas Law Review* 21, no. 1 (November 1942): 17. Also see Miller, *Ardor in the Court!* 59–60.

14. *O'Shields v. State*, 125 Ga. 310, 54 S.E. 120 (1906); *Campbell v. State*, 49 S.E. 2d 867 (Ga.Sup.Ct. 1948).

15. Carroll, "Families, Sex and the Law in Frontier Texas," 443.

16. A good place to start research on the issue of justice and the unwritten law is Alison Dendes Renteln and Alen Dundes, eds., *Folk Law: Essays in the Theory and Practice of Lex Non Scripta*, 2 vols. (Madison: University of Wisconsin Press, 1994).

17. Philip Barton Key was the son of Francis Scott Key, composer of "The Star Spangled Banner."

18. John D. Lawson, "Trial of Daniel E. Sickles for the Murder of Philip Barton Key," *American State Trials*, 17 vols., edited by John D. Lawson (St. Louis: 1914–1936): vol. 12, 530–32; and *Washington Evening Star*, March 5, 1859.

19. Robert M. Ireland, "The Libertine Must Die: Sexual Dishonor and the Unwritten Law in the Nineteenth-Century United States," *Journal of Social History* 23 (Fall, 1989): 27–44. Hendrick Hartog, "Lawyering, Husband's Rights and 'the Unwritten Law' in Nineteenth-Century America," *Journal of American History* 84, no. 1 (June 1997): 67–96.

20. Ibid.

21. Gordon Morris Bakken, "The Limits of Patriarchy: The 'Unwritten Law' in California," *California History: A Topical Approach*, edited by Gordon Morris Bakken (Wheeling, Ill.: Harlan Davidson, Inc., 2003); Gordon Morris Bakken, *Practicing Law in Frontier California, 1870–1910* (Chapel Hill: The University of North Carolina Press, 1981).

22. Charles Sydnor, "The Southerner and the Laws," *Journal of Southern History* 6 (1940): 7–8; Robert Dykstra, *The Cattle Towns* (New York: Knopf, 1968): 112–48; Dickson Bruce, *Violence and Culture in the Antebellum South* (Austin: University of Texas Press, 1979): 242.

23. See chapter one of this book: "John Hallum Tried for Shooting a Preacher."

24. Edward L. Ayers, *Vengeance & Justice: Crime and Punishment in the 19th-Century American South* (New York: Oxford University Press, 1984): 266–67.

25. Ibid.

26. Thomas J. Kernan, "The Jurisprudence of Lawlessness," *American Bar Association Report*, (1906): 451–53.

27. Michael P. Rogin, *Fathers and Children: Andrew Jackson and the Subjugation of the American Indian* (1975 reprint, New York: Vintage Books, 1976): 58.

28. Clare V. McKanna, Jr., *Homicide, Race, and Justice in the American West, 1880–1920* (Tucson: University of Arizona Press, 1997): 66–67; John Shelton Reed, "Below the Smith and Wesson Line: Reflections on Southern Violence," *Perspectives on the American South*, edited by Merle Black and John Shelton Reed (New York: Gordon and Breach Science Publishers, 1981): Vol. 1, 12.

29. Kernan, "The Jurisprudence of Lawlessness," 451–53.

30. Scholars commenting on the Code of the South and the honor defense have often overlooked the fact that women have also invoked the unwritten law to good effect. For example, see Michael Grossberg, *A Judgment for Solomon: The D'Hauteville Case and Legal Experience in Antebellum America* (New York: Cambridge University Press, 1996); Richard Wightman Fox, *Trials of Intimacy: Love and Loss in the Beecher-Tilton Scandal* (Chicago: University of Chicago Press, 1999). Also see Richard F. Hamm, *Murder, Honor, and Law: Four Virginia Homicides from Reconstruction to the Great Depression* (Charlottesville: University of Virginia Press, 2003): 216; Richard Glyn Jones, ed., *The Mammoth Book of Women Who Kill* (New York: Carroll & Graff, Publishers, 2002).

31. Bakken, "The Limits of Patriarchy," 99–102.

32. *Omaha World-Herald*, October 27, 1893; McKanna, *Homicide, Race, and Justice in the American West, 1880–1920*, 59–60.

33. Kenneth Lamott, *Who Killed Mr. Crittenden? Being a True Account of the Notorious Murder Trial That Stunned San Francisco—The Laura D. Fair Case* (New York: David McKay Company, 1963). Laura Fair's lawyers were successful in persuading the jury to find her "not guilty by reason of temporary partial moral insanity." Also see Robert M. Ireland, "Insanity and the Unwritten Law," *American Journal of Legal History* 32 (April 1988): 157–72; and Pauline M. Prior, "Murder and Madness: Gender and the Insanity Defense in Nineteenth-Century Ireland," *New Hibernia Review* 9 (Winter 2005): 19–36. In another—a much later—sensational California trial, beautiful dark-haired Nellie May Madison was not as fortunate as Laura D. Fair. On the night of March 24, 1934, in their Burbank apartment, the unconventional and enigmatic Nellie shot her abusive husband five times. The resulting murder trial brought to life a remarkable character whose plight reflected the status of women, the workings of the media and the judicial system, and the stratification of 1930s society. Her case foreshadowed the use of the battered woman defense in murder cases, but she was ahead of her time. The jury found her guilty, and she was sentenced to be hanged—the first woman to be sentenced to death in California. However, sixteen days before the hanging was to take place, the governor reduced her sentence to life imprisonment. After an extended campaign, Nellie and her supporters succeeded in having the life sentence commuted, and then finally on March 28, 1943, she was pardoned. In addition to being a fascinating true-crime story, the account also serves as a gender history: Kathleen A. Cairns, *The Enigma Woman: The Death Sentence of Nellie May Madison* (Lincoln: University of Nebraska Press, 2007).

Chapter 1

1. *Dallas Morning News*, July 30, 1896.

2. Biographical information appearing in the text and this endnote taken primarily from William Herschel Hughes, "John Hallum, Lawyer and Historian," *Arkansas Historical Quarterly* 10, no. 3 (Fayetteville: Arkansas Historical Association, Autumn 1951): 258–267. John Hallum was descended from William Hallum, who came from England about 1760 and settled at Hagerstown, Maryland. During the American Revolution he moved to South Carolina, where he became a wealthy planter and slave owner. His sons, William and Henry, emigrated to Tennessee in 1790 and located near Carthage. Bluford, a son of Henry, married Minerva Davis and settled at Ca Ira (Cairo), Sumner County, where John Hallum was born in January 1833. See also Jay Guy Cisco, *Historic Sumner County, Tennessee*, 1909; taken from http://freepages. genealogy.rootsweb.com/we3sumneritesjblcsf/halluj.htm. Accessed 3/26/08. See also *Arkansas Gazette Magazine*, November 6, 1932; and *Arkansas Gazette*, March 22, 1964.

3. Hughes, "John Hallum, Lawyer and Historian," *Arkansas Historical Quarterly*, 260. ·

4. Ibid.

5. The facts leading up to the shooting of Reverend W. A. Forbes by Colonel John W. Hallum, and incidents occurring during the trial of Colonel Hallum, as well as the entire jury argument made by Hallum, are taken from a forty-six-page pamphlet written by Hallum and entitled: *Col. John Hallum, Address to the Jury by Col. John Hallum in Self Defense in the Case of the State of Texas Against Him: An Indictment for Shooting a Minister of the Gospel, Together with the Extraordinary Facts and Remarkable Incidents Connected with the Trial and Prosecution* (Muskogee, Okla.: The Phoenix Press, 1911). Except as otherwise noted, all background facts, trial incidents, jury arguments, and quotes from Colonel Hallum are taken from this pamphlet. The only known copy of this rare 1911 edition may be found in the Jamail Center for Legal Research, Tarlton Law Library, University of Texas Law School in Austin, Texas.

6. *Daily Texarkanian*, July 29, 1896; *Dallas Morning News*, July 30, 1896.

7. *Dallas Morning News*, March 12, 1897.

8. *State of Texas v. John Hallum*, Cause No. 1113, Bowie County, Texas District Court; *Daily Texarkanian*, October 8, 1896, and March 11, 1897; *Dallas Morning News*, March 12, 1897.

9. Michael Widener and Allegra Young, "Frontier Justice: An Indictment for Shooting a Minister of the Gospel," *University of Texas Law Magazine*, Spring 2003: 64.

10. Except as otherwise noted, incidents involved in the shooting and the trial as well as jury argument quotations are taken from Colonel Hallum's pamphlet.

11. Col. Hallum's pamphlet.

12. Christopher Waldrep, "Law and Society: Structuring Legal Revolutions, 1870–1920," *Journal of the Gilded Age and Progressive Era* 5, no. 4 (October 2006): 319–20.

13. Widener, "Frontier Justice: An Indictment for Shooting a Minister of the Gospel," 64.

14. Ibid; also see Robert M. Ireland, "The Libertine Must Die: Sexual Dishonor and the Unwritten Law in the Nineteenth-Century United States," *Journal of Social History* 23 (Fall 1989).

15. John Hallum, *The Diary of an Old Lawyer: Scenes Behind the Curtain* (Nashville: Southwestern Publishing House, 1895).

16. Ibid., 86.

17. Ibid., 20.

18. Ibid., xx, 27–28.

19. Ibid., 42–43.

20. Ibid., xx.

21. Ibid., 38–42.

22. Ibid., 87.

23. Ibid., 26.

24. Ibid., 27–28.

25. The ideal of feminine delicacy was not accorded to women involved in saloon brawls, or, for that matter, even for ordinary working-class women. Thus the cloak of "knight-in-shining-armor" protection was reserved only for "higher class ladies." The Southern code of honor ethos was imported from the English Victorian notions of male/male relationships. Carolyn A. Conley, writing of the justice system in Kent County, England (circa 1859–1880), in *The Unwritten Law: Criminal Justice in Victorian Kent* (New York: Oxford University Press, 1991): 71, observed: "Chivalry and fair play demanded that the weaker sex be protected from the stronger, but the same logic implied that women were inherently inferior and must be dealt with accordingly. In order to merit protection, a woman had to be obedient, submissive, and incapable of defending herself. Chivalry was reserved for those women who both needed and deserved protection—a relatively select group." However, compare that with Professor Robert T. Pace's observations on the concept of honor in the Old South in *Halls of Honor: College Men in the Old South* (Baton Rouge: Louisiana State University Press, 2004): 4–5: "Southern honor consisted of a set of rules that advanced the *appearance* of duty, pride, power, and self-esteem; and

conformity to these rules was required if an individual were to be considered an honorable member of society. Nor were these rules confined to a particular class or social group; honor was an intricate part of the entire southern society." A definition of Southern honor is found in Bertram Wyatt-Brown's *Southern Honor: Ethics and Behavior in the Old South* (New York: Oxford University Press, 1982): xv. See also Joan E. Cashin, *A Family Venture: Men and Women on the Southern Frontier* (New York: Oxford University Press, 1991): 99, 102, 105; Necah S. Furman, "Texas Woman Versus the Texas Myth," *The Texas Heritage,* edited by Archie P. McDonald and Ben Procter (St. Louis: Forum Press, 1980): 168; and Mark M. Carroll, "Families, Sex and The Law in Frontier Texas," (doctoral dissertation, Houston, Texas: University of Houston, 1996): 386–87, 443.

26. Robert M. Ireland, "The Libertine Must Die: Sexual Dishonor and the Unwritten Law in the Nineteenth-Century United States," *Journal of Social History* 23 (Fall 1989): 27–44.

27. Hallum, *The Diary of An Old Lawyer,* 264.

Chapter 2

1. *Ogden [Utah] Daily News,* July 31, 1973.

2. Robert W. Brown, unpublished notes, dated May 15, 1970. The Honorable Phillip Ziegler, District Judge of the 52nd Judicial District Court of Coryell County in Gatesville, Texas, in an interview with Bill Neal in Gatesville on September 11, 2003, graciously made available to the author his file on the Verna Ware matter. That file contains a number of newspaper clippings, copies of miscellaneous Coryell court records, as well as the heretofore unpublished notes of Robert W. Brown. Brown, now deceased, was a Gatesville lawyer and Coryell County historian. Unless otherwise specifically cited hereinafter, all facts asserted in the story came from Brown's notes.

3. Robert W. Brown's unpublished notes.

4. Coryell County Genealogical Society, *Coryell County Families* (Austin: Eakin Press, 1996): 287.

5. Robert W. Brown's unpublished notes.

6. *State v. John J. Hanes,* Cause No. 2952, Coryell County District Court, 1909.

7. *Spendrath v. State,* 48 S.W. 192 (Tex.Ct.Crim.App. 1898).

8. *People v. Gould,* 38 N.W. 232 (Mich.Sup.Ct. 1888).

9. *Ferguson v. Georgia,* 360 U.S. 570, 577, n. 6 (1960).

10. Steven Lubet, *Murder in Tombstone: The Forgotten Trial of Wyatt Earp* (New Haven: Yale University Press, 2004): 146.

11. Gammel, *General Laws of Texas* (1898); Art. 730, Sec. 3, *Texas Code of Criminal Procedure.*

12. Gammel, *General Laws of Texas* (1903); Art. 969, *Texas Penal Code*.

13. *Wright v. State*, 20 S.W. 756 (Tex.Ct.Crim.App. 1892).

14. Robert M. Ireland, "The Libertine Must Die: Sexual Dishonor and the Unwritten Law in the Nineteenth-Century United States," *Journal of Social History* 23 (Fall 1989): 27–44.

15. Nathanial Hawthorne, *The Scarlet Letter* (New York: Simon & Schuster, Inc., 2004): 100–101.

16. *Gatesville Messenger*, February 5, 1909.

17. *State v. Verna Ware*, Cause Nos. 2963 (John J. Hanes murder), 2964 (J. J. Smith murder), and 2965 (Dave Ross murder), in the Coryell County District Court; all cases filed in 1909. See also *Gatesville Messenger*, February 12, 1909.

18. *Gatesville Messenger*, February 4, 1910. Not only newspapers of the day, but also county histories published even to this day, all take an "ostrich-head-in-the-sand" approach to anything hinting of sexual scandals in their frontier community. Any such community sex scandal was strictly taboo—it just didn't happen—and local historians studiously ignored it. For instance, no hint of the Verna Ware/John Hanes tale is to be found in any of the Coryell County historical books published to date.

19. *Gatesville Messenger*, February 4, 1910.

20. *State v. Verna Ware*, Cause No. 2321, Coryell County Court, 1909.

21. *State v. Charley Hanes*, Cause No. 2322, Coryell County Court, 1909.

22. *Ogden [Utah] Standard Examiner*, July 31, 1973.

23. The trial of Lastencia Abarta was reported in the *Los Angeles Evening Express*, April 28, 29 and 30, 1881. Also see an account of the trial in Gordon Morris Bakken, "The Limits of Patriarchy: The 'Unwritten Law' in California Legal History," *California History: A Topical Approach*, edited by Gordon Morris Bakken (Wheeling, Ill.: Harlan Davidson, Inc., 2003): 95–99. Also see Robert M. Ireland, "Frenzied and Fallen Females: Women and Sexual Dishonor in the Nineteenth-Century United States," *Journal of Women's History*, Winter 1992: 95–117. Ireland saw the period 1843–1896 as the heyday of the unwritten law, at least in California.

24. Lawrence M. Friedman and Robert V. Percival, *The Roots of Justice: Crime and Punishment in Alameda County California, 1870–1910* (Chapel Hill: University of North Carolina Press, 1981): 239–44.

Chapter 3

1. Family history of the G. W. Radford family is taken from Bill Neal, *Last Frontier—The Story of Hardeman County* (Quanah, Tex.: Southwest Offset, 1966): 178; one of many family history stories I collected originally for

the 1958 Hardeman County Centennial edition of the *Quanah Tribune-Chief* newspaper.

2. The background of the R. E. Morris family, the killing of Garland Radford, and the murder trial of Miss Winnie Jo Morris are compiled from the following sources: court records in *State v. Winnie Jo Morris*, No. 891, Hardeman County District Court, and newspaper accounts from the *Quanah Tribune-Chief*, July 5, 1915; March 23, 1916; and March 30, 1916.

3. The Grand Jury returned three murder indictments to the Hardeman County District Court in connection with the killing of Garland Radford: against Ewell Morris, Cause No. 890; against Winnie Jo Morris, Cause No. 891; and against R. E. Morris, Cause No. 892.

4. *Quanah Tribune-Chief*, March 23, 1916.

5. Billy Mitchell, "Judge A. J. Fires, Childress Pioneer," *Panhandle-Plains Historical Review* 19 (1946): 24–28. See also Leroy Reeves, "The History of Childress County" (M.A. thesis, West Texas State College, 1951); Michael Graham Ehrle, *The Childress County Story* (Childress, Tex.: Ox Bow Printing, 1971). When Judge Fires died in 1941 at age eighty-one, all flags in Childress were flown at half mast, for he was rightly known as "the Father of Childress." He was the first county judge of Childress County, sleeping in his courthouse office and boarding in a dugout. Judge Fires had a number of other Childress "firsts": he sowed the first grain of wheat in the county, helped establish the first public school, organized the first bank, built the first brick business store, and helped dig the first grave in the Childress cemetery. In his mature years, he was a one-man university for young Panhandle lawyers. Pauline Durrett Robertson and R. L. Robertson, *Panhandle Pilgrimage* (Amarillo: Paramount Publishing Co., 1976): 268.

6. In his later years, Fires served as district judge of the five-county 100th Judicial District. Even then he never hesitated to speak his mind although it might cost him politically. He was an unabashed "wet" at a time and place when "dry" was the predominant sentiment, and he stood up to, and faced down, the Ku Klux Klan in the late 1920s and early 1930s when that group had become a strong influence in the Childress community. Hon. John T. Forbis (retired district judge, 100th Judicial District of Texas), interview by Bill Neal, Childress, Texas, November 25, 2001. A. J. Fires (grandson of Judge Amos J. Fires), interview by Bill Neal, Wellington, Texas, November 16, 2001.

7. Hon. John T. Forbis, interview by Bill Neal, Childress, Texas, November 25, 2001.

8. *Quanah Tribune-Chief*, March 23, 1916.

9. Ibid.

10. Ibid.

11. Ibid.

12. *Quanah Tribune-Chief*, March 30, 1916.

13. The Hardeman County indictments were transferred to the 78th Judicial District Court of Wichita County and renumbered as follows: Ewell Morris, No. 137; R. E. Morris, No. 138. By agreement of the state and both defendants, they were tried jointly in Cause No. 137.

14. The news accounts of the trial of R. E. and Ewell Morris were carried by the *Wichita Daily Times*, May 9, 10, and 13, 1917.

15. *Wichita Daily Times*, May 13, 1917. An earlier California case mirrored the facts in Miss Winnie's story. In 1871, Laura D. Fair shot and killed Alex P. Crittenden, her married lover, when he repeatedly reneged on his promises to divorce his wife and marry her. The jury found her not guilty by reason of "temporary partial moral insanity." See Kenneth Lamott, *Who Killed Mr. Crittenden?* (New York: David McKay Co., 1963).

16. Peggy Barker Atchison, interview by Bill Neal, Quanah, Texas, June 20, 2008.

Chapter 4

1. Kathy J. Ogren, *The Jazz Revolution: Twenties America and the Meaning of Jazz* (New York: Oxford University Press, 1983): 3. Historians have long noted that the years following World War I represented a break with repressive Victorian views of gender roles, and fueled a new and less restrictive relationship between the sexes. John D'Emilio and Estelle Freedman, *Intimate Matters: A History of Sexuality in America* (New York: Harper & Rowe, 1988): 223–35; Kathleen A. Cairns, *The Enigma Woman: The Death Sentence of Nellie May Madison* (Lincoln: The University of Nebraska Press, 2007): 19.

2. Louise Kelly, *Wichita County Beginnings* (Burnet, Tex.: Eakin Press, 1982): 75

3. Lawrence Broer and John D. Walther, eds., *Dancing Fools and Weary Blues: The Great Escape of the Twenties* (Bowling Green: Bowling Green University Press, 1990).

4. An article in *The Wall Street Journal*, January 7, 2008, affords this insight into the culture of those times: "In 1922, New York alderman Peter McGuinness proposed a city ordinance to prohibit women from smoking in any public place. Alderman McGuinness argued: 'Young fellows go into our restaurants to find women folks sucking cigarettes. What happens? The young fellows lose all respect for women, and the next thing you know the young fellows, vampired by those smoking women, desert their homes, their wives and children, rob their employers and even commit murder so that they can get money to

lavish on these smoking women. A *Washington Post* editorial in 1914 declared, 'A man may take out a woman who smokes for a good time, but he won't marry her, and if he does, he won't stay married.'"

5. Nathan Miller, *New World Coming: The 1920s and the Making of Modern America* (New York: Scribners, 2003). Historian Paul H. Carlson in *Amarillo: The Story of a Western Town* (Lubbock: Texas Tech University Press, 2006): 99, described the Jazz Age this way: "Flivers, flappers, Fords, and fanatics all characterize the Jazz Age in America. So too do fast-paced and exciting new dances such as the Charleston, Prohibition and bootlegging, the Ku Klux Klan and religious fundamentalism, radios and movies, speakeasies and sexual license, and Mah Jong and crossword puzzle crazes. . . . It was a time for heroes and flagpole sitters. It was a golden age for sports and for business. And jazz music, coming out of the nightclubs and bars of the French Quarter in New Orleans, gave the 1920s a name."

6. Ron Tyler, ed., *The New Handbook of Texas* (Austin: Texas State Historical Association, 1996): Vol. 6, 952–56.

7. C. L. Douglas, *Cattle Kings of Texas* (Fort Worth: Branch-Smith, Inc., 1939): 343; J. W. Williams, *The Big Ranch Country* (Wichita Falls: Nortex Offset Publications, 1971): 229–30; John Hendrix, *If I Can Do It Horseback: A Cow-Country Sketchbook* (Austin: University of Texas Press, 1964): 87–88; Tyler, *The New Handbook of Texas*: Vol. 6, 952–54.

8. Tyler, *The New Handbook of Texas*: Vol. 6, 952–54.

9. Kelly, *Wichita County Beginnings*, 25.

10. *Wichita Falls Times Record News*, July 31, 2005, quoting from the 1926 Wichita Falls city directory.

11. Edgar Shockley, Wichita County historian, interview by Bill Neal, Wichita Falls, June 18, 2008.

12. *Wichita Falls Times Record News*, July 31, 2005, quoting from the 1926 Wichita Falls city directory.

13. Edgar Shockley interview, June 18, 2008.

14. Lita Watson, Wichita County Museum archivist, interview by Bill Neal, Wichita Falls, June 18, 2008.

15. Kelly, *Wichita County Beginnings*, 52–53; Carlton Stowers, "Legend of the World's Littlest Skyscraper," *Texas Electric Co-op Power Magazine*, July 2008.

16. *Wichita Falls Times Record News*, July 31, 2005.

17. Edgar Shockley interview, June 18, 2008.

18. Kelly, *Wichita County Beginnings*, 205.

19. *Wichita Daily Times*, August 30, 1953. For more information on Frank Collier's baseball career, see the sports column in *Wichita Daily Times*, June 29, 1941; and Kelly, *Wichita County Beginnings*, 205.

20. Edgar Shockley interview, June 18, 2008.

21. *Wichita County Beginnings*, 240.

22. Ibid., 240–41.

23. Albert Bigelow Paine, *Captain Bill McDonald, Texas Ranger* (Austin: State House Press, 1986): 13–25; Bill Neal, *From Guns to Gavels: How Justice Grew Up in the Outlaw West* (Lubbock: Texas Tech University Press, 2008): 12–16.

24. The story of the 1896 Wichita Falls bank robbery by Kid Lewis and Foster Crawford, their capture, and their subsequent lynching has been compiled from the following sources: *Fort Worth Gazette*, February 26, 27, 28, March 3, and April 29, 1896; *Dallas Morning News*, February 27, 28, and May 9, 1896; *Dallas Semi-Weekly News*, February 28 and March 3, 1896; *Wichita Daily Times*, April 9, 1908, March 21, 1920, March 5, 1950, June 10, 17, 24, and July 1, 1951; *Wichita Falls Daily Times*, March 21, 1949; Kelly, *Wichita County Beginnings*, 43–45; Jonnie R. Morgan, *The History of Wichita Falls* (Wichita Falls: Nortex Press, 1971): 87–90; Sergeant W. J. L. Sullivan, *Twelve Years in the Saddle for Law and Order on the Frontier of Texas* (originally published by W. John L. Sullivan, 1909; reprint, Lincoln: University of Nebraska Press, 2001): 227–29; Paine, *Captain Bill McDonald*, 199–213; Walter Prescott Webb, *The Texas Rangers: A Century of Frontier Defense*, Second Edition (Austin: University of Texas Press, 1935): 446–47; Glenn Shirley, *West of Hell's Fringe: Crime, Criminals and the Federal Peace Officers in Oklahoma Territory, 1889–1907* (Norman: University of Oklahoma Press, 1978): 347–48; Neal, *From Guns to Gavels*, 64–107; Neal, *Getting Away With Murder on the Texas Frontier: Notorious Killings & Celebrated Trials* (Lubbock: Texas Tech University Press, 2006):49–73.

25. *Wichita Daily Times*, March 23, 1925; *Wichita Falls Times Record News*, July 31, 2005.

26. *Wichita Daily Times*, November 21, 1926.

27. *Wichita Falls Record News*, March 23, 1925.

28. *Wichita Falls Record News*, March 28, 1926.

29. *Wichita Daily Times*, March 21, 1925.

30. *Wichita Daily Times*, March 21, 1925; *Wichita Falls Record News*, March 21, 1925.

31. *Wichita Falls Record News*, February 19, 1925.

32. *Wichita Daily Times*, March 23, 1925; *Wichita Falls Record News*, March 23, 1925.

33. *Wichita Falls Record News*, July 31, 2005; *Wichita Falls Record News*, February 19, 1925.

34. *Wichita Daily Times*, February 15, 1925; *Wichita Falls Record News*, February 15, 1925.

35. *Wichita Daily Times*, February 15, 1925.

36. *Wichita Daily Times*, February 16, 1925.

37. *Wichita Daily Times*, February 17, 1925.

38. Ibid.

39. *Wichita Daily Times*, February 16 and 17, 1925; *Wichita Falls Record News*, February 16 and 17, 1925.

40. *Wichita Daily Times*, February 18, 1925.

41. Ken Anderson, *Dan Moody: Crusader for Justice* (Georgetown, Tex.: Georgetown Press, 2008): 16–19, 158; Paul H. Carlson, *Amarillo: The Story of a Western Town* (Lubbock: Texas Tech University Press, 2006): 103; David M. Chalmers, *Hooded Americanism: The History of the Ku Klux Klan,* 2nd ed. (New York: New Viewpoints, 1981): 2–5, 39–48.

42. Accounts of the habeas corpus bail bond hearings are contained in the February 26, 1925, through March 2, 1925, editions of the *Wichita Daily Times* and the *Wichita Falls Record News*.

43. *Wichita Daily Times*, March 17, 1925.

44. *Wichita Daily Times*, March 15, 1925.

45. The murder trial of Frank Collier was Cause No. 3638 in the 89th Judicial District Court of Wichita County, Texas, and news coverage of the trial was taken from the March 15 through March 28, 1925, editions of the *Wichita Daily Times* and the *Wichita Falls Record News*.

46. *Wichita Daily Times,* March 19, 1925.

47. *Wichita Falls Record News*, March 23, 1925.

48. Neal, *From Guns to Gavels*, 36–44.

49. *Wichita Daily Times*, March 23, 1925.

50. *Wichita Falls Record News*, March 20, 1925.

51. The court's instructions to the jury in the Frank Collier murder case (Cause No. 3638 in the 89th District Court) are printed in full in *Wichita Daily Times*, March 24, 1925.

52. *Wichita Daily Times*, March 25, 1925.

53. Ibid.

54. Ibid.

55. Ibid.

56. Ibid

57. Ibid.

58. *Frank Collier v. State*, Cause No. 9596 in the Court of Criminal Appeals of Texas, January 13, 1926; *Collier v. State*, 278 S.W. 1116 (Tex.Ct.Crim.App., 1926).

59. *Wichita Falls Record News*, March 28 and 31, 1925.

60. Report of the murder trial of Dorothy Collier in the 39th Judicial District

Court of Haskell County, Texas, is taken from the May 25 through May 29,
1925, editions of the *Wichita Daily Times* and the *Wichita Falls Record News*.

61. Carolyn A. Conley, *The Unwritten Law: Criminal Justice in Victorian Kent* (New York: Oxford University Press, 1991): 69.

62. *Wichita Falls Record News,* May 25, 1925.

63. *Wichita Daily Times,* May 28 and 29, 1925; *Wichita Falls Record News,* May 28 and 29, 1925. (Emphasis added by author.)

64. Ibid.

65. Conley, *The Unwritten Law,* 69.

66. *Wichita Daily Times,* May 28 and 29, 1925; *Wichita Falls Record News,* May 28 and 29, 1925.

67. *Dorothy Collier v. State,* Cause No. 9676 in the Court of Criminal Appeals of Texas, November 3, 1926; *Collier v. State,* 287 S.W. 1095 (Tex. Ct.Crim.App., 1926).

68. Kent Biffle, *Dallas Morning News,* August 18, 2002.

69. James L. Haley, *Texas: From Spindletop Through World War II* (New York: St. Martin's Press, 1993): 144–47.

70. Ibid.

71. May Nelson Paulissen and Carl McQueary, *Miriam: The Southern Belle Who Became the First Woman Governor of Texas* (Austin: Eakin Press, 1995): 155–66; Norman D. Brown, *Hood, Bonnet, and Little Brown Jug: Texas Politics, 1921–1928* (College Station: Texas A&M University Press, 1984): 270–74; Kathleen Dean Moore, *Pardons: Justice, Mercy and the Public Interest* (New York: Oxford University Press, 1989): 63. See also Neal, *Getting Away With Murder on the Texas Frontier,* 141–43; and Neal, *From Guns to Gavels,* 242–44.

72. Pardon of Dorothy Collier, pardon No. 19868 dated November 20, 1926, Governor's Executive Record Book, Texas State Archives, Austin, Texas. *Wichita Daily Times,* November 21, 1926.

73. Ibid.

74. Pardon of Frank Collier, pardon No. 20129, dated December 27, 1926, GERB; *Wichita Daily Times,* December 27, 1926.

75. Kelly, *Wichita County Beginnings,* 205.

76. Letter dated May 6, 1997 from Jeanie Shultz Hill, daughter of Mary Frances Collier Shultz.

77. Kelly, *Wichita County Beginnings,* 205.

78. *Wichita Falls Times Record News,* August 10, 2005; Joe Brown, Wichita Falls newsman and local historian, interview by Bill Neal, Wichita Falls, Texas, June 19, 2008.

79. Myna Hicks Potts, niece of Floyd Holmes, interview by Bill Neal, Chillicothe, Texas, May 25, 2008.

Chapter 5

1. Except as otherwise noted, the story of the No. 1 McCleskey oil well and the resulting Ranger oil boom has been taken from the following sources: Don Woodard, *Black Diamonds! Black Gold! The Saga of Texas Pacific Coal and Oil Company* (Lubbock: Texas Tech University Press, 1998): 99–114; Boyce House, *Were You in Ranger?* (Dallas: Tardy Publishing Co., 1935): 4–12; Carl Coke Rister, *Oil! Titan of the Southwest* (Norman: University of Oklahoma Press, 1949): 146–48; Ruth Sheldon Knowles, *The Greatest Gamblers: The Epic of American Oil Exploration* (Norman: University of Oklahoma Press, 1978): 162, 167; Mrs. Jimmie Wagner, "The Ranger Oil Boom" (master's thesis, Southern Methodist University, August 1935).

2. Harold F. Williamson, Ralph L. Andreano, Arnold R. Daum, and Gilbert C. Klose, *The American Petroleum Industry, 1899–1959: The Age of Energy* (Evanston: Northwestern University Press, 1963): 29–30; Woodard, *Black Diamonds! Black Gold!* 106, 277.

3. House, *Were You in Ranger?* 10; Woodard, *Black Diamonds! Black Gold!* 107.

4. Rister, *Oil! Titan of the Southwest*, 148; Wagner, "The Ranger Oil Boom," 15. See also *Oil Trade Journal* 9, no. 9 (1918): 97–98.

5. Edwin T. Cox, *History of Eastland County, Texas* (San Antonio: The Naylor Company, 1950): 53.

6. "Floated to Victory on a Wave of Oil," *New York Times*, November 23, 1918; Woodard, *Black Diamonds! Black Gold!* 109; Interview of Lloyd Bruce by Leonard Marusak, 1975; and interview of Hall Walker by Randy Jacoby, 1975 (tapes in Ranger College Library, Ranger, Texas.)

7. Boyce House, *Roaring Ranger* (San Antonio: The Naylor Company, 1951): title page and 1.

8. Interview of Lloyd Bruce by Leonard Marusak, 1975 (tape in Ranger Junior College Library, Ranger, Texas); Woodard, *Black Diamonds! Black Gold!* 103.

9. Betty Dooley Aubrey and Claude Dooley with the Texas Historical Commission, *Why Stop? A Guide to Texas Historical Roadside Markers*, 4th ed. (Houston: Lone Star Books, 1999): 406. The Texas Historical Commission, in 1964, also erected a historical marker at the well site of the No. 1 McCleskey. The Ranger Preservation Society on September 21, 1996, dedicated a sixty-four-foot turn-of-the-century wooden oil drilling derrick where Big Mac blew in almost seventy-nine years earlier. Woodard, *Black Diamonds! Black Gold!* 277 n18.

10. *Fort Worth Star-Telegram*, February 14, 1919.

11. David Yergin, *The Prize: The Epic Quest for Oil, Money and Power* (New York: Touchstone, 1992): 85.

12. *The Wise County [Texas] Messenger*, February 14, 1919.

13. Ibid.

14. Fort Worth Petroleum Club, Historical Committee, *Oil Legends of Fort Worth* (Dallas: Taylor Publishing Co., 1993): 210.

15. Yergin, *The Prize*, 86.

16. House, *Were You in Ranger?* 12; Woodard, *Black Diamonds! Black Gold!* 108, 277–78.

17. Fort Worth Petroleum Club, *Oil Legends of Fort Worth*, 210; Woodard, *Black Diamonds! Black Gold!* 104.

18. Fort Worth Petroleum Club, *Oil Legends of Fort Worth*, 144.

19. Ibid.

20. *Fort Worth Record*, May 2, 1918, and January 30, 1919.

21. *Saturday Evening Post*, December 28, 1918, 22.

22. Roger M. Olien and Diana Davids Olien, *Easy Money: Oil Promoters and Investors in the Jazz Age* (Chapel Hill: University of North Carolina Press, 1990), 74.

23. Ibid., 74–75.

24. Ibid., 73–75, 130.

25. Knowles, *The Greatest Gamblers*, 167.

26. Yergin, *The Prize*, 85–86.

27. Roger M. Olien, *Easy Money*, 123–47.

28. Fort Worth Petroleum Club, *Oil Legends of Fort Worth*, 21–23.

29. Ibid., 13.

30. Nathan Miller, *New World Coming: The 1920s and the Making of Modern America* (New York: Scribner, 2003).

31. For contemporary attitudes toward public smoking by women, see chapter 4, note 4.

32. Steven L. Davis, *Texas Literary Outlaws: Six Writers in the Sixties and Beyond* (Fort Worth: Texas Christian University Press, 2004): 57; Jerry Flemmons, "The Texan Who Played Cowboy for America," in Judy Alter and James Ward Lee, eds., *Literary Fort Worth* (Fort Worth: Texas Christian University Press, 2002): 193–99. For a complete account of the life and times of Amon Carter, see Jerry Flemmons's fascinating biography, *Amon: The Texan Who Played Cowboy for America* (Lubbock: Texas Tech University Press, 1998).

33. Jerry Flemmons, *Plowboys, Cowboys, and Slanted Pigs* (Fort Worth: Texas Christian University Press, 1984): 75–91.

34. Steven L. Davis, *Texas Literary Outlaws*, 57–58.

35. Roger M. Olien, *Easy Money*, 73; Oliver Knight, *Fort Worth: Outpost on the Trinity* (Norman: University of Oklahoma Press, 1953): vii; *Fort Worth Press*, November 21, 1927.

36. Myna Hicks Potts, niece of Floyd Holmes, interview with Bill Neal, Chillicothe, Texas, April 26, 2004.

37. Fort Worth Petroleum Club, *Oil Legends of Fort Worth*, 144.

38. Ibid., 210.

39. *Fort Worth Star-Telegram* and *Fort Worth Record*, May 10, 1921 (morning and home editions).

40. *Fort Worth Star-Telegram*, February 24, 1913; *Fort Worth Star-Telegram*, November 18 and 19, 1941.

41. *Fort Worth Star-Telegram*, November 19, 1941.

42. The text story of the Boyce-Sneed feud, the killings, and the four ensuing murder trials is taken primarily from Clara Sneed's story: Clara Sneed, "Because This Is Texas: An Account of the Sneed-Boyce feud," *Panhandle-Plains Historical Review* 72 (1999): 1–99, supplemented by accounts of the four murder trials (held in 1912 and 1913) as reported in the *Fort Worth Star-Telegram*. Jury arguments cited in the text were taken from trial accounts appearing in the *Fort Worth Star-Telegram*, February 22, 23, and 24, 1912, and February 24, 1913.

43. Accounts of the trial of Floyd Holmes for killing Warren Wagner are contained in the *Fort Worth Star-Telegram*, and the *Fort Worth Record*, editions of November 14, 15, 16, and 17, 1921.

44. *Fort Worth Star-Telegram*, May 11, 1921.

45. *Fort Worth Star-Telegram* November 17, 1921.

46. The general rule is that hearsay evidence is not admissible because it violates the constitutional right of the accused under the Sixth Amendment of the U.S. Constitution to confront and cross-examine any witnesses called to testify against him. However, there are exceptions to the hearsay evidence rule in instances when hearsay evidence, because of its nature and the surrounding circumstances, is deemed important and is sufficiently reliable to be considered by the jury even though the defendant is denied the right to cross-examine the declarant. Warren Wagner's statement to the deputy prosecutor shortly after he was shot qualifies under two exceptions as the rules of evidence existed at that time. First, Wagner's statements fell under the "excited utterance" exception to the hearsay rule, which allows another witness to tell what someone said while that person was still under the immediate influence of a traumatic event. The underlying rationale is that under those circumstances, the declarant would not be likely to fabricate a falsehood. Second, Wagner's statements also qualified as a "dying declaration" exception. If a person, as did Wagner, realizes he is about to die and makes a statement, it is admissible. The underlying rationale there is that a man who knows he is about to die is deemed unlikely to lie—to go to his grave with a false accusation on his lips.

47. Section 9.31, Self-Defense, *Texas Penal Code*.

48. Thomas J. Kerman, "The Jurisprudence of Lawlessness," *American Bar Association Report*, 1906, 451–53.

49. One old-timer put it this way: "In those times, if you made open threats to kill somebody, you pretty well signed your own death warrant." C. M. Randall, interview by Joe D. Gibson, Seymour, Texas, August 4, 1971, Reels 1–3, (Southwest Collections/Special Collections Library, Texas Tech University, Lubbock, Texas).

50. Dick Everett, *The Dixie Frontier: A Social History* (Norman: University of Oklahoma Press, 1993): 232–33. (Emphasis mine.)

51. Neal, *From Guns to Gavels: How Justice Grew Up in the Outlaw West* (Lubbock: Texas Tech University Press, 2008): 269–77.

52. *Fort Worth Star-Telegram*, September 22, 1927.

53. *Fort Worth Star-Telegram*, January 12, 1942.

54. Fort Worth Petroleum Club, *Oil Legends of Fort Worth*, 112–13; Mike Cochran, *Texas vs. Davis: The Shocking True Crime Account of the Cullen Davis Murder Case* (New York: Signet, 1991): 18–21.

55. Cochran, *Texas vs. Davis*, 20.

56. *Fort Worth Star-Telegram*, January 12, 1942.

57. Cochran, *Texas vs. Davis*, 18.

58. Ibid., 23–24; Forth Worth Petroleum Club, *Oil Legends of Fort Worth*, 112–13.

Chapter 6

1. Mike Cochran, *Texas vs. Davis: The Shocking True Crime Account of the Cullen Davis Murder Case* (New York: Signet, 1991): 11–12.

2. Except as otherwise noted, the rest of the Cullen Davis story has been adapted from Cochran, *Texas vs. Davis*, and from *Fort Worth Star-Telegram* stories printed on or about the dates of the incidents referred to in the text.

3. Cochran, *Texas vs. Davis*, 32

4. Ibid.

5. Ibid.

6. Section 19.03, Capital Murder, *Texas Penal Code*. The district attorney may, but is not required to, seek the death penalty in several instances including, as in this case, where two or more people are murdered in the same transaction. Other instances in which Texas law provides a death penalty option include incidents wherein there is a murder of a peace officer, murder during the commission of certain serious felonies such as burglary, murder-for-hire, murder of a prison guard by a prisoner, murder of a child under six years of age, and others. In Texas capital felony cases the prescribed punishment is

either life imprisonment or death, and if the DA does not elect to seek the death penalty, then a life sentence is mandatory if the defendant is found guilty. Section 12.31, Capital Felony, *Texas Penal Code*.

7. Article 1.07, Right to Bail, *Texas Code of Criminal Procedure* provides, "All prisoners shall be bailable unless for capital offenses when the proof is evident."

8. Cochran, *Texas vs. Davis*, 267–68.

9. This statute was first enacted in 1856 as Article 562 of the *Texas Penal Code* and brought forward in succeeding Texas penal codes as Article 567 (1879), Article 672 (1895), Article 1102 (1911), and finally Article 1220 (1925) until it was finally repealed by acts of the Texas Legislature in 1973.

10. *E.B. v. Alabama*, 511 U.S. 127, 114 S.Ct. 1419, 128 L.Ed. 2d 89 (U.S., 1994). In quoting from prior cases on the subject, Justice Blackmun further examined the underlying basis for the exclusion of women from juries: "[There exists] . . . a need to protect women from the ugliness and depravity of trials. Women were thought to be too fragile and virginal to withstand the polluted courtroom atmosphere. . . . Criminal trials often involve testimony of the foulest kind, and they sometimes require consideration of indecent conduct, the use of filthy and loathsome words, references to intimate sex relationships, and other elements that would prove humiliating, embarrassing and degrading to a lady. . . . Reverence for all womanhood would suffer in the public spectacle of women . . . so engaged."

11. Cochran, *Texas vs. Davis*, 260.

12. Ibid., 261. (Emphasis added.)

13. Gary Cartwright, *Blood Will Tell: The Murder Trial of T. Cullen Davis* (New York: Harcourt Brace Jovanovich, 1979): 270–71.

14. Ibid.

15. Cochran, *Texas vs. Davis*, 288.

16. Ibid., 308–309.

17. Ibid., 344.

18. *Dallas Times-Herald*, November 10, 1979.

19. *Dallas Morning News*, May 5, 1980.

20. Cochran, *Texas vs. Davis*, 525.

21. Ibid., 534.

22. Ibid., 550–51.

23. Ibid., 573.

24. *Fort Worth Star-Telegram*, February 20, 2001.

25. Mike Cochran, interview by Bill Neal, Fort Worth, August 22, 2008.

26. In addition to the author's August 22, 2008, interview with Mike Cochran, sources for Epilogue II were two *Fort Worth Star-Telegram* stories by

Mike Cochran dated February 11, 2001, and June 11, 2000, and a *Fort Worth*
Star-Telegram column by Dave Lieber dated June 16, 2002.

Afterthoughts

1. Richard Maxwell Brown, *No Duty to Retreat: Violence and Values in American History and Society* (New York: Oxford University Press, 1991): preface. Also see Mark DeWolfe Howe, ed., *Holmes-Laski Letters: The Correspondence of Mr. Justice Holmes and Harold J. Laski, 1916–1935,* 2 vols. (Cambridge: Harvard University Press, 1953): 335–36; and Supreme Court Justice Oliver Wendell Holmes's opinion on the subject in *Brown v. United States,* 256 U.S. 335 (1921). See also Sections 9.31 and 9.32, *Texas Penal Code,* before and after its 2007 amendment.

2. George Wilfred Stumberg, "Defense of Person and Property under Texas Criminal Law," *University of Texas Law Review* 21, no. 1 (1942): 21; William R. Ravkind, Justifiable Homicide in Texas," *Southwestern Law Journal* 13, no. 2 (1959): 521.

3. *Whitten v. State*: 29 Tex.Crim.Rep. 504, 16 S.W. 296 (1891).

4. *Lilly v. State*, 20 Tex.App. 1 (Tex.Ct.App. 1885).

5. Albert Bigelow Paine, *Captain Bill McDonald, Texas Ranger* (Austin: State House Press, 1986): 154–58.

6. Laura V. Hamner, *Light'n Hitch* (Dallas: American Guild Press, 1958): 115–16.

7. Stumberg, "Defense of Persons and Property under Texas Criminal Law," *Texas Law Review,* 33–35.

8. Ravkind, "Justifiable Homicide in Texas," *Southwestern Law Journal,* 124.

9. Necah S. Furman, "Texas Women Versus the Texas Myth," in Archie P. McDonald and Ben Proctor, eds., *The Texas Heritage* (St. Louis: Forum Press, 1980): 168; Joan E. Cashin, *A Family Venture: Men and Women on the Southern Frontier* (New York: Oxford University Press, 1991): 99, 102, 105; Sandra L. Myres, *Westering Women and the Frontier Experience, 1800–1915* (Albuquerque: University of New Mexico Press, 1982): 122–31; Margaret S. Henson, *Anglo-American Women in Texas, 1820–1850* (Boston: American Press, 1982); Ann Patton Malone, *Women on the Texas Frontier: A Cross-Cultural Perspective* (El Paso: Texas Western Press, 1983): 28–52; Jane Dysart, "Mexican Women in San Antonio: The Assimilation Process, 1830–1860," *Western Historical Quarterly* 7 (October, 1976): 437–47; Mark M. Carroll, "Families, Sex, and the Law in Frontier Texas," (doctoral dissertation, Houston, Texas: University of Houston, 1996): 386–87, 442–48. Novelist Jane Gilmore Rushing, a West Texas writer, accurately depicted the way life really was for frontier women.

For a perceptive summary of her life and writings, see Lou Halsell Rodenberger, *Jane Gilmore Rushing: A West Texas Writer and Her Work* (Lubbock: Texas Tech University Press, 2006).

10. Cornelia Otis Skinner in Bergen Evans, *Dictionary of Quotations* (New York: Avenel Books, 1978), 445.

11. Dorothy Scarborough, in her celebrated 1925 novel *The Wind*, paints a grim picture of a frail, sensitive, and lonely woman desperately fighting to retain her sanity in a desolate, windblown shack on the West Texas prairie. Dorothy Scarborough, *The Wind* (Austin: University of Texas Press, 1986, reprint). For a nonfiction account of the extreme loneliness endured by pioneer women, see Louise Fairchild, *The Lonesome Plains: Death and Revival on an American Frontier* (College Station: Texas A&M University Press, 2002).

12. *Dallas Morning News*, June 25, 2000.

13. Ibid.

14. Bill Neal, *From Guns to Gavels: How Justice Grew Up in the Outlaw West* (Lubbock: Texas Tech University Press, 2008): 64–107; 303–309; also see Richard Maxwell Brown, *Strains of Violence: Historical Studies of American Violence and Vigilantism* (New York: Oxford University Press, 1975); and Richard Maxwell Brown, "The American Vigilante Tradition," in *Violence in America: Historical and Comparative Perspectives*, ed. Hugh Davis Graham and Ted Robert Gurr (Washington and New York: Frederick A. Praeger, and Government Printing Office, 1969).

15. Gordon Morris Bakken, "The Limits of Patriarchy," in Gordon Morris Bakken, ed., *California History: A Topical Approach* (Wheeling, Ill: Harlan Davidson, 2003): 102.

BIBLIOGRAPHY

Books

Alter, Judy and James Ward Lee, eds. *Literary Fort Worth.* Fort Worth: Texas Christian University Press, 2002.

Anderson, Ken. *Dan Moody: Crusader for Justice.* Georgetown, Tex.: Georgetown Press, 2008.

Aubrey, Betty Dooley, and Claude Dooley with the Texas Historical Commission. *Why Stop? A Guide to Texas Historical Roadside Markers,* fourth edition. Houston: Lone Star Books, 1999.

Ayers, Edward L. *Vengeance and Justice: Crime and Punishment in the 19th Century American South.* New York: Oxford University Press, 1984.

Bakken, Gordon Morris. *Law in the Western United States.* Norman: University of Oklahoma Press, 2000.

—————. "The Limits of Patriarchy: The Unwritten Law in California." In *California History: A Topical Approach,* edited by Gordon Morris Bakken. Wheeling, Ill.: Harlan Davison, Inc., 2003.

—————. *Practicing Law in Frontier California, 1870–1910.* Lincoln: University of Nebraska Press, 1991. First published 1981 by University of North Carolina Press.

Blackstone, William. *Commentaries on the Laws of England, 1765–69.* 4 vols. Chicago: University of Chicago Press, 1979.

Broer, Lawrence, and John D. Walther, eds. *Dancing Fools and Weary Blues: The Great Escape of the Twenties.* Bowling Green: Bowling Green University Press, 1990.

Brown, Norman D. *Hood, Bonnet, and Little Brown Jug: Texas Politics, 1921–1928.* College Station: Texas A&M University Press, 1984.

Brown, Richard Maxwell. *Strains of Violence: Historical Studies of American Violence and Vigilantism.* New York: Oxford University Press, 1975.

262 ――――. "The American Vigilante Tradition." In *Violence in America: Histori-cal and Comparative Perspectives,* edited by Hugh Davis Graham and Ted Robert Gurr. New York: Frederick A. Praeger and Government Printing Office, 1969.

――――. *No Duty to Retreat: Violence and Values in American History and Society.* New York: Oxford University Press, 1991.

Bruce, Dickson. *Violence and Culture in the Antebellum South.* Austin: University of Texas Press, 1979.

Cairns, Kathleen A. *The Enigma Woman: The Death Sentence of Nellie May Madison.* Lincoln: University of Nebraska Press, 2007.

Carlson, Paul H. *Amarillo: The Story of a Western Town.* Lubbock: Texas Tech University Press, 2006.

Cartwright, Gary. *Blood Will Tell: The Murder Trial of T. Cullen Davis.* New York: Harcourt Brace Jovanovich, 1979.

Cashin, Joan E. *A Family Venture: Men and Women on the Southern Frontier.* New York: Oxford University Press, 1991.

Chalmers, David M. *Hooded Americanism: The History of the Ku Klux Klan,* second edition. New York: New Viewpoints, 1981.

Cochran, Mike. *Texas vs. Davis: The Shocking True Crime Account of the Cullen Davis Murder Case.* New York: Signet, 1991.

Conley, Carolyn A. *The Unwritten Law: Criminal Justice in Victorian Kent.* New York: Oxford University Press, 1991.

Coryell County Genealogical Society. *Coryell County Families.* Austin: Eakin Press, 1996.

Cox, Edwin T. *History of Eastland County, Texas.* San Antonio: The Naylor Company, 1950.

Davis, Steven L. *Texas Literary Outlaws: Six Writers in the Sixties and Beyond.* Fort Worth: Texas Christian University Press, 2004.

D'Emilio, John. *Intimate Matters: A History of Sexuality in America.* New York: Harper & Rowe, 1988.

Douglas, C. L. *Cattle Kings of Texas.* Fort Worth: Branch-Smith, Inc., 1939.

Dykstra, Robert. *The Cattle Towns.* New York: Knopf, 1968.

Ehrle, Michael Graham. *The Childress County Story.* Childress, Tex.: Ox Bow Printing, 1971.

Everett, Dick. *The Dixie Frontier: A Social History.* Norman: University of Oklahoma Press, 1993.

Fairchild, Louise. *The Lonesome Plains: Death and Revival on an American Fron-tier.* College Station: Texas A&M University Press, 2002.

Flemmons, Jerry. *Plowboys, Cowboys and Slanted Pigs.* Fort Worth: Texas Chris-tian University Press, 1984.

————. *Amon: The Texan Who Played Cowboy for America.* Lubbock: Texas
Tech University Press, 1998.

————. "Smiting a Sinful World." In *Literary Fort Worth,* edited by Judy
Alter and James Ward Lee. Fort Worth: Texas Christian University Press,
2002.

Fort Worth Petroleum Club, Historical Committee. *Oil Legends of Fort Worth.*
Dallas: Taylor Publishing Co., 1993.

Fox, Richard Wightman. *Trials of Intimacy: Love and Loss in the Beecher-Tilton
Scandal.* Chicago: The University of Chicago Press, 1999.

Friedman, Lawrence. *Crime and Punishment in American History.* New York:
Basic Books, 1993.

————, and Robert V. Percival. *The Roots of Justice: Crime and Punishment in
Alameda County California, 1870–1910.* Chapel Hill: University of North
Carolina Press, 1981.

Furman, Necah S. "Texas Women Versus the Texas Myth." In *The Texas Heritage,* edited by Archie P. McDonald and Ben Proctor. St. Louis: Forum
Press, 1980.

Grossberg, Michael. *A Judgment for Solomon: The D'Hauteville Case and Legal
Experience in Antebellum America.* New York: Cambridge University Press,
1996.

Haley, James L. *Texas: From Spindletop Through World War II.* New York: St.
Martin's Press, 1993.

Hallum, John. *Col. John Hallum, Address to the Jury by Col. John Hallum in
Self-Defense in the Case of the State of Texas Against Him: An Indictment for
Shooting a Minister of the Gospel, Together with the Extraordinary Facts and
Remarkable Incidents Connected with the Trial and Prosecution.* Muskogee,
Okla.: The Phoenix Press, 1911.

————. *The Diary of an Old Lawyer: Scenes Behind the Curtain.* Nashville, Tenn.:
Southwestern Publishing House, 1895.

Hamm, Richard F. *Murder, Honor and Law: Four Virginia Homicides from
Reconstruction to the Great Depression.* Charlottesville: University of Virginia
Press, 2003.

Hamner, Laura V. *Light'n Hitch.* Dallas: American Guild Press, 1958.

Hawthorne, Nathaniel. *The Scarlet Letter.* New York: Simon & Schuster, Inc.,
2004.

Hendrix, John. *If I Can Do It Horseback: A Cow-Country Sketchbook.* Austin:
University of Texas Press, 1964.

Henson, Margaret S. *Anglo-American Women in Texas, 1820–1850.* Boston:
American Press, 1982.

House, Boyce. *Were You in Ranger?* Dallas: Tardy Publishing Co., 1935.

————. *Roaring Ranger*. San Antonio: The Naylor Company, 1951.

Howe, Mark DeWolfe, ed. *Holmes-Laski Letters: The Correspondence of Mr. Justice Holmes and Harold J. Laski, 1916–1935*. Cambridge, Mass.: Harvard University Press, 1953.

Jones, Richard Glyn. *The Mammoth Book of Women Who Kill*. New York: Carroll & Graff Publishers, 2002.

Kelly, Louise. *Wichita County Beginnings*. Burnett, Tex.: Eakin Press, 1982.

Kens, Paul. "Don't Mess Around in Texas: Adultery and Justifiable Homicide in the Lone Star State." In *Law in the Western United States*, edited by Gordon Morris Bakken. Norman: University of Oklahoma Press, 2000.

Knight, Oliver. *Fort Worth: Outpost on the Trinity*. Norman: University of Oklahoma Press, 1953.

Knowles, Ruth Sheldon. *The Greatest Gamblers: The Epic of American Oil Exploration*. Norman: University of Oklahoma Press, 1978.

Lamott, Kenneth. *Who Killed Mr. Crittenden?: Being a True Account of the Notorious Murder Trial That Stunned San Francisco—The Laura D. Fair Case*. New York: David McKay Co., 1963.

Lawson, John D. "Trial of Daniel E. Sickles for the Murder of Philip Barton Key." In *American State Trials*, Vol. 12, edited by John D. Lawson. St Louis: n.p., 1914–1936.

Lubet, Steven. *Murder in Tombstone: The Forgotten Trial of Wyatt Earp*. New Haven: Yale University Press, 2004.

Malone, Ann Patton. *Women on the Texas Frontier: A Cross-Cultural Perspective*. El Paso: Texas Western Press, 1983.

McDonald, Archie P., and Ben Procter, eds. *The Texas Heritage*. St. Louis: Forum Press, 1980.

McKanna, Clare V., Jr., *Homicide, Race, and Justice in the American West, 1880–1920*. Tucson: University of Arizona Press, 1997.

Miller, Jeffrey. *Ardor in the Court! Sex and the Law*. Toronto: ECW Press, 2002.

Miller, Nathan. *New World Coming; The 1920s and the Making of Modern America*. New York: Scribners, 2003.

Moore, Kathleen Dean. *Pardons: Justice, Mercy and the Public Interest*. New York: Oxford University Press, 1989.

Morgan, Jonnie R. *The History of Wichita Falls*. Wichita Falls: Nortex Press 1971.

Myers, Sandra L. *Westering Women and the Frontier Experience, 1800–1915*. Albuquerque: University of New Mexico Press, 1982.

Neal, Bill. *Last Frontier: The Story of Hardeman County*. Quanah, Tex.: Southwest Offset, Inc., 1966.

————. *From Guns to Gavels: How Justice Grew Up in the Outlaw West*. Lubbock: Texas Tech University Press, 2008.

————. *Getting Away With Murder on the Texas Frontier: Notorious Killings and Celebrated Trials*. Lubbock: Texas Tech University Press, 2006.

Orgren, Kathy J. *The Jazz Revolution: Twenties America and the Meaning of Jazz*. New York: Oxford University Press, 1983.

Olien, Roger M., and Diana Davids Olien. *Easy Money: Oil Promoters and Investors in the Jazz Age*. Chapel Hill: University of North Carolina Press, 1990.

Pace, Robert F. *Halls of Honor: College Men in the Old South*. Baton Rouge: Louisiana State University Press, 2004.

Paine, Albert Bigelow. *Captain Bill McDonald, Texas Ranger*. Austin: State House Press, 1986.

Paulissen, May N., and Carl McQueary. *Miriam, The Southern Belle Who Became the First Woman Governor of Texas*. Austin: Eakin Press, 1995.

Reed, John Shelton. "Below the Smith and Wesson Line: Reflections on Southern Violence." In *Perspectives on the American South*, Vol. 1, edited by Merle Black and John Shelton Reed. New York: Gordon and Breach Science Publishers, 1981.

Renteln, Alison Dundes, and Alan Dundes, eds. *Folk Law: Essays in the Theory and Practice of Lex Non Scripta*, two volumes. Madison: University of Wisconsin Press, 1994.

Rister, Carl Coke. *Oil! Titan of the Southwest*. Norman: University of Oklahoma Press, 1949.

Robertson, R. L., and Pauline Durrett. *Panhandle Pilgrimage*. Amarillo: Paramount Publishing Co., 1976.

Rodenberger, Lou Halsell. *Jane Gilmore Rushing: A West Texas Writer and Her Work*. Lubbock: Texas Tech University Press, 2006.

Rogin, Michael P. *Fathers and Children: Andrew Jackson and the Subjugation of the American Indian*, 1975 reprint. New York: Vintage Books, 1975.

Scarborough, Dorothy. *The Wind*. Austin: University of Texas Press, 1986.

Shirley, Glenn. *West of Hell's Fringe: Crime, Criminals and the Federal Peace Officers in Oklahoma Territory, 1889–1907*. Norman: University of Oklahoma Press, 1978.

Skinner, Cornelia Otis. In *Dictionary of Quotations*, edited by Bergen Evans. New York: Avenel Books, 1978.

Sullivan, W. J. L. *Twelve Years in the Saddle for Law and Order on the Frontier of Texas*. Originally published by W. John L. Sullivan, 1909; reprint, Lincoln: University of Nebraska Press, 2001.

Tyler, Ron. *The New Handbook of Texas*, Vol. 6. Austin: The Texas State Historical Association, 1996.

266   Webb, Walter Prescott. *The Texas Rangers: A Century of Frontier Defense*. Austin: University of Texas Press, 1935.

Williams, J. W. *The Big Ranch Country*. Lubbock, Tex.: Texas Tech University Press, 1999. First published 1971 by Nortex Offset Publications, Inc.

Williamson, Harold F., Ralph Andreano, Arnold R. Daum, and Gilbert C. Klose. *The American Petroleum Industry, 1899–1959: The Age of Energy*. Evanston: Northwestern University Press, 1963.

Woodard, Don. *Black Diamonds! Black Gold! The Saga of Texas Pacific Coal and Oil Company*. Lubbock: Texas Tech University Press, 1998.

Wyatt-Brown, Bertram. *Southern Honor: Ethics and Behavior in the Old South*. New York: Oxford University Press, 1982.

Yergin, David. *The Prize: The Epic Quest for Oil, Money and Power*. New York: Touchstone, 1992.

Periodicals

Dysart, Jane. "Mexican Women in San Antonio: The Assimilation Process, 1830–1860." *Western Historical Quarterly* 7 (October 1976): 437–47.

Hartog, Hendrick. "Lawyering, Husband's Rights and 'the Unwritten Law' in Nineteenth-Century America." *Journal of American History* 84, No. 1 (June 1997): 67–96.

Hughes, William Herchel. "John Hallum, Lawyer and Historian." *Arkansas Historical Quarterly* 10, no. 3 (Autumn 1951): 258–67.

Ireland, Robert M. "Frenzied and Fallen Females." *Journal of Women's History* 3 (Winter 1992): 95.

———. "Insanity and the Unwritten Law." *American Journal of Legal History* 32 (April 1988): 157–72.

———. "The Libertine Must Die: Sexual Dishonor and the Unwritten Law in Nineteenth-Century United States." *Journal of Social History* 23 (Fall 1989): 27–44.

Kernan, Thomas J. "The Jurisprudence of Lawlessness." *American Bar Association Report*, 1906: 451–53.

Mitchell, Billy. "Judge A. J. Fires, Childress Pioneer." *Panhandle-Plains Historical Review* 19 (1946): 24–28.

Potts, C. S. "Is the Husband's Act in Killing Wife Taken in Act of Adultery Justifiable Homicide in Texas?" *Texas Law Review* 2, No. 1 (1923): 111.

Prior, Pauline M. "Murder and Madness: Gender and the Insanity Defense in Nineteenth-Century Ireland." *New Hibernia Review* 9 (Winter 2005): 19–36.

Ravkind, William M. "Justifiable Homicide in Texas." *Southwestern Law Journal* 13, No. 2 (1959): 50–11.

Sneed, Clara. "Because This Is Texas: An Account of the Sneed-Boyce Feud." *Panhandle-Plains Historical Review* 72 (1999): 1–99.

Stowers, Carlton. "Legend of the World's Littlest Skyscraper." *Texas Electric Co-Op Power Magazine,* July 2008.

Stumberg, William. "Defense of Person and Property under the Texas Criminal Law." *Texas Law Review* 21, No. 1 (November 1942): 17.

Sydnor, Charles. "The Southerner and the Laws." *Journal of Southern History* 6 (1940): 7–8.

Waldrop, Christopher. "Law and Society: Structuring Legal Revolutions, 1870–1920." *The Journal of the Gilded Age and Progressive Era* 5, no. 4 (October 2006): 319–20.

Widener, Michael, and Allegra Young. "Frontier Justice: An Indictment for Shooting A Minister of the Gospel." *University of Texas Law Magazine,* Spring 2003: 64.

Documents

COURT CASES

State of Texas v. John Hallum, Cause No. 1113 in the District Court of Bowie County, Texas (1897).

State of Texas v. John J. Hanes, Cause No. 2952 in the District Court of Coryell County, Texas (1909).

State of Texas v. Verna Ware, Cause No. 2963 in the District Court of Coryell County, Texas (1909).

State of Texas v. Verna Ware, Cause No. 2964 in the District Court of Coryell County, Texas (1909).

State of Texas v. Verna Ware, Cause No. 2965 in the District Court of Coryell County, Texas (1909).

State of Texas v. Verna Ware, Cause No. 2321 in the County Court of Coryell County, Texas (1909).

State of Texas v. Charley Hanes, Cause No. 2322 in the County Court of Coryell County, Texas (1909).

State of Texas v. Winnie Jo Morris, Cause No. 891 in the District Court of Hardeman County, Texas (1916).

State of Texas v. Ewell Morris, Cause No. 137 in the 78th District Court of Wichita County, Texas (1917).

State of Texas v. R. E. Morris, Cause No. 138 in the 78th District Court of Wichita County, Texas (1917).

State of Texas v. Frank Collier, Cause No. 3638 in the 89th District Court of Wichita County, Texas (1926).

State of Texas v. Dorothy Collier, Cause No. 1626 in the 39th District Court of Haskell County, Texas (1926).

APPELLATE COURT CASES

Brown v. United States, 256 U.S. 335 (U.S.SupremeCourt 1921).

Burger v. State, 231 S.E. 2d 769 (Ga.Sup.Ct. 1977).

Campbell v. State, 49 S.E. 2nd 867 (Ga.Sup.Ct. 1948).

Collier v. State, 278 S.W. 1116 (Tex.Ct.Crim.App. 1926).

Collier v. State, 287 S.W. 1095 (Tex.Ct.Crim.App. 1926).

Ferguson v. Georgia, 360 U.S. 570 (U.S.SupremeCt. 1960).

Gregory v. State, 94 S.W. 1041 (Tex.Ct.Crim.App. 1906).

J. E. B. v. Alabama, 511 U.S. 127 (U.S.SupremeCt. 1994).

Lilly v. State, 20 Tex. App. 1 (Tex.Ct.Crim.App. 1885).

Oliver v. State, 159 S.W. 235 (Tex.Ct.Crim.App. 1913).

O'Shields v. State, 125 Ga. 310, 54 S. E. 120 (Ga.Sup.Ct. 1906).

People v. Gould, 38 N.W. 232 (Mich.Sup.Ct. 1888).

Price v. State, 18 Tex. App. 474 (Tex.Ct.CrimApp. 1885).

Reed v. State, 59 S.W. 2d 122 (Tex.Ct.Crim.App. 1933).

Reed v. State, 11 Tex. App. 509 (Tex.Ct.Crim.App. 1882).

Sensobaugh v. State, 244 S.W. 379 (Tex.Ct.Crim.App. 1922).

Spendrath v. State, 48 S.W. 192 (Tex.Ct.Crim.App. 1898).

Tarrant v. State, 25 S.W. 2d 836 (Tex.Ct.Crim.App. 1930).

Whitten v. State, 16 S.W. 296 (Tex.Ct.Crim.App. 1891).

Williams v. State, 165 S.W. 583 (Tex.Ct.Crim.App. 1914).

Wright v. State, 20 S.W. 756 (Tex.Ct.Crim.App. 1892).

OLD ENGLISH COURT CASE

R. v. Brown, 24 Q. B. 357d (1890).

Maddy's Case, 2 Keb. 829, 1 VENT. 158 (1671).

Interviews

A. J. Fires (grandson of Judge Amos J. Fires), interviewed by Bill Neal, Wellington, Texas (November 16, 2001).

C. M. Randall, interviewed by Joe D. Gibson, audio tapes, Reels 1–3, Southwest Collections/Special Collections Library, Texas Tech University, Lubbock, Texas (August 4, 1971).

Edgar Shockley, Wichita County historian, interviewed by Bill Neal, Wichita Falls, Texas (June 18, 2008).

Hall Walker, interviewed by Randy Jacoby, audio tapes, Ranger College Library, Ranger, Texas (1975).

Honorable John T. Forbis (retired district judge, 100th Judicial District of Texas), interviewed by Bill Neal, Childress, Texas (November 25, 2001).

Joe Brown, newsman and Wichita County, Texas, historian, interviewed by Bill Neal, Wichita Falls, Texas (June 19, 2008).

Lita Watson, Wichita County Museum archivist, interviewed by Bill Neal, Wichita Falls, Texas (June 18, 2008).

Mike Cochran, author and retired Associated Press reporter, interviewed by Bill Neal, Fort Worth, Texas (August 22, 2008).

Lloyd Bruce, interviewed by Leonard Marusak, audio tapes, Ranger College Library, Ranger, Texas (1975).

Myna Hicks Potts, niece of Floyd Holmes, interviewed by Bill Neal, Chillicothe, Texas (April 26, 2004, and May 25, 2008).

Peggy Barker Atchison, interviewed by Bill Neal, Quanah, Texas (June 20, 2008).

Honorable Phillip Ziegler (retired district judge, 52nd Judicial District of Texas), interviewed by Bill Neal, Gatesville, Texas (September 11, 2003).

Theses and Unpublished Works

Carroll, Mark M. "Families, Sex, and the Law in Frontier Texas." Doctoral dissertation, University of Houston, Houston, Texas, 1996.

Brown, Robert W. Unpublished notes, given to author by Hon. Phillip Ziegler, Gatesville, Texas (September 11, 2003).

Reeves, Leroy. "The History of Childress County." MA thesis, West Texas State College, 1951.

Wagner, Mrs. Jimmie. "The Ranger Oil Boom." MA thesis, Southern Methodist University, 1935.

Laws

Laws of New Mexico, Section 35–315, N. Mex. Stat.Ann. (Courtright, 1929).

Laws of Texas, Article 730, Section 3, *Texas Code of Criminal Procedure,* Gammel (1898).

Laws of Texas, Article 969, *Texas Code of Criminal Procedure,* Gammel (1903).

Texas Penal Code, Article 562 (1856), *Repealed by acts of the Texas Legislature* (1973).

Texas Penal Code, Article 567 (1879), *Repealed by acts of the Texas Legislature* (1973).

Texas Penal Code, Article 672 (1895), *Repealed by acts of the Texas Legislature* (1973).

Texas Penal Code, Article 1102 (1911), *Repealed by acts of the Texas Legislature* (1973).

Texas Penal Code, Article 1220 (1925), *Repealed by acts of the Texas Legislature* (1973).

Texas Penal Code, Section 9.31, Self-Defense.

Texas Penal Code, Section 19.03, Capital Murder.

Texas Penal Code, Section 12.31, Capital Felony.

Texas Code of Criminal Procedure, Article 1.07, right to bail.

Records

Handwritten notes of editor Rhea Howard, in the *Wichita Falls Times Record News* file on the 1896 Foster Crawford and Elmer "Kid" Lewis lynching in Wichita Falls, Texas.

Governor's Executive Record Book, Pardon No. 19868, *Dorothy Collier,* 20 November 1926. Austin: TSA.

Governor's Executive Record Book, Pardon No. 20129, *Frank Collier,* 27 December 1926. Austin: TSA.

Letter from Jeanie Shultz Hill, daughter of Mary Frances Collier Shultz, May 6, 1997.

Internet

Jay Guy Cisco. "Historic Sumner County, Tennessee," 1909. RootsWeb.com and its subsidiaries (Ancestry.com), March 26, 2008.

INDEX